Hugh Seymour-Davies has travelled widely in North America, Mexico, the Caribbean and North Africa. He has written about some of these experiences in articles for *Country Life*. In 1973 he bought a house in Andalusia, and has been a regular visitor there ever since. When not in Spain, he lives in London with his wife and two sons. He is an occasional journalist and literary critic, but *The Bottlebrush Tree* is his first book.

THE BOTTLEBRUSH TREE

A VILLAGE IN ANDALUSIA

Hugh Seymour-Davies

BLACK SWAN

THE BOTTLEBRUSH TREE
A BLACK SWAN BOOK : 0 552 99658 0

Originally published in Great Britain by
Constable and Company Ltd

PRINTING HISTORY
Constable edition published 1988
Black Swan edition published 1996

Set in 11/12pt Linotype Melior by
Phoenix Typesetting, Ilkley, West Yorkshire.

Black Swan Books are published by Transworld Publishers Ltd,
61–63 Uxbridge Road, London W5 5SA,
in Australia by Transworld Publishers (Australia) Pty Ltd,
15–25 Helles Avenue, Moorebank, NSW 2170,
and in New Zealand by Transworld Publishers (NZ) Ltd,
3 William Pickering Drive, Albany, Auckland.

Reproduced, printed and bound in Great Britain by
Cox & Wyman Ltd, Reading, Berks.

To Georgina, Adam and Daniel.
Also to Rosalia and Jesus, Angel and Ana, Consuela,
José, José and José

ACKNOWLEDGEMENTS

Some short elements of this book have appeared in the *Sunday Times Travel Book 1986*, and in *Country Life*.

The plant book referred to on page 177 is *The Collins Guide to Tropical Plants*.

The reader will not find the name Dalmácija on any map of Andalusia. The names of some neighbouring villages and towns have also been changed.

H S-D

1987

CONTENTS

1

ANDALUSIA

And citizens dream of the south and west,
And so do I.

Thomas Hardy

Looking at the Mediterranean Sea in my school atlas, I used to think it resembled a dragon, facing west and swimming – to judge from the upflung arm of the Adriatic – in a racing crawl. Its eyes, the Balearics, were of unequal sizes, and it had lost its tail, as sometimes do the little dragons of the region, the geckoes, when seized by predators. The outline of its littoral was picked out on the map with a layer of bright blue, as though its whole form were glowing with St Elmo's fire: and this radiance, together with the fabulous significance of its shape, gave the Mediterranean an aura of enchantment, which grew and grew in my mind, the more I learnt of its history. Wars, quests, odysseys, crusades, the clash of empires, the efflorescence of art and the evolution of political and religious systems . . . so much of interest and importance had taken place around or upon this wonderful sea.

So captivated was I, that I was soon drawn towards the dragon, irresistibly and repeatedly. Before it began to devour me – to ingest great pieces of my life – I made a number of darting approaches to it which, so to speak, scratched its hide at various points. But these brief visits merely made me greedy for a closer relationship with the Mediterranean. Instead of a passing acquaintanceship with various different places, I wanted to develop a deeper knowledge of one. The only way to achieve this, it seemed clear, was to live there. I would buy a house.

It must be a cheap house, and an old house. It must be in a countryside of great natural beauty, and scant human habitation. It must be a sunny house, and an accessible house, so that I could flee to it whenever the grey skies of England threatened to congeal my soul. I would spend whole winters there – become a migrant like the warblers. While my friends were buttoning their overcoats to the neck, I would be marinading in warmth and wine. Somewhere in the far south I would achieve the Gilbertian idyll, and ripen at my ease, growing on the sunny side . . .

But where would this house be? On the tip of the dragon's left ear, perhaps, in one of the vertiginous villages of the Cinqueterre: or in the earhole itself, the porphyry massif of Corsica, so powerfully fragrant with the gummy incense of the maquis that it could be smelt fifty miles out at sea. Or perhaps in the beast's armpit, among the stone igloo-dwellings of Puglia: or on the elbow, on a Dalmatian hillside above a walled town with the lion of St Mark carved above its gateway. There were many memories to confuse my choice, together with tangible relics of other places, too. On my dining-room wall were two round-bellied amphorae, whorled with the incrustations of sixteen centuries of marine life, from the dragon's lumbar region, the coast of Caria. And in an old leather stud-box on my dressing-table were two Roman coins and three tesserae – white, black and ochre – from a mosaic-floored villa situated near the Adam's apple (if dragons have such things) at Thurburbo Maius, whose ruins stand in golden isolation among the wispy cornfields of Tunisia.

In the end I chose none of these places. Instead I alighted, like a fly, on the dragon's nostril. This spot, the fabled shore of southern Spain, had the warmest winters in Europe, the clearest skies west of the Aegean, and mountains higher than any except the Alps. Inland lived a peasantry whose way of life had barely been touched by the passage of centuries. As a whole, the country had a flavour of its own, as pungent and elusive as that of the olives which grew there. If my intention had been to look deeper into a foreign nature, then the Spanish temper – a source of fascination and admiration for scores of writers and travellers – would provide a fertile subject. The Spaniards were complex, subtle, in many ways self-contradictory. 'When I speak of Spain,' wrote one of its poets, 'I speak of Man.'

And Spain met another of my requirements. I was looking for an extreme. I wanted somewhere as different from England as possible. If I was to find sunshine, it must be scorching sunshine. If there were to be hills, they must be rough and brown – I could find smooth green hills nearer home. The flowers must be rampant exotica, not roses: even the weeds must be acanthus and wild herbs, not nettles. Spain had all these things. Despite its accessibility, it was at the edge of Europe: and countries at the extremities are indeed the most extreme, the least European. Turkey is Asian, the Balkans are Siberian, and Spain is African, especially southern Spain – African in its appearance, and African through its history.

'When I named the countries of the West,' wrote Victorian traveller Charles Doughty, 'Amin enquired if there were not Moslemin living in some of them. I told him that long ago a rabble of Moghrebies had invaded and possessed themselves of the florid country of Andalus – Andalusia was a glorious province of Islam. The Arabian plant grew in the Titanic soil of Europe to more excellent temper and stature, and there were many bulbul voices among them, in that land of the setting sun gladdened with the genial vine. Yet the Arabs decayed in the fruition of that golden soil, and the robust nephews of them whom

13

their forefathers had dispossessed, descending from the mountains, reconquered their own country. As I said this, "*Wellah guwiym*! then they must be strong people," answered Amin Mohamud.'

Andalusia bears the imprint of all the civilizations which have resided there, but of none more than the Arabs. The 'rabble of Moghrebies' was anything but a rabble. Superbly led, fired with the new faith of Muhammad, they were the froth on the crest of a wave which had swept east through Persia, south through Arabia, and west through Egypt along the whole northern coast of Africa, pervasive as a swarm of locusts. Reaching the Atlantic, their general Okba rode into the ocean up to the girth of his camel and cried, 'Allah, if these waters did not stop me, I would bear yet further the knowledge of thy name!'

Although legend blames the Arab invasion of Spain on treachery and a slighted woman, it was inevitable that this explosive young nation would have spilled over into the decadent kingdom of the Visigoths. There, across a mere ten miles of water, was a mirror-image of the hard African coastline on which they stood — but transformed by a 500-year time-warp back into the fertility of the Roman era, when Africa was the granary of the empire and the corn around Thurburbo Maius grew twice the height it is today. Then, the territories along the shore were rich in trees and crops and flowers: the final flourishing of a benevolent climatic era when, as depicted in the Tassili cave-paintings in southern Algeria, giraffes and antelopes abounded in the vast hinterland. Since that time, North African life had become harder. The rains had gone, together with everything that depended on them, as the sands of the Sahara encroached relentlessly northwards. But Andalusia was, by comparison, a paradise, a million-acre oasis, a place where the Arab conception of heaven touched earth. In his advance publicity for the invasion its instigator, Sheikh Mousa, had described southern Spain as 'Syria for the beauty of sky and soil; Yemen for climate; India for flowers and perfume; Egypt for fruit; China for precious metals.' The bait was irresistible. Crossing the straits of Gibraltar in 711, the Moors took three days to crush the vastly larger army of the Visigoths and only two years to accomplish what had taken the Romans two hundred, and conquer the whole of the Iberian peninsula apart from a few isolated pockets. That first major confrontation, on the banks of the Guadalete, was one of the most decisive battles in history.

The Moors settled into Spain for seven centuries. Their stay there, and the protracted campaign by the Christians to eject them, provided the most continuous confrontation between Christianity and Islam, and the most fruitful opportunity for the former to learn from the arts and sciences of the latter. Through the interface of Spain, the ideas of the Middle East were able to filter into comparatively backward Europe. The Moors were architects, engineers, philosophers, mathematicians, gardeners, artists and musicians. Their farmers irrigated the land as it has never been irrigated since, and imported crops which were unknown in the west: rice and sugar, figs and cotton, oranges and lemons. Their merchants built up flourishing industries in minerals, wool, silk, glass, paper, weapons and leather. Their scholars transmitted the learning of the Greeks, and their courtiers passed on new styles in dress, music and decoration. Spain, and especially Andalusia where the Moors survived longest, became the most cultured, liberal and luxurious state of the Mediterranean world: and its largest city, Córdoba, grew to be second in size only to Constantinople.

The Moorish irruption was not, of course, the first. The earliest invaders had come from the same direction, but on foot, across what was then an isthmus at Gibraltar. Palaeolithic man left many relics in Andalusia, spanning several centuries. (The Pileta caves at Benaoján are 25,000 years old, predating the more famous cave-paintings at Altamira.) Next came the insatiably questing Phoenicians – and with them the growth of legend. To these visitors from the eastern Mediterranean, and to those that followed them, Andalusia was the uttermost achievable settlement of the world. Beyond it, outside the Pillars of Hercules, lay the icy, perilous, monster-infested waters of the Outer Ocean, into which the setting sun sank with a hiss as of hot metal. It was an enchanted land. Just as the Arabs, later, saw it as an earthly paradise, so the ancient world associated it with the after-life. This was where Homer sited the Elysian fields, the last resting-place of heroes and patriots. The Guadalete – site of the Moorish victory – is an Arabization of River Lethe, the river of the underworld whose waters brought eternal sleep.

The first tourist on the Costa del Sol was Ulysses, who, like many since, was having trouble with his return ticket. Hercules also passed this way, but he was on a business trip – rustling the cattle of Geryon from Erytheia, now the Isla Leon near Cádiz. As for Cádiz itself, it typifies the way in which, here on the rim of the Mediterranean world, myth has meshed with history. According to Pliny this city was a fragment of the lost Atlantis, which was submerged beneath the sea in the same cataclysm that dried up the Sahara. It was also equated with the fabled Tartessus, capital of a vanished kingdom famed for its silver mines. This was the Tarshish of the Bible, whence sailed the argosies that bore Solomon his three-yearly tribute of gold and silver, amber and ivory, apes and peacocks. For a millennium Cádiz – or Tartessus or Tarshish – was one of the great markets of the Mediterranean; and under the Romans it became the second largest city of the Empire, the Paris of its time, *Gades Jocosae*, where men came to savour, in the words of Rose Macaulay, its 'dancing girls, its erotic music and rich varieties of fish, its fabulous oriental luxury, its sea air and hot sun, its public entertainments, its mystic religious miracles and rites, its ebbing and flowing wells, its temples and altars to the god Hercules or Melkarth, to the maritime Aphrodite, to the forces of nature and time, life and death.'

Throughout this period the domination of Andalusia changed hands many times. The Tartessians were succeeded by the Phoenicians, who were followed by the Greeks. These two invading races fought it out for centuries, and finally compromised. The Phoenicians settled Málaga, Almuñécar and most of the Andalusian shore. The Greeks retreated to the Costa Blanca and the Balearics. Little of their influence now remains, except for their importation of the vine (thank heavens) and the olive. Next came the Carthaginians, who became lords of Andalusia for three hundred years, until they were beaten out of it by the Romans.

The Romans made Spain the western corner of their empire: the breeding ground of emperors, philosophers and the stoutest legions in their army. They were the first invaders to dominate the whole peninsula – not merely the accessible shorelines, but also the austere and inhospitable interior. In so doing they made two important bequests: settled civilization, and the Christian religion. The former was disrupted by the next invasion – from the north this time – by the Vandals and Visigoths: but Christianity survived, and provided the ideological underpinning for the subsequent campaign to eject the last invaders, the Moors.

The Reconquest – the only ultimately successful crusade – ground on for two centuries, gradually scouring every cranny of the hinterland clean of Arab domination, moving on slowly and bitterly from valley to valley and from town to town, until only the kingdom of Granada remained. But this continued to flourish for another two hundred years. At last the Catholic Monarchs trundled forward their newly acquired lombards (the first use in Spain of siege artillery) and smashed down the Arab fortresses one by one. The final campaign, described by Washington Irving with Homeric rumbustiousness, lasted ten years – the length of the Trojan War – and culminated in the surrender of Granada. Boabdil, the last of the Moorish kings, was compelled to abdicate his earthly paradise, and departed over the Sospirio del Moro, the pass of sighs. The Arab occupation of Spain was over.

After the Reconquest, the geo-political power of Spain expanded. (It was in the same year as the final recapture of Granada, indeed the very same month, that Columbus was dispatched to open his Pandora's box in the west and make Spain an immediate world power.) Yet in many ways it was the achievement of the Moors that represented the apogee of Spanish civilization, and their departure led to a cultural decline. This was immediate. Writing only thirty-four years later, the Venetian ambassador observed of the province of Granada that the farms of the Moors were already in ruins: 'for the Moorish population is diminishing, and it is they who kept everything in order; the Spaniards here, as in other parts of Spain, are not industrious and disdain work.' The *mañana* syndrome appears to have set in early. The delighted spirits of the Arabs, their intellect and energy and aesthetic vision, became submerged by the more plodding and backward mentality of the north.

But some of the Moorish character (together with their architecture) lived on among the Andalusians. 'They are an insolent, frivolous people, fond of dancing and song. The person in most esteem among them is invariably the greatest *majo*, and to acquire that character it is necessary to appear in the dress of a Merry Andrew, to bully, swagger and smoke continually, to dance passably and to strum the guitar.' Such was George Borrow's opinion, in 1843, of my future neighbours.

But I had encountered few Andalusian mannerisms of this kind on my own previous visits. The reality of the place seemed very different from its image. This, I later realized, was because the image had been largely concocted. The south of Spain has indeed been different from the rest ever since the Reconquest, and Castilians regard Andalusians with a mixture of amused tolerance and half-envy: but increasingly over the last century and a half Andalusia has subsumed a wider reputation and has come to represent, to foreigners, the very essence of Spain. Guitars and castanets . . . tiled patios and splashing fountains . . . gypsy dancers and bull-fighters . . . laughter and love . . . Figaro and Carmen and Don Juan. Much of this was the creation of the French – Gautier, Merimée, Bizet, Barrès – who elevated the more romantic Andalusian traits into national characteristics. And latterly the tour operators have taken over. The Costa del Sol – itself a catchpenny title coined by some latter-day publicist – now stands for a two-week sun-tan and cheap wine.

In any case there would be no great prevalence of *pasa dobles* and Merry Andrews where I was going. I would not be residing in any of the old Moorish cities, nor among the meretricious entertainments of the coastal resorts. I would be looking for a house in the hills, as remote as practicality permitted. I would be living among peasants. And their life, I knew, would be hard.

There are many peasants in Andalusia. A fifth of the people there are still engaged in agriculture, compared with western Europe's average of just over a twentieth. The fragmented terrain of Spain, and a communications network that has not radically improved since the Romans left, have ensured that rural life has remained unchanged to a degree which is barely credible in twentieth-century Europe. Richard Ford's comment in 1861 – 'The mule has always been much used in Spain, and the demand for them very great' – would be equally true today in most Spanish hill villages. The rural economy is still mule-based.

And it is not merely new technology which has been slow to advance, but also new doctrines. Deep in the wrinkled countryside, primitive beliefs survive. Spain is a land of magic. Gerald Brenan, who like me had gone house-hunting in the Andalusian uplands and lived there through the 1920s, had much to say on the subject of witches: until shortly before his arrival, they used to fly about in the dark, singing sweet music, stark naked and anointed with fat. Girls who learnt witchcraft commonly gave their young men a potion which transformed them into donkeys, on which they rode about in the air all night. The incidence of such practices, he said, increased with altitude. Clearly I had better check the contour-lines before I set out.

Similarly Nicholas Luard, writing of his life in Andalusia in the 1960s, claimed that every village has at least one witch and more probably two – a black and a white. The latter was more witch-doctor than witch. It was to her, instead of to the priest, that the villagers went for advice on all matters of practical importance – the slaughtering of pigs, for instance. It was vital to pick the right day. If the killing took place when the moon was thin, then the pig's blood would be thin too, and the black puddings a disaster. The most propitious time was when the moon was well rounded and waxing, at dawn after a night when the dew was light. Then the yield of sausages would be doubled.

Nor were bloodless sausages the only potential problem. There was also the matter of the Evil Eye. Brenan, again, confirmed its local prevalence. His servant had taken part in at least fifty ceremonies of exorcism. Beautiful children were particularly at risk: if 'looked at' the crowns of their heads would fall in and they would wither away. The cure was for a virgin called Mary to lay the afflicted child upon some twigs of *torvisco*, a local daphne which was sacred to the Devil.

The Evil Eye had been a menace for centuries. George Borrow, in his book *The Gypsies of Spain*, expatiated on the same matter at length. He too appended some precautions and cures. One could quote an appropriate verse from the Talmud, while grasping one's right thumb in the left hand: or one could apply the spittle of the person who had cast the spell, 'If it can be obtained'.

Evidently there were unexpected hazards to living in Andalusia, but I was not to be deterred. My dreams had long been full of the warm south, and Andalusia was where they must be realized. Bestirring myself, I decided the time had come for action, if my ambition was not to weaken and evaporate as ambitions are apt to do. Hold fast to the dreams of thy youth, wrote Herman Melville. I held fast and tightened my grip – helped by a second pair of hands. By now I had married. The quest for a piece of Andalusia would henceforth be a joint one.

Georgina, my wife, and I had several very clear ideas of what our Spanish house would be like, almost none of which was fulfilled by subsequent events. It would stand on a hill, in its own land. Around it the vineyards – our vineyards – would fall away in every direction, opening up immeasurable vistas of mountain scenery. On a clear day, which would mean any day, the perennial snows of the Sierra Nevada would gleam in the far distance beyond the intervening peaks and valleys. The solitude would be absolute. No other human habitation would be visible except, a few hundred yards down the slope, the white cottage of Manuel, our only neighbour. Manuel would tend our vines in our absence, and press the pungent life-enhancing wine which would fill the portly barrels in the *bodega* under the house. From time to time, on winter evenings, he would stroll up to our house with his guitar, and as we sat before blazing logs of olive and eucalyptus, his high sandpapery voice would juggle the tumbling and cascading notes of the *cante jondo*, the gipsy music of the south. Perhaps his daughter Carmen, as slim and sleek as an elver, would dance for us. I had a very clear vision of Carmen in my mind. Georgina wasn't so sure that Manuel would have a daughter.

The house itself would be tall, old, graceful. High doors would open on to the terrace, veiled by heavy wooden shutters in summer, so that only narrow frets of sunshine would penetrate the cool interior, half lighting the tiled floor . . . the massive roof timbers . . . the big hooded fireplace . . . the dark coffered furniture . . . the spines of a thousand books . . . the elaborately framed mirror that hung on the whitewashed wall like a cyclopean eye in a pale face . . .

Beyond this room a further door would lead into an interior patio, open to the azure sky, where we would sit in cold weather, secure from the mountain breezes, wrapped in the heavy perfume of the jasmine that decked the encircling walls. Big Ali Baba pots would stand filled with rare lilies that contributed their own varieties of fragrance. A fountain would play in the centre, embroidered with bright tiles. Somewhere within earshot a brace or two of Doughty's bulbuls would be trilling, or chirping, or whatever bulbuls do.

Further research cast some doubt on the likely prevalence of bulbuls. My bird book marked them 'accidental Spain', being predominantly an Asian and African species. But in compensation the book suggested that the oleander thickets and orange groves around our house would be infested with hoopoes, bee-eaters, rollers, perhaps even an errant parakeet. Andalusia was reputedly rich in wild life. To the west, in the delta of the Guadalquivir, lay the Coto Doñana, the largest bird sanctuary in Europe, inhabited also by deer, boar, genets, wild camels and lynxes. In the east of the province were the plunging valleys and castle-crowned crags of the Sierra de Cazorla, another game reserve where hunters came to shoot wild goat, stag and moufflon. There were several rare birds, I read, at Cazorla, including the *quebranta-huesos*, the bone-breaker, with a wing-span of ten feet. The name derives from the bird's habit of dropping bones from a great height on to rocks, in order to break them open so it can extract the marrow. Predators have long used this hazardous technique: Aeschylus was killed by a tortoise dropped on his head by an eagle. The eagle mistook his bald pate for a rock.

There is a specific reason for Andalusia's large population of birds. Twice a year millions migrate from Africa to Europe and back again. Most of them take two routes only, in order to avoid a long sea passage which would deprive them of the necessary thermals. One is via the Bosphorus, the other is across the Straits of Gibraltar. During the migration seasons, when the conditions are right, the sky north of the Straits is dense with birds, day and night: not merely swallows and warblers, but also birds of prey: eagles and hawks, falcons and kites and harriers.

However, we would be house-hunting in an area some way east of there. Most of Andalusia is a vast basin centred on the Guadalquivir and Genil rivers, shelving up towards the mountains of the east, and containing the greatest of the Arab cities, Seville and Córdoba and Granada. But south of this, between the coastal mountains and the sea, lies another strip of land, so narrow that it barely registers on the map. Here the climate is more equable, being fanned by the sea breezes in summer and protected from the north winds of winter by the Sierra de Tejeda, the Sierra de Almijara and finally by the Sierra Nevada, whose highest peaks are dusted with the sand of the Sahara. It is this shore-line which carries the most continuous legacy of history, much of it still visible. Between the concrete wens of the tourist developments the old Phoenician towns – now in Arab dress – still pile their white houses on to knuckles of rock, castle-crowned, that jut like islands from seas of sugar cane. Elsewhere the coast is puckered into narrow coves, too small for hotels, where fishermen's cottages line the gritty beaches and Moorish watch-towers stand on the encircling promontories. Behind them rise the mountains, always in view. These mountains were our goal.

To the eye of the visitor looking up from the shore, the foothills of these Sierras are studded with small white villages that shine like grains of rice on steeply crumpled baize. Somewhere up there would be people who would help us find our house. But there are dozens of such villages, scattered above the entire southern coastline from Gibraltar to Almeria. Their character varies from end to end, as does the terrain. To the west is the Marbella gold-coast, where the Arabs have returned with a vengeance. To the east the hills crumble to desert, a favourite shooting-ground for cowboy movies. Georgina and I could not possibly cover this whole extent, nor would we want to.

We picked a certain sector of the coast. The main highway ran along the shore, and from it jutted short spurs of road or track which headed inland until they hit the mountains and stopped. These little roads would be our access to the upland villages. There were only half a dozen such roads in our chosen sector, and each touched only two or three villages. Thus our task was a finite one. So was the time we allowed ourselves. We would need a high strike rate, in terms of local contacts, and we were not sure how to achieve it. We would try to enlist the support of local estate agents, but we suspected they would not deal in the kind of houses we wanted. We would have to talk to the villagers direct.

This would not be easy: how did one meet villagers? It would require a certain social finesse to inaugurate a business conversation with a total stranger in some precipitous alleyway. We decided that the only possible course of action would be to find the bar in every village on our planned itinerary, and make enquiries of the bartender and his clientele. This prospect cheered us considerably. We bought our air tickets, and began to make ambitious marks on our road map. We rummaged in drawers for mosquito-repellent and sun-tan cream: it was early autumn, and Andalusia might still be hot. We assembled a sum of money, a small sum: we had heard rumours of houses in the Spanish hinterland which could be bought for £50. We told few of our friends what we were about, in case we failed. We packed Brenan and Laurie Lee and Jan Morris and a large dictionary. At a rigorously early hour typical of the cheaper charter flights we boarded a plane, bleary with sleep but filled with hope. The game was afoot. The time for the fulfilment of dreams was at hand.

2

THE SEARCH

A cloudless sky and glowing sun may offer great and deserved attractions to the invalid, whose hopes are all centred on climate: but let no-one be tempted to fix on Málaga, as a residence, for any other reason. Society there is none: and with the exception of the theatre, there are no amusements whatever which could contribute to make time pass agreeably, and no objects of interest to attract the attention of the traveller.

Lady Louisa Tenison, 1853

As we drove away from the airport in the mid-afternoon, the terrain was indistinct, as though viewed through mosquito netting. The heat-haze veiled the distant features and softened the near ones, leaving us with an unfulfilled impression of empty mountains behind a teeming plain. The latter was the medium for a variety of activities, agricultural and industrial. We passed fields of sugar-cane and tomatoes and beans, a brick works and a beer factory, and a shanty town that merged into the suburbs of the city which lay ahead. Before we reached it we crossed a river of deep still water lined with eucalyptus trees, which disconcerted us by its absolute resemblance to an African swamp. The incongruity was, in local terms, even more marked than we then realized: this was the only river we were to see in the next fortnight which had any water in it.

The city was tall and tawdry, the colour of dust, enhanced only by Moorish towers and castle walls scaling a pine-green hill, and by a sober strip of park – a long Edwardian-style promenade – which ran beside the harbour. The hot, still air lapped in through the windows of the car. When Joseph Townsend visited the city in 1786, he was told that the summer heat kept the entire population indoors until dusk, when they would rush into the sea and bathe for hours. (The women were segregated in the water by musket-toting guards: but the more persistent of the men would run the blockade by disguising themselves as female attendants.)

Passing through the city without stopping, we entered what appeared to be an endless vacation-land, equipoised between dream and nightmare, one's judgement dependent on the style of one's ambitions. On the rolling slopes above the highway burgeoned a thickly planted crop of villas, some wealthily isolated on palm-crested knolls, others clustered into conurbations which mimicked, more extensively and symmetrically, the hill villages which were our goal. Every wall was white, every entrance arched, every roof tiled. Wrought-iron caged the windows, and from the artfully angled gables tapering chimneys sprouted like young shoots of asparagus. The gardens were planted with shrubs and creepers that bore, to our eyes, outlandish blossoms: magenta bougainvillea, scarlet hibiscus, sky-blue plumbago, pink and white oleander. The capitals of the palm trees exploded in the shimmering air like fireworks, yuccas and aloes bristled with dagger-leaves sharp enough to transfix flesh, and long creamy trumpet flowers dangled from daturas, the Moon-trees whose sap causes blindness.

For a while the road deviated away from these excesses and ran along the beach, where the scenery was less aggressive. Painted fishing boats were drawn up on the shore amid coils of rope and glinting glass floats, and at frequent intervals stood thatched restaurants, like cheerful oases in the sand, each with its cluster of chequered table-cloths, and with a stack of firewood piled in readiness for the evening barbecues. On the

27

landward side of the road fishermen sat in the doorways of a continuous row of low white hovels which had so far survived the tourist invasion.

By now the sun was low, and after a few miles we decided to stop for the night, picking at random a small and superannuated hotel which stood a trifle uneasily among the pert new villas, as though aware that it had been eclipsed by the multi-storey megaliths we had passed along the way. It was late in the season and there were few other guests, but this did not noticeably improve the quality of our welcome. Highway-based hostelries the world over tend to be possessed of a kind of numbed malevolence, and this place was no exception. The flabbiness of the grilled fish belied the presence of the fishing boats a few yards away. A persistent dusting of sand had blown under the ill-fitting door of our bedroom, and nothing emerged from the hot-water tap except a small centipede.

When we strolled, blinking, into the sunlight the following morning the air had cleared. Inland, the big hills now stood out sharply, and like the psalmist we lifted up our eyes to them, as to a better world. But before venturing towards them, we decided to look for advice. An estate agent, surely, would be able to point us in certain directions: perhaps would even have some suitable farmhouses on his books. Luckily such practitioners were easy to find in this rent-a-villa landscape. In the next town along the road we saw an office which did not look too grandiose, and went in.

It was small, spry and modern. The window-bay was filled with a large model of a new residential development. Shining white blocks of flats rose up like wedding cakes, and between them mossy expanses of garden, thickly studded with toy trees, sloped down to a vitreous lagoon where miniature sail-boats stood reflected in the glass. I wondered if the proprietor played with them in the evenings, behind lowered blinds, tacking his Lilliputian flotilla to and fro in obedience to an insensible sirocco.

He raised his eyes from the morning paper as we entered. He was a large elderly man in a short-sleeved white shirt, pale-complexioned despite the weather outside his office window, with a jutting jaw and eyes of the same blue as the looking-glass lake which served to peddle his wares. He did not look Spanish, nor was he. He was, as we later discovered, a Dutchman who had spent all his working life in East Africa before semi-retiring to Spain. Now he dabbled in real estate.

We told him our intentions. We were looking for a house in the foothills, preferably old, remote and cheap. The man flinched, and his eyes flickered despairingly towards the toy apartment blocks, which were self-evidently modern, accessible and expensive. He didn't deal with country property, he said. It was hard to find, few customers were interested in it, and there was a multitude of problems in buying it. What problems? we asked, dismayed. He motioned to us to sit down, and settled back, in avuncular fashion, in his plastic-padded chair. Behind him a desk fan swung its moon-face to and fro, like a tennis spectator.

The remote country houses, he explained, were mostly *cortijos*, small shacks which were only used during the harvest season. Because they were not permanent habitations, they had neither water nor electricity. The absence of the latter could be circumvented by the use of bottled gas for the cooker and fridge and by a petrol-driven generator for light (and solar electricity was beginning to be available) – but the real problem was water. The buyer could try sinking a well beside the house, but he could only do this *after* making the purchase, with no guarantee of success. Or water could be pumped up from a well in a stream-bed – if there was one nearby: if not, sufficient land would need to be bought to include one, which would sharply raise the price.

Moreover, he said, warming to his theme, there were local water regulations. In some communities, one was only allowed to pump water to an outside tap, not into the house. Why? we asked. Because water was scarce, he said. This regulation meant that a household's consumption was limited by a woman's capacity to carry buckets indoors. Farmers didn't like the idea of a foreigner squandering their precious water supply by taking half a dozen showers a day.

Was land expensive? we asked, faced with the possibility of needing to buy some to secure our water supply. How much was it per square metre? There was only one answer to that, he replied: buy the land, measure it, and then we could work out how much it cost per square metre. Spanish peasants didn't know the precise area of their land, only that it ran from this olive tree to that white stone and round to the edge of the gully over there. One farmer had said to him, 'Square metres? I don't have any square metres on my land.' In any case, prices tended to relate to pride and to farming values, rather than to the realities of development. A peasant would base his asking price on the size of his grapes or almonds – despite the fact that the land was being sold as a building site.

And what about legalities? we asked. Would we be able to buy a house on our own, without the services of an estate agent? Were there any pitfalls? Well, we'd find it rather different from buying an English house, replied our friend. His eyes twinkled and his false teeth rattled with relish at the thought of the complications that confronted us.

First there was the question of the ownership of the property, he said, extending his fingers carefully to emphasize each point, as though covering the stops of an invisible clarinet. A house might belong jointly to five brothers – including one in Madrid and another in

Argentina. It would be essential to ensure the agreement of all five before buying. Or sometimes a single room in a house would belong to the next-door resident, through an old agreement. In that case we could find, after moving in, that our neighbour was entitled to stable his mule in our sitting-room.

There were various levels of document to ensure security of tenure. Some emptors were inclined to skip much of the paperwork, he said disapprovingly, but short-cuts were foolish. We must sew up every legality. We wouldn't want some bandy-legged gaucho knocking on our door in five years' time, claiming ownership of our house.

There was silence in the little office after this discourse, except for the variometric whisper of the fan. Nothing about this venture looked promising so far, and I began to wonder when the next flight left for London. The agent stood up. Business was slack at this time of year, he said, so why didn't we close the office down and go and have a drink. He'd give us some advice about Andalusian builders. If we ever found a house in the hinterland, we would need to modernize it. As for the legalities, we needn't worry about them. He'd handle them for us. He couldn't help us to find what we were looking for, but he'd help us to buy it.

We picked an outdoor table at a nearby bar, and sat down in the shade of a huge yucca, whose leaves sprouted at the top of a twenty-foot trunk like a jagged tiara around the rich coiffure of its blossom, white against the intense blue of the sky.

The Dutchman, Jacob, relaxed over his beer, and his strong corrugated face reflected an avuncular interest in our quest. He was a kindly man, and we came to know him well over the next few years. During his retirement here he had developed an interest in the history of the region, and was something of a scholar. He lived in a fragrant pinewood on a steep knoll above the coastal highway. The house had a curving verandah with a comprehensive view down the shore to Málaga and on towards Gibraltar: but when we called on him there, on a subsequent visit, it was plain that the grander assets of his home were never used. For all his amusement at our search for rural property, Jacob himself lived like a rustic. He and his wife shunned the verandah with its well-upholstered lounging chairs, and spent all their leisure in a little patio round the back, crudely scraped out of the hillside, and roofed with cracked and irregular sheets of transparent plastic, weighted with rocks against the onshore breezes. Its floor was paved – evidently by Jacob himself – with what looked like left-over scraps of building materials. Tools and broken bits of furniture lay scattered among the flower-pots, and the counter-weight for a ramshackle sliding door was a beer bottle filled with sand hanging from a pyjama cord. The old Hollander had acquired the self-sufficient mentality of an Andalusian villager.

As such he was well qualified to advise us, now, on the local idiosyncrasies we would encounter in renovating a house. The problems, he said as he poured another beer, were two-fold, relating first to Andalusian houses and second to Andalusian builders. (Again his fingers sounded two notes on the dialectical clarinet.) The old houses, he explained, were mostly built of rubble, cemented together like a Christmas pudding. This method allowed the peasants to use local materials – rocks off the hillsides – and the resulting buildings were admirably suited to the climate: the crude walls, as thick as a medieval barbican, kept out the heat of summer and the cold of winter. But such masonry was hazardous to work with. Opening an aperture for a new window or door, or even a water pipe, risked bringing the whole wall tumbling down.

Unfortunately we would not be able to rely on a builder's counsel in such circumstances. Due to the innate sunniness and optimism of his nature, an

Andalusian would far rather agree with his client's proposal – any proposal – than put a damper on proceedings by raising objections. It was friendlier to say yes than no. And pride was a factor, too: no builder would admit that a job was impracticable, any more than an official would admit to ignorance of local regulations.

As for time-scales, Jacob hoped that we would not be expecting too precise a schedule, or too close an approximation to the length of time quoted at the outset. The problem was not so much the *mañana* mentality: contrary to popular belief Spanish labourers were generally hard-working. But if they were part of a rural community, as they were likely to be in our case, they would be bound by wider loyalties. Foreigners were amazed, said Jacob, that construction workers would down tools in the middle of a relatively well-paid job in order to help their neighbours – free – with the harvesting of the grapes or almonds or olives. Financially it made no sense, but in terms of the survival of the countryside it was essential. If the crops were not gathered in, the farmers would lose their livelihood and the villages would wither.

What about the standard of workmanship? we asked. Could local builders be relied upon to do a competent job? Jacob smiled. It was the smile of a parent parrying an awkward question from a child. Yes, he replied, most builders were competent. The Spaniards were a manually practical race. Every man could mend a car or build a house. But, he added, one might occasionally find that they were working to broader tolerances than we would regard as normal. Meaning what? we queried. Meaning, he explained, that they were apt to be, well, over-relaxed about any little problems that might emerge after the work was finished. He gave us an example. An American of his acquaintance had renovated a local house and moved in. After a few months in residence, he had paid a furious visit to

the builder who had done the work. The place was
uninhabitable, he cried. What was the matter? asked
the builder courteously. The roof leaked, complained
the American: every time there was a cloudburst a
stream of water flowed across his sitting-room floor.
How often did this happen? asked the Spaniard. It
had happened three times in the past winter, said the
American. And for how long each time? Well, at least
a couple of hours. The builder looked at his enraged
client with genuine puzzlement: was it possible, he
asked, that the *Señor* was so concerned about a roof
which only gave trouble for six hours a year?

With this Parthian shot, Jacob rose from his chair. He
must return to his office, he said. But if we succeeded
in finding a suitable house – the inflexion of his voice
implied he was prepared to offer long odds against it
– then he would be glad to give us all the help we
needed in securing the sale, and in making the place
habitable. Georgina and I eyed his retreating figure with
both relief and regret. We felt we had made a friend, but
his departure left us with a sense of isolation. From now
on our quest was ours alone, and nothing Jacob had said
suggested it would be an easy one.

We drove out of the town, along the coastal road.
After a couple of miles a side-road appeared, leading
inland. We stopped to examine the map. The road
wound among the foothills for half a dozen miles,
before stopping at a small village. Another village lay
along the way. Both were amongst our targets for the
search. We turned up the road.

For a few hundred yards we passed ornate driveways
where the noon sun flashed from the paintwork of well-
polished cars. Fat men in shorts brandished hose-pipes
over little lawns of hard spiky grass. There was no
shortage of water here, nor of money. The place looked
like a tropical Surbiton. Juvenal said that poverty makes
man ridiculous: wealth can have the same effect. But

suddenly we were through, and the twentieth century vanished as abruptly as if a door had closed behind us. Now the road meandered beside a dried-up river-bed, through empty country. As far as the eye could see, from the fractured rim of the ill-made road to the tall horizon of hills, there was not a single blade of grass. The land was planted with almonds and olives, between which the earth was bare except for some half-dried thistles, like stubble on an unshaven chin, and occasional tall clumps of bleached fennel. Even the almond trees had shed many of their leaves in the heat of summer, and were attenuated to black-barked skeletons. Only the olives retained their sea-green foliage. Otherwise the pervading colours were those of a Nash landscape, umbers and ochres and greys. Even the distant blue of the Sierras had vanished behind the diminishing horizon. The African antecedents of this place were suddenly very strong in our minds. We felt as though we had strayed to the fringe of the Sahara.

On the far side of the river-bed we could see occasional examples of the little white *cortijos* which Jacob had described to us. Some were finely situated on shoulders of hillside, but none was approachable by any road. We wondered wildly if we would have to invest in a mule. On our side of the ravine there was no sign of human habitation, partly because our view was obscured by the steepness of the slope above us, and by long hedges of prickly-pear cacti which brandished their flanges against the sky like huge fleshy hands, on which the bright fruits gleamed like exotic jewellery. Weaving our way through this austere countryside, we rounded a bend of the road and saw, ahead of us, the first of the two villages. It lay below the level of the road, spilling out into the valley like an overturned bag of sugar. The outermost of the white houses extended along a narrow finger of rock in a graceful composition which was as far removed from the rectilinear grid-plan of a modern town as is a haiku from an instruction manual.

We drove down into a small square which opened off the road. On three sides it was surrounded by two-storey buildings, with wrought-iron balconies which gave the impression of boxes in a miniature theatre overlooking a dusty stage. The fourth side was open, a narrower extension of the square, from which a street led away between two ranks of irregularly connected houses, diminishing as it went until it passed beneath an arch. That way, we guessed, lay the jutting outcrop of the village which we had seen from above. Two other paths led out of the square, up steep flights of steps which threaded between the houses. A further stair-case climbed up to one of the balconies. All the rough geometry of white masonry was given sharp definition by the fierce sun. There were no people to be seen. Screwing up our eyes against the stabbing brightness, we climbed out of the car and went in search of a bar.

Eventually we found one down a side street. Apart from a soft-drinks sign beside the door it looked like any other house. Drawing aside the sheet which hung across the doorway, we went in. After the glare of the sun, the interior was as dark as if we had walked into a cupboard. Peering across the room we detected a tile-topped bar. There were no bar stools, and nothing on the counter. This was unusual. A Spanish bar of any size and pretentions would have had a selection of snacks – *tapas* – laid out for inspection: anchovies in olive oil, prawns, olives, slices of country sausage. Here, however, there was a more substantial alternative. On a table behind the bar stood a metal stand like a small set of stocks, in which was held a ham, partly sliced. Half a dozen others hung from the ceiling, the famous Serrano hams, matured in caves in the Sierras. They were whole legs – complete with trotters – and the leathery hide of pinkish sepia which covered their haunches gave them a look of mummified permanence apparently incompatible with anything as transitory as eating.

At the other end of the ceiling hung a bunch of laurel leaves. It appeared to serve no purpose, being too desiccated to offer much in the way of decoration – but Georgina's eye, attuned now to the gloom, detected an odd silhouette among the leaves. A chameleon hung there. It was motionless apart from the occasional swivelling of an eye, like a ball-in-socket ventilator on an aeroplane. There was no way the creature could climb down from its perch, nor was it intended to. It had a job to do. It was a living fly-trap. Any fly landing on the laurel leaves was within range of its long, sticky, whiplash tongue.

When we looked back at the bar there was a man standing behind it, short and broad-shouldered, typical of the stock which for many generations had contributed legions to the Roman army. (The local women are built along similar lines, and look equally capable of toting a 60 lb pack or swinging a *gladius*.) He shuffled along the bar towards us, limping, perhaps as a result of more recent legionary service: there was a faded photograph of him as a youth in military uniform on the wall, next to a poster for a forthcoming football match.

We asked for wine. Wine of the region? Yes, please. He stooped behind the bar and reappeared with a plastic jug from which he filled two tumblers with a liquid the colour of pale honey. This was our first encounter with the local wine – not the La Mancha red which had fuelled Sancho Panza and now filled the supermarkets along the coast, nor the nobler Rioja from north of Madrid, nor the treacle from Málaga, but the wine from this small group of villages, squeezed out on a handful of private presses and not to be found more than a few kilometres from its source, since it was drawn straight from the barrel and never bottled. The first swill of it hit my palate with something between a caress and a slap. It was aromatic, rich, druggy, with a flavour suggesting a compound of nectar and cough mixture in equal proportions. It was a flavour with which, in its many manifestations – sweet or medium-sweet or searingly dry – we were to become very familiar over the years ahead.

The man watched us as we drank. It was up to us to open the conversation. What a pretty village, we volunteered, for openers. He shrugged. We liked this part of Spain, we continued, slipping creakingly into our pre-rehearsed patter. We liked it so much that we would like to spend more time here. Longer holidays? he asked, with the polite indifference of someone who didn't take holidays himself. Not exactly longer holidays, I said: the fact was, we had a plan. A flicker of alarm crossed the man's face. He was clearly unused to foreigners arriving in his bar with plans: plans were apt to entail action . . . perhaps even on his part. Our plan, I continued boldly, taking a large gulp of wine, was to buy a house. Here. Did he know of anyone with a house for sale?

The bartender slowly removed his straw hat and turned it round in his hand, as though examining it for structural deficiencies, before replacing it on his head. Then he repeated my words back to me, one by one, weighing them to see if they made any more sense the second time round. We wanted to buy a house? Here? I realized that my lifelong ambition needed more justification than I had anticipated. We liked the sunshine, I explained a trifle defensively, and the tranquillity. This merely served to bemuse him further: the sunshine is the Spanish peasant's enemy for much of the year, and as for tranquillity, the young villagers were drifting away to the towns, looking for less tranquillity and more employment. A house *here*? he repeated, looking around as though we were planning to redecorate his bar. Here or hereabouts, I maintained stoutly: and in the meantime could we have two more glasses of wine and some *tapas* of the ham?

The tawny slivers came off the bone like axe-chippings from a California redwood. Unlike prosciutto, through which one can see the pattern of the plate, this Serrano ham was opaque, dense, and as fibrous as tarpaulin. It was the best ham I had ever tasted. And I was learning to coexist with the wine. We had a third round, and were beginning to construct the rudiments of a conversation with the bartender when there was a quick gleam of light from the doorway as the sheet was pulled aside, and in came a young man in a checked shirt and a well-pressed pair of cotton trousers. He leant on the counter and ordered a beer. After a couple of swallows he swivelled round in our direction. Were we looking for a house? he asked. If so, he could help us.

This was curious, as we had not seen the bartender leave the room. But there was no mistaking the offer — it was repeated and endorsed, and after finishing our respective drinks we left the bar, and the three of us climbed into our car.

A mile outside the village our guide motioned to us to turn off the road on to a track that ran alongside a gully. It was unpaved, and the dust rose to the level of the open windows, mingling in our nostrils with the pungent garlic-flavoured emanations from our passenger. In the flat gully-bottom, where the soil retained a trace of moisture, there were miniature plantations of beans and tomatoes, fenced with impromptu barricades of cactus. Above, on either side, the naked land, uncultivated except for the olive trees, sloped gently up to low ridges where the dun horizon met the cobalt sky.

We bumped along the track for half a mile or so, until the man told us to stop. We all got out. This was it, he said, here was our house. We looked around. Apart from some terracing among the olives, not one stone was to be seen standing upon another. We were surrounded, Ozymandias-like, by a most complete desolation, flickering in the afternoon heat and crackling with cicadas. A house, we said . . .

where? Here, he replied, stamping his leather sandal on the ground and raising a puff of dust. I had wild recollections of the troglodyte dwellings of Guadix a few dozen miles to the east, and began to peer anxiously around for signs of a subterranean entrance, or maybe a chimney sprouting through the tilth. Here was the place, repeated our guide, with a rush of pride: he stamped again, and began to strut around in widening circles. This land, it was his. Here was where we should build our house. He'd sell us a decent-sized plot.

There was a short silence – even the cicadas held their breath – while Georgina and I looked at each other and the man and the empty hillside. Then we explained that we had been looking for something a bit more – well – complete in the way of accommodation. He accepted this cheerfully enough, and chattered sociably all the way back to the village. But a dank gloom, stronger than the heat, settled on Georgina and me as we drove slowly back towards the coast, lacking the resolution to make an assault that day on the village that lay further up the road.

Things had not started well: first the baleful warnings of our Dutch Cassandra, and now this. We gloomily checked into an elderly hotel in a town a mile or two behind the coastline. The proprietress sat in a rocking chair at the entrance amid a dense jungle of potted palms and sprawling monsteras. She was dark and feline and almost invisible among the fronds. I had a fearful vision of her extended watchfully along a branch during the midnight hours, eyes glowing. The bedrooms gave on to an echoing, galleried central well, at the top of which, when we retired to bed, we could see the stars. Their uncertain flickering gave a muted message of hope.

But the next day saw us no nearer our goal. Following an abortive visit to the other village on the same road as the previous day, the afternoon saw us again bouncing along an earthen track with another guide, further along the coast. We were heading for a village on the far side of a small valley where there was reputedly a house for sale. After an atrociously rough mile the road suddenly widened and levelled. We commented on this to our guide. Yes, he said, it was because we were now driving along the bed of a dried-up river. Just as well it was dried-up, I said, with a flash of wit, a hint of Merry Andrew. Just as well it was summer, the man agreed. Why, what happened in winter? I asked, with growing apprehension. *¡Hombre!* – in winter the water was up to here, he replied, indicating the roof of the car. It was his turn to laugh, which he did immoderately. And the village, I asked, with no answering smile: how did one reach the village in winter? By swimming, perhaps, he replied, pantomiming an extravagant breast-stroke. Or by mule – there was a ford further upstream: and he gestured optimistically into the middle distance. But not by car, not for a couple of months each year. However, he explained encouragingly, this was not important. Nobody in the village had a car.

I stopped in the middle of the river-bed and did a lurching turn, avoiding various boulders with some skill. The man looked at us with surprise: why were we going back already? Georgina and I were brief with our excuses, knowing that they would seem effete to a local peasant. We tried to regard the débâcle philosophically, but there was no disguising the fact that our strike-rate so far was poor. Two tries, two failures.

The next day we actually found a house. It wasn't much of one, but it was the first time we had found ourselves face to face with bricks and mortar – well, rubble and mortar – which was accessible and for sale. The foray began on the beach. Georgina and I were sitting in one of the open-air restaurants, toes in the sand, shaded by a roof of bamboo slats, eating squid and sardines, when a man walked over from the bar and began to talk to us.

He was a fisherman, drinking his meagre profits. One of the yellow-and-green boats on the beach was his, and so no doubt were the squid. He wore a pair of khaki trousers bleached almost white by the sun and salt, and a shirt so heavily darned that its original colour was indeterminable. The same elements which had lightened his clothes had darkened his face to the colour of our table-top. It bore the wrinkles of fifty or sixty years, and also a disconcerting defect: the end of his nose was sliced off at an angle, revealing the septum and some bristly grey hairs. A shark? A dog? A knife? A congenital defect? One's mind raced through the possible causes, while one's eyes sought to avoid settling on the result.

Which hotel were we staying at? he asked. We explained that we were transient, and then – word-perfect by now – told him that we were looking for a house to buy. A house? A house in the countryside? His nose, what was left of it, pointed like a gun-dog's at its quarry. He had a house for sale, he said. The perfect house for us. A fine position. Some land. Water. Papers. Papers? Yes, the ownership was documented. There would be no complications in buying it. And was this house his? we asked, thinking it curious that a fisherman should also be a land-owner. Well, not exactly his, he admitted. In fact not his at all. But it belonged to a friend of his. He would act as intermediary.

The thought of an agent's fee was clearly acting on him as a powerful stimulant. He leant over our table and began to accompany his proposals with mime, in order to hammer them through the language barrier. Would we like to see the house? He pulled down the lower lid of one eye, revealing a rheumy interior. Afterwards we could meet his friend to talk the matter over – and he stuck out a leathery tongue, tapping the tip of it several times. We rapidly agreed, before he could make any more anatomically-endorsed suggestions. In that case, he said, when we had finished our meal, perhaps we

42

would like to come to his house, which he indicated to us.

It was one of a row of single-storey fisherman's cottages built along the beach. The man let us in through a tin gate, and we found ourselves in a long narrow yard. A very small dog with a large curling tail, like a four-legged Toby jug, waddled up and pee'd delicately on Georgina's shoe. Down one side of the yard was a raised vegetable bed planted with broad beans and onions, and with a large crop of camomile which, like Peter Rabbit's mother, the man used for making tea. There was an assortment of trees – an orange, an almond, a fig and a loquat – and a small cemented area roofed with a vine. Most of the available space, apart from a well-head, was filled with bicycle parts, an outboard motor, broken flower-pots, oil-cans, bedsprings and some coils of rope. On one of the posts supporting the vine hung a fishing net, which our friend had been mending.

He brought out two chairs, one with a leg missing. Could we wait a few minutes? He wanted to shave. Disappearing into a shack at the back of the yard, he reappeared after a short while, transfigured. Gone were the battered slacks and shirt. He now sported an elegant pair of linen trousers, a tweed jacket and a beret. Obviously the real-estate business required a certain standard of dress.

Off we went in our car along the coast road, turning on to a smaller road which we had already travelled that morning, in a fruitless visit to a village which lay along it. This time we passed the village, and turned off again on to a dirt track which wound up the hillside. Our passenger maintained a constant commentary on the scenery outside the car windows. Olives, he said, as though we had not seen such trees before. Fine olives. Almonds. A fig tree, see there, several fig trees. He gestured excitedly, at some peril to Georgina's driving.

Crossing a ridge, we found the countryside suddenly transformed by intensive farming. Bulldozers had ripped huge terraces out of the bare slopes, and the earth was covered, as though gift-wrapped, with acres of plastic through which sprouted rows of various crops. Tomatoes, cried our friend. See how they redden. Broad beans. Runner beans. Avocados. More avocados, very strong, giving much money. It was as though he owned them all personally.

A fine view, he said, as we surveyed the sheeted landscape, glistening in the afternoon sun. Very fine, we agreed, but this road was not so fine. The track had degenerated by now to a boulder-strewn ledge reminiscent of some of the less hospitable corners of Utah. The road was good, he maintained reproachfully: nevertheless it might be advisable if he got out and guided us down this next stretch, where he would suggest a little care. We slithered down a slope, and began to wonder where we were. We had evidently circumscribed a wide circle, and the sea now lay somewhere ahead. Stop here, said the man. Georgina edged the car between a rock and an antediluvian olive tree, and we disembarked.

We walked down a ridge past a patch of courgettes, and stopped outside a house which at first sight seemed about the size of a telephone kiosk. It was not exactly the extensive *hacienda* of our dreams. Standing in the doorway, and filling it, was a woman in black with a shock of grey hair like wire-wool. She could have walked into a cast for *Macbeth* without an audition. She raised a broom in welcome. I think it was a welcome.

Our guide ignored her, after a brief flurry of explanation, and bustled around indicating the extent of the land that went with the house. Most of it was on a 45-degree slope, but his vision was more exuberant than ours. A bulldozer could be brought in, he said, for no more than 20,000 pesetas, and all this could be terraced – he made a series of horizontal chopping gestures, like a karate black belt in training – and we could grow avocados. We listened, impressed. It seemed as hazardous as growing avocados on the north face of the Eiger. Spanish bulldozers must be as agile as moufflon. Those prickly pears would naturally have to go, he added, eliminating them with a sweep of the arm. On the other hand – as an alternative thought struck him – the fruits of prickly pears were worth money: he looked warily at us, assessing our attitude to prickly pears. And look at these fine almonds, he cried, moving further down the slope. And loquats. And this excellent carob tree. But the most important thing of all (this was clearly the peroration) was that there was water. Plenty of water, year round.

He jumped heavily down from the last of the ruined stone terrace walls to the level bed of the gully at the bottom. There was a miniature vegetable garden here, and he strode through it like Attila, plucking bean pods here and uprooting onions there, to demonstrate the excellence of the produce. Water, he repeated, as much as we needed, and very pure. We had arrived at a well-head, and all of us peered over the edge, as though to surprise the contents. Three faces peered back from ten feet below. They disappeared abruptly as the man threw down a large rusty tin attached to the end of a rope and pulled it up again, spraying water from several holes. He took a sip, hollowed his cheeks like a vintner assessing a Château Latour, and passed the tin to us. The water certainly tasted good, apart from the rust. And could this be pumped up to the house? we asked. Of course, he replied, nothing easier. We would put a cistern up *there*, from which we would draw water for the house, and also irrigate the avocado terraces *there* and *there.* His forefinger flickered across the slope above us as though landscaping the Hanging Gardens of Babylon.

We climbed back up the dusty path and asked if we could see inside the house. Sidling nervously past the witch, we went in. The interior consisted of two rooms, of which the larger, at the front of the house, had been subdivided into three. One of these, separated by a curtain, was evidently used as a kitchen. That is to say, it contained an open fireplace, where a blackened pot stood propped on a charred log. An earthenware water-jug sat plumply in a hollow-bottomed recess in a wall – a common feature of these peasant houses, as we were to discover over the next few days. A plastic bowl and some empty tins lay on the floor. There was no furniture except a single rush-bottomed chair, not even a table.

On the other side of the entrance a head-high partition with no door fenced off a small cell full of almonds. A perfect bedroom for our children, suggested our guide. The back room was already a bedroom, and was almost filled by a bed, at which we did not look too closely. The whole house measured about twenty feet square. It had a lean-to roof and a total of two windows and a door. It would have made a rather inadequate two-car garage.

It was a fine house but, we explained cautiously, we had been looking for something a little bigger. No problem, exclaimed the man, we could build an extension. He led us outside and showed us a rough stone enclosure at one end of the house, a kind of goat-yard surrounded by loose rocks piled casually upon one another. There, he said, the job was already half done. We could build on another bedroom and bathroom. A kitchen the house already had, as we had seen. The place was ideal for us. Did we have paper and pencil? Look, here was the house, and he boldly inscribed it CASA in case our dull foreign comprehension was lagging. And here would be the garden. JARDÍN. And the swimming pool? we asked facetiously. His face lit up. Yes, of course, here. PISCINA. He handed the paper back to us. The blueprint was complete. And the price was a mere 2¼ million pesetas. Or less, he quickly added, studying our faces anxiously, and making diminishing gestures with the palm of his hand, as though patting a dog on the head.

We groped for excuses. The place was remote, we said, and the road here – he would surely agree – was somewhat demanding. No, no, he said, that wasn't the way to the house at all. From here it was barely a kilometre down an easy track to the sea. And so it proved to be. The previous extensive and intimidating excursion had been merely a conducted tour of our environs, a preview of the delights of our neighbourhood-to-be. Or possibly a softening-up process to lower our resistance to his sales pitch.

Down on the main road the pitch continued. *Mutatis mutandis*, the cadences were identical to those of any Sussex Coast estate agent. The man extolled the proximity of our house to the sea, the ready availability of shops, the virtues of the nearest bar. Soon we were back at his own bar, where we had met him. We bought him a beer. Then, feeling guilty that this would be his only reward for two hours of his time, we said that we would need to devote serious thought to the matter of the house: and to give verisimilitude to this promise we asked for his name and address. I wrote them down carefully at his dictation. Firmly he took the notebook from me, crossed out what I had written and wrote it again, similarly spelt but larger. He was evidently proud of his ability to use a pen.

Another day, another bar, another peasant, another road. This one climbed steeply behind the village where we had met our new would-be salesman, and wound up a slope which was plentifully scattered with *cortijos* similar to the one we had seen the previous day. Each was like a child's drawing of a house: one door, two windows, a tiled roof, a chimney, and usually a vine arbour in front, propped on two white pillars. All were tiny, and most were accessible only on two feet or four hooves. The one we were visiting, however, had a road leading to it, we were told, and was evidently larger. Our guide graced it with a more expansive name – a *finca*. A farm. This sounded more like what we'd told our friends we'd be buying. We glowed with anticipatory pride.

The road passed through a narrow cleft at the top of the hill, and the view changed as suddenly and dramatically as if a proscenium curtain had been raised. We had crossed a 2,000-foot ridge and ahead of us was a huge valley divided by smaller ridges and backed by the massif of the Sierra de Tejeda, which ran away to right and left, to each jagged horizon. Deeply eroded water-courses ran between the dividing spines, marked with the white flecks of well-heads. Every slope was planted with vines or olives, and throughout this shining landscape the *cortijos* and *fincas* were scattered like confetti: small individual hovels, or larger clusters of variably pitched roofs. One of these, according to our guide's extended forefinger, was our goal.

We drove jerkily around the rim of the valley for a couple of miles, and then branched off on to a track that led out along a ridge, gently sloping down to the end where the house stood. When we stopped the car and switched off the engine the silence was as sudden as if a hand had been pressed over each ear. We climbed out and looked around. We had been hoping for a house with a spectacular view, but now, in the event, the impact of the scenery was almost bruising on the senses. It was hard to conceive of actually living here and being subjected every day to such variety and vastness of outlook. On three sides of the house the slopes fell away, dusted with the delicate tracery of the almond trees. On the near side the slope was visible all the way down to a narrow water-course, marked with occasional patches of deep-pink oleanders, behind which rose the steep vine-covered ridge we had crossed on our way here, now dark against the lowering sun. To the right, in the opposite direction, towered a mountain, 6,000 feet high, long and furrowed in the transverse light, with two white villages sprouting like tufts of iberis from crevices in its cliff-face. Ahead, looking down the valley, the eye fell first on the wrinkles of lower ridges: then on a higher foothill, rough with the silhouettes of olive trees, encircling the lower end of the valley: and behind, in the distance, on line after line of hills, delineated in diminishing intensities of tone against the evening sky, grey and roseate and lavender, terminating at the uttermost horizon in the barely perceptible pinkish silver of a wood-pigeon's breast.

Our guide watched our admiration in silence. He knew it was worth money. But when we broke from our trance and started looking around at the amenities, the sales patter began. Come and look at the water, he said. This was the only *finca* hereabouts with plenty of water. The others had to tote it up from the valley bottom. And water there certainly was, a 10,000-gallon cistern of it. He had tapped the water main supplying the village whence our quest had started. (As we heard later, this was by a private arrangement with the mayor which was most unlikely to be repeated if we bought the place.) He brandished a running hose-pipe, spraying the flashing drops around like a child. There was no plumbing in the house, he said, but he had used the water to irrigate a little garden, a miniature oasis on the rocky knoll. There was a lemon tree, a cherry and a loquat. There were tomatoes and gourds. There was even, as we deduced from the appropriate gestures, a loofah plant.

The house, we were compelled to admit at once, lacked style, or even charm. It was a single-storey accretion of blank white walls, with a massively jutting chimney as the only feature of interest. Inside, the largest room was a new garage containing an electricity generator and a Land-Rover: evidently the vendor was no subsistence-level labourer. The other rooms were small. The sitting-room had the only window, and a huge open fireplace. Behind it, in semi-darkness, lay two bedrooms. The further was characterized by a pair of unmade beds and a smell so aggressive that it rocked us back on our heels. It was attributable, as we later discovered, to a lean-to goat shed on the other side of the bedroom wall. Its effect was as if an assailant had crept behind one and suddenly enveloped one's head in a sack which had recently contained a particularly virulent type of ordure. Hercules must have had much the same experience in the Augean stables. It was the worst smell I have ever smelt.

Our host spent some time extolling the virtues of this memorable room, and proudly fingering a shotgun which lay on one end of a bed, but Georgina and I were already outside, filling our lungs with good Andalusian air. After a short convalescence we were ready to continue the tour of inspection. Various sheds and stalls backed against the central house. There was also a two-room extension, which would have provided useful extra living-space had it not been in ruins. We commented on its dilapidation. It need not concern us, he said, since it belonged to a lady in Granada. So he wasn't selling us the whole *finca*? But yes, everything except that ruined extension. And of course the goat shed, which belonged to his brother.

So that was it. We had discovered the most magnificently sited house in Andalusia, but it had two fellow-owners, a purloined water supply, no mains electricity, a long and rigorous approach road, and, as we next discovered, an asking price which represented about four times its true value. We sat drinking the wine which the man had poured us from a leather bottle dangling from the vine arbour outside the house, and watched the sun go down behind the endless hills. Sadly, we knew we would not be coming here again.

And so, for a week, the search continued. Recalled to mind now, after several years, it suggests the dedication and multiplicity of a knightly quest, although the encounters and pursuits took place not through the groves of an enchanted forest, nor across the perilous expanses

of Lyonesse, but up and down stony hillsides embroidered with vines and olives, along arid water-courses
and through terraced plantations of almond trees. The
villages we visited, all of them small and white and
remote, merge in the recollection, although the special
characteristics of a few of them stand out.

One, on the very top of a bare hill, was infested with
flies, as though with some unwelcoming *genius loci*.
It appeared to be empty of humans. Curly-tailed dogs
snarled from doorways, and we could find no bar in
which to make contact with the invisible population.

Another consisted simply of a long street, which in
the space of two hundred yards pursued every vari-
ation of which a street is capable. It threaded through
narrow canyons between buttressed walls, it opened
out into cobbled squares, it plunged through arches,
it marched up flights of steps, it sidled past fountains
where mules were slaking their thirst. Along both sides
of it the houses showed their own variations: one-storey,
two-storey, tile-fronted, flower-bedecked: flat-topped
or with the many-angled russet-tiled roof-lines which
are the glory of southern Europe. Wrought-iron balconies overhung our heads as we walked by, and the
many planes of whitewashed walls cast reflections
that overlaid the indigo shadows. But other people
had appreciated these charms before us. Modern villas
had sprouted in the environs, and the unmistakable
lineaments of expatriate Englishmen were to be seen
on the street. We made no enquiries there: the place
was poised on the rim of change.

Another village, the most beautiful of all, was sited
high on the flank of the region's biggest mountain –
the 6,000-foot ridge which we had already seen from a
distance. The road up to it meandered first among vines
and almonds and then, as we climbed higher, through
gum-scented pines, and at last debouched into the village square. At the head of the square was the town
hall, façaded with solemn little arches, giving grace to

an otherwise haphazard collection of buildings. Beside it was a fountain, with four shining brass taps pouring perpetual streams of water into a stone trough. Down the centre of the square was a double row of standard hibiscus bushes, like miniatures of the pollarded limes one sees in small provincial French towns, but covered with lilac-coloured blossoms. From the foot of the square a dog-leg of alleyways led past a squat church to a belvedere at the bottom of the village. Here, in the afternoon sun, we leant on the warm stone balustrade, looking out over the last of the rooftops and across the valley. Against the stupefying brightness the plunging landscape looked insubstantial, and the strenuous realities of peasant life were veiled in the luminous haze. Somewhere out there the population was at work. The man in the bar on the square could offer us no help in house buying. Come back after the almond harvest, he said, when the people are back in their homes.

The houses that we were shown elsewhere were a varied collection. Some were two-room shacks beside a road or up a mountainside. Others were *fincas*, often handsomely situated, but waterless in an arid terrain and expensive because of the value of the land. Our preconceptions of our house – the gracious mansion embowered in its hilltop garden – were being steadily eroded. We began to look at houses within some of the villages. One or two of these were urban equivalents of the *cortijos*, low and small and primitive. Others were styled as town houses, narrow and vertical like medieval Yemeni dwellings, stacks of small dark rooms piled one upon the other, inducing a growing claustrophobia until one emerged blinking on to a flat roof and could look out at the hills around. For various reasons – size or situation or sheer lack of charm – none of these houses appealed to us, and we were confronted, by now, with the prospect of the failure of our project. We were midway through the second of our two weeks. Time was drying up.

Every evening we would review the day and plan the targets for the morrow. Some of the nights were spent in small local hotels. One of these was on a cliff above the sea looking out towards Africa, the parent in so many ways of the culture we were now experiencing. Another was in a hill town, the only one of any size in the region where we were travelling. Our room looked out on the town square. In front of it, seemingly near enough to touch, was the belfry of the church. Here, as elsewhere in southern Europe and Latin America, the clock struck each hour twice, so that the workers in the fields, wristwatch-less and transistor-less, could have a double chance to hear the time.

Alternating with our nights in hotels, we slept out. We had brought sleeping bags with us, and in this climate had no need of a tent. The ground was no harder than many of the hotel beds, and the sun woke us early, giving us a long day for our prospecting.

The last of these alfresco nights began one evening as we were driving along a road overlooking the coastal plain. Rounding a corner, we saw a track leading off the road and out along a short ridge, ending at a ruined house. The approach was dignified with a row of eucalyptus trees and the view was spectacular. A flush of rose-tinted optimism, undimmed by the disappointments of the past few days, convinced us that this ruin was a desirable residence-to-be. We decided to camp there, and search for its owner the next day. After a plate of ham and crisp, juicy onions at the nearest village, we returned and unrolled our sleeping bags on the remains of a stone terrace beside the house. I kicked away the more belligerent of the thistles, releasing a dusty fragrance from the herbs among the paving stones. Far below us twinkled the lights along the shore.

A gale blew up in the night and the sky flashed with a continuous – but soundless – blaze of sheet lightning. No rain fell and the wind, although it inflated our sleeping bags like barrage balloons and threatened to launch us airborne above the plain, was warm and died away before dawn. Awaking early, Georgina and I lay there for an hour or more, looking out on the countryside below, cosseted in our bags and sipping brandy and black coffee from a flask we had filled at the village the preceding evening. The scene below us was a simplified version of Breughel's *Fall of Icarus*, but lit by the early sunshine with a freshness beyond the power of paint. A short way down the slope a man was guiding a plough behind a mule, corrugating a patch among the almond trees no bigger than a tennis court. Every few yards the mule turned, apparently without command, and the primitive plough, shaped like a child's geometry instrument, assumed a will of its own as the man wrestled it through the rocky soil. From time to time he would stop and conduct a conversation – effortlessly clear in the upland air – with a friend half a mile away, who was pruning his almond trees and stacking the severed twigs carefully for future use. In the distance lay the sea, and round a headland stammered a small boat, a fisherman returning from his night's work.

Rousing ourselves, we climbed back into the car and bumped down a rough track nearby towards a large whitewashed farmhouse, hoping to find the owner of our ruin. The smell of the farm, carried by the onshore breeze, hit us fifty feet before we reached the place: one of the most evocative smells in the world, second only to wood-smoke. Wine. Boxes of grapes were stacked beside the gateway of the farmyard, and inside the air was dense with wasps. As we drove up a man emerged, elderly but erect, too busy for small talk but civil enough to ask our business. That ruin up the hill? No, it was not for sale. But his brother-in-law owned an empty house in a village up the valley, the village of Dalmácija, and he might be willing to sell it. The man wrote something on a piece of paper and gave it to us, with instructions to deliver it to an Angel Perez Moreno. I have the paper still. The message is laconic enough: 'These people want to buy a house.'

We were not aware of the existence of Dalmácija. The signpost down in the valley had indicated another village up this road, but Dalmácija was evidently beyond it, according to the old man's directions. We set out to find it. The road up the valley clung to the hillsides, snaking around every projection and doubling back where each re-entrant held a dry water-course. It was as well not to look down. Over the road's edge, innocent of protective fencing, the slopes fell steeply to a narrow river-bed far below, waterless but lined with a bright ribbon of oleander. Above the road, against the morning sun, the insubstantial plantations of leafless almond trees hung along the hillsides like smoke. The white cubes of several *cortijos* shone out against the prevailing browns and greys, scattered up and down from hilltop to valley bottom. Some of those below possessed little gardens scratched out from the valley floor. Those above made one sweat at the very thought of climbing up to them.

Across the plunging valley was a round-shouldered hill, cicatriced all over with old Arab terraces. On its top could be seen the remains of a castle. As the valley circled round the hill, traces of masonry revealed themselves, a tower here, a stretch of wall there. In the years to come we were to know this castle well. Now we looked up at it and wondered about its history.

After half a dozen kilometres we reached the first village, and our road ran around the bottom of it. In the shade of a half-built house by the roadside sat a group of old men, holding their sticks and wearing straw hats. The product of a society with a practical and sedentary attitude to leisure, they were ruminating and watching, although there was nothing to watch. Apart from ourselves, the road was empty. Moreover at this point it almost ceased to exist. The hard-top ended and was replaced by scoured and pitted dust. We jolted along it for a further two kilometres. Then, as we rounded yet another bend, we saw ahead of us, half-way up a mountainside, a tiny village, surely the smallest village in all Spain. Dalmácija.

It had a stumpy church-tower at the centre, surrounded by a dusting of white houses. Encircling it, and more conspicuous than the tiny settlement itself, lay the means of its livelihood, the raisin racks. In this region, every *finca* and large *cortijo* had them. They were neat rectangles marked out on a south-facing slope, each with a white triangular wall at top and bottom, like pyramidal bed-ends, to hold a canopy in the rare event of rain at raisin time. Within these rectangles every August and September were laid the layers of grapes, to dry and shrivel and discolour and change their nature. The Arabs had been forbidden by Allah to turn their grapes into wine, so they turned them into raisins.

The road ended at Dalmácija. Nor did the village have any streets of its own: the houses, loosely clustered, were set on a steep slope, and between them ran dusty alleyways not much larger than goat-tracks. We parked the car in a level space between the road and the first of the houses, and looked up. The white walls, foreshortened, looked ready to slide down the hill and engulf us. Along the top of the little arena where we were standing ran a low terrace planted with a continuous row of geraniums which tumbled down the wall towards us like a tapestry. At one end of it was a fountain, where a black-garbed woman was filling a bucket from a brass tap. We asked her for the likely whereabouts of Angel Perez Moreno, and she directed us towards a track which curled left-handed up the hill among the houses. It was unpaved and steep, and as we climbed slowly up it our nostrils were filled with the smells of an African kraal . . . dust and dung and spicy cooking.

Half-way up the slope, beside the church, was a tiny square, or rather a broadening of the track. In the centre stood an acacia, a welcome flourish of green among the relentless whiteness of the walls, and beyond it was another fountain. Long lines of wasps were sucking moisture from the runnels of water which had over-flowed the stone basin and trickled down the hill. Beside the fountain was a flight of steps on which sat an old man with a crutch resting beside him, feed-ing dried sunflower seeds to a little girl. I stooped and asked her name. The man told me, but I failed to catch it. A foreign name, he said, from far away, and he gestured broadly down the hillside. The parents had got it from the television.

We climbed the steps, following the old man's instructions, and emerged at the top of the village. Walking along the hillside above the houses we came to a small *cortijo*, close enough to the village to form part of the settlement. It consisted of one room, guarded by a massive timber door, and it was extended outside by an open loggia where white stone pillars supported a roof of thatch. In the shade sat a man, amid a litter of wooden boxes. Yes, he said, he was Angel Perez Moreno.

He was short and thick-set, aged about sixty, wearing a thick cotton shirt and a pair of ancient trousers tied round his waist with rope. His blue eyes were set deep in an infinitely wrinkled face. He took the message and read it, slowly deciphering the seven words. So we were looking for a house? It was true that he owned an empty house, here in the village, a good house. He would show it to us, if we could be troubled to wait a few minutes. He had to finish his raisins. The lorry was coming for them that afternoon.

He took each box from his right-hand side and went through it meticulously, extracting any raisins that were undersized or mildewed and throwing them on to a pile on the floor together with any excess bits of stalk. The survivors were packed carefully into other boxes stacked neatly on his left, ready to go. It was slow, finicky work, and the resulting produce – the dark-brown nuggets of fruit, as wizened as the corpses of bees – hardly looked worth the trouble. Yet they were the village's main livelihood.

Georgina and I sat on the floor while the man worked. The view from the loggia looked down the valley up which we had driven. It was cool under the thatch, and silent except for the occasional scraping of the boxes on the wooden floor, and the rustling of the raisins, and the humming of flies. None of us talked. Georgina and I were half asleep, and Señor Perez was busy. After half an hour he had finished. He got up from his chair and smiled for the first time. Would we like to see the house?

He led us back into the village, along an alleyway behind the church and down a steep little street lined on one side with geraniums and morning glories spilling from a narrow flower-bed above. At the last house he stopped, asked us to wait, and disappeared through the door like a rabbit into its hole. He reappeared with a key which would not have disgraced St Peter. Bearing it before him like a sceptre, he led us back to the little square beside the church. Next to the fountain were two or three steps leading up to a faded blue door. This was the house.

It grew out of the house above it, like a cell on the edge of a wasp's nest, and owing to the steep slope of the village was disconcertingly elusive. It was impossible to see more than a part of it from any direction. From below, it stood too high above the alleyway: one could see a couple of jutting walls, but not the full façade, and none of the roof. From above, the next house blocked the view. The only place, as we later found, whence one could see the building as a whole was from across the little valley. From there one could, with care, pick out the house next to the church, but only as one fragment in the mosaic of the village's roofs and walls. Thus unlike most houses it had no individual exterior which one could study and appreciate: only an interior.

Angel Perez turned the key, put his shoulder to the door, and led us in. The entrance opened into a strange half-lit room. There were no windows, and the womb-like appearance was accentuated by the fact that there were no straight lines. Four doorways and a staircase led out of the room, but none of these apertures had square corners. Crude plasterwork and a hundred coats of whitewash had rounded every angle. The opening to the staircase was almost an oval, the fireplace was arched like a railway tunnel, and the shelf over it was so round-edged and so integral with the wall that it looked like a half-melted ledge on an iceberg. The ceiling was low, and formed in the ancient manner: a number of crude beams straddled the room at irregular intervals, some with traces of bark still on them, and across these were laid canes, bound to the beams with cords. The canes, sealed with a daub of mud and lime, supported the floor tiles of the room above. Beams and canes and cords were all coated, like the walls, with the thick layer of whitewash that united every component and made the room an entity.

Beside the fireplace was a round-topped recess, and there was another half-way along the side wall with two shelves and two depressions at the bottom, like piscinae, to hold water jugs. Otherwise the room was without decoration. It was all white except for the earthenware tiles on the floor, and glowed like old ivory in the shaft of sunlight from the door. There was nothing in it except for some sacks and coils of rope on the floor.

Off this central room, behind heavy wooden doors, were two smaller rooms, one a step higher, the other down three steps so sheer that it was like stepping down into the bilge of a boat. All the ground floor of the house was on different levels: different terraces on the hillside on which the various rooms had been built. At the far end, through a round-eyebrowed archway which mirrored the recess on the other side of the fireplace, were further steps leading down to the *bodega*, the wine shed. Every house in the village, as we discovered later, had its *bodega*. This one was a long narrow lean-to, with similiar beams and canes above, containing a stone manger and four enormous barrels. The barrels, said Señor Perez, were not for sale. In any case, he added regretfully, they were empty.

The stone staircase, surfaced with tiles, was the steepest I had ever climbed. There were ten steps where a modern house would have had twenty, and each was of a different height. Above was a room that ran the length of the house, lit only by an unglazed, shuttered window a foot square. (Spanish rural architecture eschews windows. They serve only to admit the heat in summer and the cold in winter. Light is of lesser importance where the main indoor activities are resting, eating and talking.) Through the gloom we peered at what seemed to be piles of fairy gold heaped upon the floor. They were almonds, drying out, waiting to be bagged and sold. Off this long room was another, tiny and square, where the roof timbers were so low that we could not stand erect at their further end. Calculating swiftly, we realized that this house could give us four bedrooms. Although some of the subsidiary rooms were small, there were plenty of them. It was the biggest house we had yet seen.

Having inspected the interior, we walked through the *bodega* and out into a tiny chicken-yard enclosed by a wall, with a little stone shed at one end. A wooden door in the wall led out on to a path with trees on the far side. The house was, we saw, at the edge of the village, with other houses above and below, but with an open hillside at the end of it. This was not the country mansion we had come to Spain to find, but the countryside was there beside us. We stood outside and looked at the surrounding hills. They were empty. Dalmácija lay in a bare beige saucer without even a single *cortijo* to be seen. If we had been looking for remoteness, we had found it. We would not be alone in it: our house here, if we bought it, would not be surrounded by oleanders and palms and orange trees, as we had preconceived, but by a couple of dozen Spanish families. Looking at Señor Perez as he stood beside us, proud of his house and patient in his expectation of our response, this seemed no bad exchange.

We told him we liked his house, and asked the price. The price? he said, as if the question of money had not occurred to him: he would need to think about it. We should return tomorrow, when we would tell him if we wished to buy the house and he would tell us the price. We should meet in the bar, in the evening. He would be working throughout the day. And he had to return to his work now, with our permission. We shook hands.

The bar was half-way down the slope we had ascended, below the acacia tree. It was unidentified except for a Coca Cola roundel over the door. As we passed it, an irresistible force drew us aside and up a short flight of steps on to a stone platform outside the bar's doorway. It was past midday, and hot, and we felt a prickle of celebration in the air. The proprietor, a mountain of a man, served us a couple of beers. He was civil but diffident, and left us sitting alone on the little terrace. We were out of the sun but could sense the heat lapping at the edges of our small island of shade. A long black dog shared it with us, curled up against the angle of the wall. Otherwise there was no sign of life in the village. Our car stood solitary in the arena below. The only sound was the rhythmic panting of the dog. Georgina and I looked at each other, and at the shimmering white walls around us, and the terraced hillsides beyond. We said nothing, as we sipped the icy beer, but our silence was instinct with the shared conviction that our quest was at an end.

*   *   *

It was dark when we returned to Dalmácija next day. As always the darkness stimulated the other senses. The velvety warmth of the night wrapped around us like a cloak, and the rich herbal smell of mule dung marked the track up the hill. There was a street lamp at the bottom of the village and another at the top: each created its zone of radiance, where the walls shone bluish-gold and the corners threw black shadows, but in between was a heart of darkness, and we stumbled as we climbed. Only the top of the church tower above us reflected enough light for us to see the steps up to the bar. The door was open, but a sheet hung across the entrance. From inside came a low murmur of voices.

As we entered we were confronted with the rotund silhouette of the barman, Luis, who greeted us shyly but expectantly. Behind him, in the centre of the little room, was a round table, over which hung a solitary light-bulb. At the table sat Señor Perez, with a glass of wine in front of him. Luis drew up chairs for Georgina and me. At the far end of the room, away from the direct light of the bulb, were several more chairs. Most of them were occupied by small dark-skinned men whose chatter fell silent at our entry. Like Luis, they reflected an air of expectation. Their shirts and the whites of their eyes gleamed in the shadows. They were like a theatre audience awaiting the rising of the curtain. The wine in my glass shook slightly as I gulped it, and gulped it again. I had no experience of house-buying in circumstances like these. I told Señor Perez that we had seen many other houses – I tried to imply that some of them, too, were possible purchases – but his was the best. What was the price of it?

He emptied his glass and leaned back in his chair. He named a price for the house. It was almost exactly double the price I had anticipated. I allowed my face to fall, and wondered how to signal to Georgina to burst into tears. Suddenly the hitherto taciturn Luis entered the discussion. Did the price seem too high?

he asked me, in the sympathetic tone of a dentist asking if the drill is hurting. But it was a good house, the best in the village, and a good price: what price did I propose? After a moment's hesitation I gave a figure slightly above the one I had preconceived: about two-thirds of what Señor Perez was asking. Luis pirouetted with unexpected speed, for his size, and looked into Señor Perez's face, scrutinizing his reaction. There was none. He sat motionless, looking at me. In the uttermost depths of his blue eyes glinted the suggestion of a twinkle, but he said nothing. There was silence in the little room. A slight oscillation of the light-bulb gave a swaying motion to the shadows of the figures around the table, as though we were all afloat. A trickle of perspiration ran down between my shoulder blades. I decided the moment had come for a gesture I had prepared in advance, an intended *coup de théâtre*.

I reached into my pocket and brought out a wad of peseta notes as thick as a pack of playing cards. There, I cried, letting them fall on the table with a flourish, there was a deposit on the house. Nothing like the sight of raw cash, I thought. And indeed the spectacle of the fluttering paper galvanized the hitherto silent figures in the shadows round the room. A frisson ran through the audience, and a man darted forward to pick up one of the notes which had fallen on the floor and scrutinized it – perhaps to ensure it was not some dubious foreign currency – before restoring it reluctantly to the table. Luis, too, ran a large moist tongue over his lips as he looked down over his belly at the multi-coloured pile of money. The only person who remained unmoved was Señor Perez.

What was this money? he asked. A deposit, I repeated. A down-payment on the house. One third of the price now, one third when the legalities were completed, and the final third when I moved in. How about it? Agreed? I pushed the pile of notes towards him, as though to a big winner at Las Vegas. He shook his head decisively.

That was not the way to buy a house, he said. The way to buy a house was this: I would give him the money – all the money – and he would give me the key.

I heard a murmur of agreement from the spectators behind me. Or perhaps it was the creaking of my own respiratory system: I was dangerously near choking, now that the crisis-point of our venture was upon us. Georgina was no help. She was looking at me expectantly, waiting for my next trick. It was Luis, the roly-poly diplomat, who moved first to resolve the impasse. There were only a few thousand pesetas, he said, between Señor Perez's price and mine: was it not possible to agree a price in between? It was true that we were haggling over the sort of sum which was less than the price of a small car back in England. There was more pride at stake than money. I raised my price. Señor Perez lowered his. Split the difference . . . split the difference, cried Luis, flitting from one side of the table to the other like an inflated leprechaun. We split the difference. It was a deal. I jumped to my feet and seized Angel Perez's hand. He held on to it much longer than business formality required.

Dalmácija lay only fourteen kilometres by road from the sea, but the corkscrew bends required a half-hour drive. This situation seemed to us the perfect combination. We were within easy reach of the beach and of the airport, yet the village's relative inaccessibility and tiny size should protect it from being infected by the coastal blight. Sure enough, we soon found nobody had heard of the place. On a subsequent visit, when we were opening an account at a bank in the nearest town on the coast, the clerk asked for our address. We named Dalmácija, but it meant nothing to him. He then asked for our street address there. We told him there were no streets. He looked sharply at us, suspecting either a joke or a subterfuge.

The legalities of the house-purchase would have to be undertaken in our absence, and we entrusted them to Jacob, the Dutch estate agent. He also promised to advise us on plumbers and electricians when we next came to Spain. A builder we would probably be able to find in the village or nearby.

We returned to study the house in more detail, on our penultimate day in Spain: partly through pride in future ownership and partly to assess what modernization work would be necessary before we could take up residence. The roof seemed sound enough, except for the section over the *bodega*. The quarry-tiled floors were crazed but serviceable. One of the small downstairs rooms could be a kitchen. The chicken-house was blueprinted for a bathroom, and the remaining spare rooms would be bedrooms. All the plumbing would need to be installed – there was no water in the house (nor in the other houses). But unlike the mountain eyries we had previously visited, the supply was at hand: one of the village fountains was only ten feet away. And electricity already came to the house, although the place would have to be properly wired. As for redecoration, a tub of whitewash would serve for that.

Much of this labour would need to be done while we were in England. How would the workmen gain access? Angel would not be able to admit them. His own house was at the other side of the village, and he spent much of each day in the fields. We asked him if he could introduce us to a neighbour with whom we could leave the key.

The doorway opposite ours, across the alleyway, opened into a cubbyhole occupied by a sparrow-like septuagenarian crone and her oafish son who was to be seen hobbling around with a stick and a whiff of alcohol. These two were evidently regarded by Angel as inappropriate custodians of our key. He led us round the corner to the next house. This stood on the little square beneath the acacia tree. Angel's shout through the open doorway activated a shuffling of feet in a back room and the eventual appearance on the doorstep of a stocky middle-aged woman in a faded checked apron. He introduced her to us as Rosalia. She wiped her palms on the apron before shaking hands with us. She had been preparing the evening meal, she said. Squid with saffron. The fish-man had visited the village that day.

Rosalia was built to generous proportions. Her robust trunk was squeezed into a black cotton dress, and arms like a shot-putter's protruded from the short sleeves. None of this bulk looked like otiose flab. It looked very much like muscle. Rosalia would constitute a formidable chatelaine if she accepted the post.

She listened without comment as Angel explained that these two foreigners were planning to buy his house, but would not be living there except for a few weeks each year. We would be living there, I quickly interjected, when I was old and no longer needed to work. I didn't want to sound too much like an absentee landlord. Rosalia received this information cautiously, as though evaluating our desirability as neighbours, whether intermittent or permanent. Indeed I had the disconcerting impression that I was being interviewed for a job. Rosalia's eyes were the optical equivalent of the iron hand in the velvet glove: they were large and of a warm hazel colour, yet the glances they flashed at Georgina and me impinged with a metallic sharpness which was almost tangible. Her voice had a similar ambivalence, soft but vigorous. She said she would wait to hear when the sale was completed. Angel would tell her. Then she would discuss with her husband whether to take charge of the key. She would like to help us, but it would mean extra responsibility for her. She bade us good-bye, and it seemed that the interview was at an end. But she turned back to face us again. She was glad we were buying the house, she said. Many of the people of Dalmácija were leaving it, to seek work in the towns.

It would be good for a new family to arrive. Especially a foreign family. She had never met a foreigner before.

The next day we flew back to England, having signed various bits of paper for Jacob. We returned the following spring, by which time the house was legally ours. We visited it, to see if it looked as we remembered it. It was smaller and damper, and without the almonds and the wine barrels. The thought of living in such a place, in such a village, generated a delighted fascination, tinged at the edges with alarm, almost fear. We swept the floors as a token proprietorial gesture, and left the key with Rosalia, who had agreed to look after it. She received it with the gracious impassivity of a princeling accepting tribute.

And now the whole affair moved into a Spanish tempo, in contrast to the diligent haste of the previous summer. The search for a plumber outlasted our visit and was only concluded a year later, which meant that the plumbing was only actually installed a year after that. The plumber lived down in the coastal plain, and needed much cajoling to agree to drive up the narrow valley to Dalmácija. He was aided in the installation by a builder from the village itself. Both of them were to feature in our subsequent life there. As for the wiring, we opened negotiations with a couple of successive electricians, without securing from either a commitment to a further meeting, let alone to the work itself. In desperation, we entrusted the problem to Jacob. He too failed to find a practitioner. In the end he wired the house himself, holding – he said – a how-to-do-it manual in one hand while he installed junction boxes with the other. The resulting system seemed to work. It still does.

And so, stage by stage, crisis by crisis, and year by year, the little house at Dalmácija was prepared for our occupation. We bought a bed from the plumber, with fine brass ornamentation at head and foot, which jangled like a distant percussion band every time Georgina or I turned over. The springs appeared to be from a different bed, and had to be lashed to the frame with several feet of rope. The mattress didn't bear close inspection. We also bought a table from a local carpenter. The builder donated a chest of drawers too dilapidated for his own use, and Jacob's wife a cooker that appeared to pre-date the Reconquest. We ferried out supernumerary pots and plates from England, on our interim visits. We invested in a paella pan. We were ready to move in. We booked flights for the following April, and alerted Rosalia to our imminent arrival, thereby giving her time to remove the almonds, farming equipment and spare relations which we assumed filled our house in our absence. The Dalmácija era was about to begin.

3

SPRING

The Admiral says that today and ever thereafter they had very mild breezes, that the savour of the mornings was a great delight, that the only thing wanting was to hear nightingales. Says he, 'The weather was like April in Andalusia.'

Journal of Christopher Columbus

11 April
The first sound on the first morning in the house at Dalmácija was of Remedios shooting back the bolt of her front door. Remedios lived behind a faded curtain covering a doorway in the alleyway below our house. She was a tiny, shrivelled woman of seventy-six — yet the bolt resounded with a Herculean clangour that echoed off the hard, bare walls. Her voice, the second sound, was more in keeping with the frailty of its author: thin, creaking and tremulous. 'Loli . . . Loli . . . Loli.' She was calling her cat, who in feline equivalence was about as old as she. Gradually her voice was joined by others, all female, muffled by the thickness of the wooden shutter over our window, but building in volume and complexity, as solo followed solo, giving way to duets and trios, until one sensed that the little chorus was fully assembled on the narrow stage outside.

Georgina and I continued to lie in the big brass bed, motionless, swaddled against the chill, listening to the sounds of village life as they developed further. Soon came the dusty stamp of a mule: Jesus, Rosalia's husband, was saddling it up, exchanging confidences with it as he tightened the straps. In unmechanized Dalmácija, this activity was a more leisured and animate version of a man starting his car to go to work. We heard him give a final pat to a furry flank, and the six legs set off down the alleyway, heading for the open hillsides. As they rounded the invisible corner at the end of our house the footsteps died away. The voices, meanwhile, had concluded their aubade and their owners had retired within the massive, sound-enclosing walls of their houses, leaving Georgina and me becalmed on an ocean of silence.

I opened my eyes. Two feet above me was one of the roof timbers, which sloped down almost to the bed-head. Across these rough-hewn supporting beams stretched a layer of glossy canes, each the thickness of a thumb, tied to the beams with strands of finely plaited esparto grass. Compared with factory-produced plastic string the workmanship of these braids was dainty, meticulous, barely credible. I stared up at the beams and the cords like Sartre scrutinizing tree bark, searching for existential significance. Finding none, I decided it was time to get up. Enveloping myself in a thick dressing-gown I went downstairs to greet the day.

Stepping out of doors, early in the morning, is like reading the first page of a new book – an assessment of the quality of the hours to come, sometimes accurate, often misleading, always exciting. On this occasion, entering our little patio at the rear of our house was like opening the door of a refrigerator. Dalmácija is 1,500 feet up, and an April day there starts cool. But overhead the zenith of the sky was already of that intense and radiant Mediterranean blue which so enchants a northerner's eye, and to the west, barely visible over the patio wall, the hillside was tinged a strange foxy red by the early sun. Gulping the pure cold air, like a swimmer about to plunge underwater, I turned back into the house and made haste to light a gas heater in the dank little cubby-hole of a kitchen.

As I wrestled with the coffee-grinder I became aware of another sound, increasing in volume. Someone was beating at our front entrance. Conscious of the social inadequacy of my dressing-gown, I opened the door a crack, but was immediately propelled back into the room by the forceful arrival of an irresistible object. It was Rosalia. What time had we arrived last night? she asked, accusation in her voice. Late, I said, apologetically, as though personally responsible for airline schedules. She hadn't heard us, she said, in a tone which implied some deficiency on our part. Then, mellowing, she welcomed me to the village, clasped me warmly by the hand, and asked if we had breakfasted: she had brought us some bread. Rosalia and I had met many times before, during our exploratory visits to the house, but now, for a moment, we reassessed each other. Black-clad, apron-girt, four-square, she exuded personality as a Sumo wrestler exudes sweat. The hazel eyes, set in a face free from wrinkles, smiled at me with a steely possessiveness. Her custody of our house-key in our absence gave her status among the villagers, and in our presence it encouraged regular access to this new phenomenon, a pair of foreigners in their midst. It was entirely appropriate that she should play a part in our first hour of residence, since she was to pervade all our future life in Dalmácija.

After a glance at my goose-pimpled knees and a longer examination of the contents of the suitcases that lay open on the floor, she wished me good appetite and reluctantly took her leave. I sped back to the comparative warmth of the kitchen and bolstered my resolution with a mug of coffee, freshly ground, pungent and dark as Erebus. Then I broke open Rosalia's loaf. It was light, crisp and ambrosial, as fresh as the day. The necessities of life were shaping well.

I took a mug of coffee to Georgina, up the misshapen and break-neck stairway. In the gloom the brass bed, portentously tall under the low sloping roof, and the only furniture in the room, towered like a catafalque. I put the steaming coffee on the floor beside Georgina's faintly stirring form, and left the fragrance to do its work. The house was still gelid with the cold of night, but outside, as I recrossed the patio on my way to shave, the first tender warmth was perceptible in the air. The sun was hidden behind the tall, blue-shadowed wall of the house, but soon it would be upon us.

After Georgina had breakfasted we took our coffee outside the front door on to the earthenware-tiled terrace that ran along the house for a few yards, overlooking the little sloping square that lay between Rosalia's house and the church. Beneath our house wall ran a long tiled ledge, and here we sat, blinking in the sun which on this side of the house was high and unopposed. Behind our backs the rough whitewashed masonry was already absorbing the warmth of the day and returning it to our gratefully thawing shoulders. In front of us, on the other side of the terrace, a row of geraniums was carrying a varied crop of Remedios' laundry, laid out to dry. The multiplicity of her underwear would have constituted a star exhibit in a clothing museum . . . whalebone corsets, bodices, spencers, pantaloons, in a variety of shades from black to off-white. They detracted a little from the effect of the geranium blossoms: but Remedios was too short to reach a washing-line.

Outside Rosalia's house at one side of the square stood an acacia, carrying the first racemes of its white blossom. Behind it, half-visible through its branches, the roofs of the houses fell away, and in the blue distance the far side of the valley rose to the bare mountain, void of habitation, that stood between Dalmácija and the sea. Gazing at the acacia in its setting I was reminded of an old Chinese proverb which states that if one wants to enjoy the possession of an oak tree one must plant it in the village of nowhere in the province of nothingness, and only then can one lie down and repose in its shade without care and anxiety.

But Georgina and I had reposed enough. All was right with the world, and we wanted to see more of this little corner of it into which we had found ourselves translated. We walked across to the church. Its flank confronted our house, a low rough wall topped by a long and irregular slope of ancient tiles, mossy and weed-grown, more like a hillside than a roof, which led the eye up to the stumpy tower behind, where a single bell peered like a sentry through a narrow and defensive aperture. Round the front, in the centre of a bare façade, the big double doors were shut, and Georgina and I stood a while on the platform outside, looking down on the lower half of the village where the white walls and ochre roofs spilled down the slope to the dirt road below.

The road, leading down the valley to the sea and to civilization – of a sort – was empty. So, it seemed, was the village around us. Strolling down the alley on the far side of the church, beneath the tall tapestry of purple morning glory that hung from the terrace outside the house of Angel, we saw no-one. The heavy wooden doors along the path, scabby with the puckered remains of sun-bleached paint, were closed. A little geranium-decked patio below us was empty. At this hour of the day the women were indoors, cleaning their houses or preparing the midday meal, and the men were working in the vineyards and almond groves. Yet the hillsides, when we looked up at them from the end of the path, seemed empty too. On three sides the fold of the valley wall enclosed the village, shielding it from the north winds that blew down in winter from the great mountains behind. Every slope was scarred with terraces of rough stone, half-mantled at this time of year with a froth of dainty green almond foliage, and pricked with the first springing of the vines. Somewhere out there were men, pruning and weeding and pasturing their mules, but we could not see them. The village of nowhere had become as lifeless as a ghost town in Montana.

Back in our house we finished our unpacking and took stock of our requirements. The place was almost unfurnished, and over the coming days and months we would have much to buy. And there was still the conversion of the *bodega* to be done. This was now a ramshackle lean-to at the far end of the house, and we planned to transform it into a bedroom with a roof terrace above. We hoped to inaugurate the project during this visit. The most pressing requirement at the present moment, however, was to buy some food. The nearest supermarket or modern shop of any kind was eleven kilometres away. Two kilometres away, in the next village, Álamos, there were shops of a sort, providing most basic requirements. But for today we would not even need to go to Álamos. Here in Dalmácija there was a single shop, in the alley immediately below our house. We decided to test its capabilities.

It was closed. It was, as we later discovered, almost always closed: but conversely was always opened on demand. The village was too small to generate constant commercial traffic, so any would-be shopper, on each occasion, had to go and seek the shop-lady in her house. We did so now. We found her in residence, a lady of about fifty named Consuela. Like many of the village ladies, she was of an immense girth, and in her skin-tight black dress, tightly corseted, she had the configuration of a bumble bee. Above the ovoid trunk, in an ovoid face, topped by henna'ed hair piled up like a cottage loaf, large brown eyes glittered good-humouredly as we introduced ourselves and explained

74

our presence: but there was a knowing competence, too, in her regard, as befitted a personage who, we came to discover, wielded considerable power in the village. She owned two or three other buildings besides her house and the shop, and various plots of land in the surrounding countryside, and she had her plump finger in several pies. By giving credit, she was effectively the village money-lender: and her shop, when open, served as a kind of women's club, filled with a softly chattering gaggle of customers, while children played outside on its steps, sucking the lollies which were one of her stocks-in-trade. If, as we had read, every Andalusian village has a white and a black witch, we soon came to believe that Consuela was our white one.

We followed her from her house to the shop round the corner. She hobbled up the path on two trunk-like legs so blotched and stiffened by various circulatory diseases that locomotion was evidently a major problem. Yet when, a few days later, we sought her help in shifting some building impedimenta, we found that she was possessed of a demoniac strength when needed, and with a flick of her massive wrist could levitate weights that would send any six-foot Englishman straight to his osteopath. The same, unbelievably, was true of the tiny Remedios. The year before, when Georgina and I had been struggling up the hill with a refrigerator, Remedios had emerged from her nook, brushed Georgina aside and briskly propelled the refrigerator up the one-in four slope, over the pot-holed cobbles, leaving me puffing in her wake.

Consuela's shop, which she unlocked for us with a gigantic key, consisted of a single room with further storage behind the rear wall. Floor space and wall space alike – even air space – were dense with merchandise of every kind . . . cans of tomatoes, rolls of lavatory paper, olive oil, washing powder, flea powder, onions, brooms, toffees, brass ladles, great truncheons of salami, crates of red peppers, jeroboams of lemonade.

Stalactites of plaited garlic hung from the bare beams of the roof and ziggurats of plastic buckets rose from the floor.

It soon transpired that Consuela could supply all the basic goods we required, even a chicken. We half expected the latter to be produced, squawking, from under the counter like a rabbit from a hat, but in this case the arrangements were made off-stage, and the squawking was later audible further up the village, followed by a light snowstorm of feathers drifting in the breeze.

The goods piled up on the counter. Those we had ordered were soon joined by others which Consuela felt should be added to the list. Her saleswomanship was of the direct kind. What, we had no flyspray? . . . and she reached for an aerosol the size of a torpedo. And there was a new kind of fly device, very modern, very scientific; you applied it to the wall, and flies stuck to it. It looked like standard fly-paper to us, very ancient, very primitive, but Consuela was adamant; why, she used it herself, there by the door of the shop. Indeed two foolscap-sized pieces of sticky paper were affixed to the door-posts. Neither contained a single fly.

For weighing out comestibles, Consuela used a little brass weighing machine. The weights for it were kept in a block of wood, butter-smooth with age and handling, drilled with round sockets of increasing size to accommodate the bright brass cylinders as snugly as gold coins in a display case. It was the kind of artefact which sells for large sums in the Portobello Road and I coveted it at once. Consuela's dexterity with it was bemusing. Her fingers flickered to and fro in a brown blur, manipulating different combinations of the weights to counterbalance the goods in the brass saucer dangling from the other end of the rocker arm, adding goods to the weights and weights to the goods until the mind reeled. Finally, the purchases were carefully wrapped for the journey home – all ten yards of it. This was common practice locally. On a later visit I bought stamps in a tobacconist in the next village, and they too were wrapped for me, in a tiny dolls'-house package. I half expected them to be tied up with ribbon.

We lunched off Rosalia's bread and Consuela's cheese and salami. Afterwards we took a bottle of brandy out into our little patio where we basked in the early afternoon sun. If it was like this tomorrow, we thought, we'd take a picnic up to the ruined castle on the hill across the valley. But by early evening we were driven indoors by the chill, only to find that the temperature in the sitting-room was lower than that outside. The damp of decades impregnated the thick old walls. Shivering, we pulled on sweaters and set to work to light a fire in the open fireplace, utilizing every combustible *objet trouvé* . . . cardboard boxes and packing material from our luggage, olive prunings hastily garnered from the hillside beyond our rear patio, a fallen timber from the crumbling *bodega* roof. Pyromaniacally I flapped the reluctant blaze with the lid from an old tin of sprats. Smoke poured out into the room and charred fragments of *The Times* danced across the floor. At last the flames began to lick gratifyingly up the chimney, and I sank back into a chair, dusting the ash from my hair and the bark from my sweater. It was time for a large drink of cheap gin. The moment it was poured – the precise split-second that we raised the glasses to our lips – the door opened and Rosalia entered.

This time she had her husband with her, Jesus, who held his hat in his hand and remained by the door, smiling apprehensively and stammering a form of greeting. Rosalia, already proprietorial, advanced across the room and lowered herself into the rocking chair, which creaked like a brigantine rounding the Horn. Refusing a drink, she settled down comfortably, evidently for a long stay. Jesus, coaxed to the fireside, took a small glass of wine. Both looked expectantly across the room at Georgina and me. They'd had a hard day, and now they were ready to be entertained.

Ill-equipped for soirées of this kind, we reached clumsily into our quiverful of clichés. The weather had been good, had it not? The sun had been very warm. Tomorrow we might go for a picnic. At what hour? asked Rosalia, who evidently liked to pin these things down, and where? Up at the castle, we said. Ah, the castle, said Jesus, speaking for the first time: he had some land up there, some vines. We stared at him. The castle was 2,000 feet up, on the far side of the valley with an intervening ridge to be crossed. Why was his land so far away? And how, with no more than a mule to help him, could he retrieve his produce from so great a distance?

He shrugged. Everyone in the village had parcels of land scattered far around the countryside, inherited, often, from an in-law in the next village. As for working the more distant plots, he would stay out all day. Rosalia would give him bread to take with him. And when the harvest came, up at his vineyard by the castle, he would leave the village before dawn in order to make two trips in the day, carrying the grapes home on his mule. A hard life, I said, lamely. He smiled at us with disconcertingly blue eyes and opened his hands in front of him, as though his whole existence could be read in their calloused palms.

Meanwhile Rosalia, while monopolizing the entire output of heat from the fire, was eyeing the blaze with curiosity. What a big fire, she said. We accepted the comment modestly, and asked if hers was burning well. She had no fire, she said. Then how did she keep warm? Why, with her *brasero*, of course. Her *brasero*? In explanation she pointed at the table purchased on our last visit, which was visible through the door of the kitchen: did we see the round hole underneath? It was true that the shelf joining the legs had a circular hole cut in it, about fifteen inches in diameter. We had assumed it to be some kind of ornamentation. No, said Rosalia, it was to hold a *brasero*, a pan of hot ash. She would show us how to use it, she said, noting our look of consternation, and would tell us where to buy one.

Meanwhile she continued to act like a well-upholstered firescreen, leaning closer to the flames and kneading one of her massive legs. She suffered from rheumatism, she said. It was hard work which caused rheumatism, she continued, looking accusingly at Georgina's shapely limbs. Georgina tucked them nervously under her chair, while I poured more drink. It was now ten o'clock and Consuela's chicken was sending out distress signals from the casserole on the cooker: but medical small talk continued to take precedence over eating.

At length Rosalia raised herself out of her chair, biceps straining against the sleeves of her black dress. Would we like her to get our bread for us tomorrow? she asked. A bread van came up every day, early, from the next village down the valley. We thanked her with genuine gratitude: early rising is not one of our virtues. But it wasn't too much trouble for her? No, she said, she was glad to help us. We were neighbours, friends.

And so we were. As Georgina and I later sat in front of the diminishing embers of the fire, while the strange little round-shouldered room looked more and more – in the half-light – like a cave fashioned out of some deep reef of chalk, we reflected that here in Dalmácija we had acquired more than a house. We had acquired a village, and all its inhabitants, and from now on they would play an increasing part in our life.

12 April
I was sitting on the loo when Rosalia arrived the next morning. The bathroom was the former chicken-shed, opening on to the little patio at the back of the house. Until now I had regarded its ground-floor accessibility as an asset.

At first Rosalia's voice was audible at the far end of the house, like surf beating on a distant shore, with

Georgina making small Canute-like noises. Gradually the flow of words grew nearer, until I heard the shuffling of feet outside the door. Rosalia wants to talk to you, said Georgina. Now? Now.

¡Buenos dias Hugo! I swear I could feel her hot breath through the key-hole. *¡Buenos dias* Rosalia! I replied, trying to sound nonchalant, and wondering what emergency could have brought her to the bathroom door so early. Central to my growing apprehension was the fact that the door could not be locked. It was a new one, not built to the medieval specifications of the house's original slab-like portals, and it had already warped. I leant a bare elbow against it. Great heavens, surely that wasn't a contrary pressure being exerted from outside?

When were we going on our picnic up the mountain? asked Rosalia through the crack. Around noon, I replied, increasing my elbow's weight against the door. Were we aware that the road up there was impassable? Jesus had said nothing about this last night, but I was in no condition now to debate inconsistencies. I swivelled round, and extended my leg across the doorway.

It would be necessary to walk the last mile, Rosalia continued. Was it an easy walk? I asked, beginning to pant a little from the physical discomfort of my position. It was steep, she replied with satisfaction, and then proceeded to move on to matters of greater interest: the commissariat. What were we going to take to eat?

Merciful God, was this the place to discuss a menu? Georgina will tell you, I cried, trying to shift the centre of responsibility, but to no avail. There was a dusty shuffling on the paving stones as she adjusted her weight, evidently settling in for a long conversation. I could see her shadow underneath the door.

But then, as we proceeded to discuss the merits of alternative forms of sausage, *salchichón* versus *chorizo*, in the context of an alfresco meal, a diversion occurred.

¡Hola! came a cry from the other end of the house. This was too much for Rosalia. Who could possibly be calling on the foreigners at this hour, with poor Hugo still in the bathroom? She strode off to investigate. Sun streamed under the door again. Birds sang. I withdrew my leg from the threshold and tried to straighten it. The crisis had passed. I was my own man again.

Later in the morning, after a mug apiece of Consuela's wine to stiffen us for the predicted rigours of the journey, Georgina and I set out on our picnic. We drove down towards Álamos, the next village, and turned on to a track which plunged off the road into the bed of the stream running down the valley. At this time of year there was a diffident trickle of water in it, through which we splashed and drove up the far slope. After a few hundred yards we reached the crest of a ridge, and dog-legged back to drive along the spine. Already the view was magnificent. Behind us, across the valley, lay Dalmácija, looking so remote that it was hard to imagine people living there, let alone ourselves. Behind it, visible over the foothill which shelters the village, loomed the huge granite shelf of the Sierra de Tejeda, now beginning to lose its substance in the flattening glare of the midday sun.

To our left, down the opposite side of the ridge, the land fell away steeply to the next valley, dominated by a conical hill as precisely defined as a volcano, beneath which could be seen another village, another splash of white, another pocket of human habitation in an otherwise almost uninhabited landscape. Below this village the valley opened towards the coast, and at the end could be seen the gleam of the sea. All around us the hillsides were planted with almonds and olives and vines, occasionally punctuated with the more solid bulk of a carob – an oil-painter's tree rather than a water-colourist's – which we marked down as a haven of shade for future picnics in the hotter months to come. Ahead of us the ridge dipped until it met the wall of the mountain now confronting us. We could see our track rearing up. Suddenly it looked steep, and we remembered Rosalia's warning.

The little car trundled down the final slope, past a ruined *cortijo* with a long-abandoned rose bush beside it, and up the other side. The track was indeed steep. Even a mule would have raised a sweat. Worse than that, it was extremely rough. Georgina drove, circumagitating the gear lever like a Scotswoman stirring porridge, while I hopped out every few yards to remove a boulder. Meanwhile the angle of ascent grew more acute.

At last the track reached another ridge, over which it disappeared, as though with a sigh of relief, down to the coast. We parked the car under a clump of umbrella pines, and carried our picnic up the final slope. At this altitude there was little cultivation, although the old Arab terraces corrugated every yard of the hillsides below us. Now they were hosts to the wild flowers of the Andalusian spring. Huge thickets of cistus, hundreds of feet long, flaunted blossoms of pink and white. On the intervening slopes and ledges grew lavender – the Mediterranean species *stoechas*, with flowers like bumble-bees – and myrtle and sheets of purple viper's bugloss. In crevices grew tiny vetches, and bicoloured sweetpeas, and bright carmine tendrils of convolvulus which belied their kinship with the English gardener's Public Enemy Number One. Giant fennels towered like young trees: their yellow seeds, later in the year, release an explosion of anise in the mouth when chewed, and are used to flavour the lethal local *aguardiente.*

Across the little footpath ahead of us stood a tower jutting from a ruined wall. We scrambled through a hole in the golden, lichen-encrusted masonry, and entered the castle. Once, it had been a mighty power in the region. The stones, carried up on the backs of Christian slaves, had formed a mile of walls enclosing an Arab settlement which had dominated this part of the coast.

When Ferdinand and Isabella passed nearby in 1487 to lay siege to Málaga, prior to the final Christian assault on Granada, this fortress played its part in the campaign. To it came the Moorish veteran El Zagal with an army from Granada, and in a night attack fell upon the Christians encamped in the valley below. The attack failed, and next day an unaccountable panic swept through the Moors: 'They were terrified, they knew not why, or at what,' says Washington Irving's account. 'They threw away swords, lances, breastplates, cross-bows, everything that could burden or impede their flight, and, spreading themselves wildly over the mountains, fled headlong down the defiles. They fled without pursuers, from the glimpse of each other's arms, from the sound of each other's footsteps.' When a small Christian patrol cautiously reached the heights, they found them abandoned and strewn with cuirasses, scimitars and crossbows. The road to Málaga lay open.

Now, little of the fastness remained. The sagging corpse of a gate-tower, a strip of curtain wall, the foundations of a few internal walls and cisterns, nothing more. Within the outline of the old bailey the terrain was flat across the cranium of the mountain and planted with almond trees. We looked for a picnic spot. Between the glaucous foliage of the almonds, hardly substantial enough to throw a shadow, the ground was bright with flowers: lying down, Georgina disappeared from sight among their sappy stems and insect-crowded blossoms. How often, it seems, are war and flowers associated . . . the poppies of Flanders, the white roses of Minden, the drenching perfume of honeysuckle all across the killing-ground of Vicksburg. But our minds were set on less morbid matters. We spread a cloth among the blossoms and unpacked the bread and cheese and wine. It was like picnicking inside one of the Cluny unicorn tapestries, but sunnier.

Later, much later, we roused ourselves for a walk around the castle's perimeter. Standing on the northern rim we could again see Dalmácija, and behind it the long particulate wall of the Sierras, weightless in the afternoon haze, extending in diminishing layers to the narrow plain in the west: and in the east, the sharper peaks that pointed the way to Granada. Southwards, the land fell away to the coast and the mercifully indistinct tower blocks of the late twentieth century. Beyond them the silver sea sloped up to meet the sky with no horizon. Africa, we had been told, was visible from here. But not today.

We strolled around the ruins. Were these the store-chambers for corn, or were they the cisterns that had gathered the rainwater for the watering of so many hundred throats? Was this a court where some local Jamshyd had gloried? And the janissaries – somewhere among these walls they must have pitched their silken tents on the eve of that nocturnal eruption down the slope . . . silent but for the susurration of their white robes . . . heron plumes nodding above their tall turbans . . . starlight glinting on arquebus and scimitar . . . in their bid to turn back the hard, sweaty hordes from the north, before the Frankish flood could lap across the meticulously tended gardens and cornfields of the Andalusian plateau and up against the walls of Granada itself, the last stronghold of Islam in this earthly paradise.

The sun on our backs was warm enough to induce daydreams. (At this time of year one could strip to a swimsuit at midday but sleep under two blankets at night – the climate of paradise, indeed.) But an hour later the air, thinned by the altitude, began to take on an underlying prickle of chill, like bubbles in a glass of *vinho verde.* It was time to gather up the detritus of our picnic and return home.

We told Rosalia that we had succeeded in driving to the top of the mountain, and she hid her disappointment well. She and Jesus had arrived again just as the foam at the rim of the first gin and tonic was beginning to subside. Evidently this was to be a daily social event: cocktails with the Seymour-Davieses. There was no need for an invitation, nor for an agreed hour, as Rosalia clearly had ESP as far as evening drinks were concerned. Either that, or she could smell gin at forty paces through two front doors.

Tonight she wasted little time on small talk and plunged straight into matters of substance. How much did potatoes cost in England? And bread? And what about almonds? They knew, of course, how much they sold almonds for here, at source, so that when we told them the London price the mark-up was immediately calculable. It was enormous, as one would expect, but my fractured Spanish was not up to explaining the technicalities of distribution costs, wholesalers' and retailers' margins, and the like. Hence all that was apparent to these almond-producers was the injustice of the system. They sold their produce for a pittance, and tightened their belts. Shopkeepers in England sold the same nuts for a fortune, and grew rich. Everyone in England was rich. Rich enough to buy houses in Spain.

13 April

By this, the third day of our occupancy, it had become necessary for us to drive down to Valdez, the town in the plain below our valley, in order to buy various essential goods. In addition to foodstuffs which even the Aladdin's cave of Consuela could not provide, we needed a number of items of furniture and equipment for the house. Including the *brasero*. We also wanted to explore the wider resources of the neighbourhood.

Valdez was eleven kilometres away down the serpentine road that hugged the hillsides above the oleander-filled ravine. The tortuousness of this approach to Dalmácija was its defence against the outside world, but today, after our experiences on the track to the castle, the hairpin bends had the easy fluency of a motorway. On our arrival in Valdez we parked in a square half-way up the town, decked with standard hibiscus trees and canna lilies, and went into the covered market. This was a huge echoing building lit by clerestory windows set high in the walls, which gave it the cool shadowiness of a cathedral. The central aisles were lined with stalls of fruit and vegetables and flowers, at each of which the vendor harangued the passerby and hawked his wares: while at the door a seller of lottery tickets added a strident *obbligato* to the mellower *tutti*. We bought a large bag of local oranges for conversion into juice, and a generous supply of those Spanish onions which, when eaten raw in a salad, are as sweet and juicy as if they had been hybridized with some tropical fruit. Strawberries were already in season, tasting like no strawberries I could remember . . . quintessential Platonic strawberries . . . Wordsworthian strawberries, charged with some past glory. The asparagus, conversely, was wiry and emaciated and tasted of chickweed.

Along two sides of the market were butchers' stalls. On their counters were displayed obscure portions of a pig's anatomy: multi-coloured gobbets of flesh and bone and gut. The dangling sausages were purple or scarlet. Even familiar objects like chicken carcasses were transmogrified. Hanging from hooks, these chickens were incredibly elongated, Giacometti chickens with the legs of storks. Yet like the strawberries, they proved to have a flavour which harked back to a pre-supermarket age.

Adjoining the main building was the fish market. This was even noisier, owing to the reverberation of the voices off the hard tiled surfaces. The marble counters glistened with the silver currency of sardines and anchovies . . . *chanquetes* half the size of whitebait . . . mullet, hake, and the disconcertingly named *rape* . . . semi-transparent octopus and squid . . . clams in two or three different sizes and colours. Red-faced men in rubber boots strode to and fro across the sodden floor, sweeping the fallen debris out into the street to the waiting cats. We bought some thumbnail-sized black clams – for eating raw, like oysters – and an octopus. The latter had a reproachful look, and we wondered how to cook him.

We got lost on the next leg of our expedition, but this gave us the chance to see something of the town. Valdez is said to have been founded by Hercules and to be one of the oldest towns in Andalusia. According to Strabo, a party of Phoenicians from Tyre were bidden by an oracle to establish a settlement at Heraclea – Gibraltar – but failing to find the expected altar there on which to make their inaugural sacrifice, they came to Valdez instead and sacrificed to Hercules at his shrine here. Ulysses and other Greek heroes of the Trojan War are also said to have passed this way, and later, probably around the eighth century BC, Greeks founded the city of Mainake, now vanished but known to have been somewhere nearby.

Today the visitor to Valdez will find nothing Herculean. The single surviving tower of the castle juts above the town as imperiously as a traffic policeman raising his hand, backed by the authority of the mountains behind. In the upper reaches of the town are two large churches: one late Gothic, the other with arcading and ceiling in the Mudéjar style – built in the Christian period with decorative features inherited from the Moors. But the lower streets, through which we were now threading, were of a more recent drabness, apart from some older buildings – eighteenth century, perhaps – which retained the projecting Arab windows, shielded by fretted shutters, from which invisible Muslim womenfolk used to watch the street below. Valdez was no beauty as a town, but we learnt to love it for its Spanishness and for its hustling practicality. The place was one huge bazaar wherein could be bought all the more basic domestic artefacts, many of them produced on the spot.

Chairs, for example. We found the chair shop, after several enquiries, at the bottom of a steep cobbled street. It was little more than a hole in the wall: a direct descendant of a stall in a North African souk. In it sat a man, cross-legged on the floor amid a deep-litter of wood shavings, plaiting the rush seat of a chair. He had evidently just completed half a dozen frames, turning the legs and backs on a primitive lathe which also contributed the decorative rings and bosses on each upright, then whittling the slats and stretchers with a formidable knife. The place was fragrant with sawdust and freshly sun-dried rushes: a woodman's potpourri.

After strapping four new-minted chairs on to the roof of the car, we strolled across the road to a pottery shop. In it were shelves loaded with plates and bowls decorated in the local style: birds and pomegranates and roses loosely hand-scrawled in sub-aqueous blues and greens. On the floor were stacked flowerpots, together with some waist-high Ali Baba jars with rims crimped like an apple pie. We bought a couple, together with some bird-decked plates for the mantelpiece of our sitting-room. Then we went in search of the *brasero* specified by Rosalia.

We found it at an ironmonger's. It was like a large inverted World War One tin hat, with a handle on each side. We put it in the car, now laden like a camel with our purchases, and drove back to a little square in the middle of town, on the main road, where we sat down at a table under a large acacia tree. We drank beer and chewed enormous rolls filled with ham. Across the road was a Carmelite monastery, showing only a huge blank honey-coloured wall pierced with a single beetling gateway. It had the air of a stronghold: an outpost of the Church Militant. It contained, we later learned, a legendary emerald chalice, reputedly studded with 365 jewels. Traffic roared past, and pedestrians trickled around us, squat, brown and relaxed, more synchronized with their rhythm of life, it seemed, than would have been their English counterparts even in a small country town. It was not an ideal lunch spot, but the sun was drowsily warm through the diffusing acacia leaves, and we were proud of our indigenous purchases. We had coffee and a couple of glasses of rich, purposeful brandy, more like souped-up dessert wine than cognac. Then we drove back up through the hills, round the mighty flank of yesterday's mountain, its terracing now sharply etched in the transverse sun of afternoon. These terraces, in Arab times and after, used to be planted with mulberry trees. This area was one of the centres of the silk industry, providing raiment for caliphs and kings and grandees, for courtiers and courtesans, and the material for tents and pennons and boudoir hangings, all across the Mediterranean world, until superseded by the looms of Languedoc.

Back home we had no need to search for Rosalia to get her instructions on the *brasero*. Parking our car at the bottom of the village had the same effect as pouring a pre-prandial gin and tonic – she instantly materialized at our door like a large black genie and started to cross-examine us about our shopping trip. (In actual fact, Rosalia is not large. She *seems* large: something to do with a combination of personality and sheer muscle. But stand her next to Georgina and she comes up to Georgina's shoulder – and Georgina is only 5′2″.)

The *brasero* was laid like a votary offering on the ground outside our front door. Into it Rosalia tossed some feathery fragments of dried Spanish broom, *Spartium junceum*, which gilds the uncultivated shoulders of the hillsides here in May. On top of this she shredded a macedoine of almond-tree prunings and olive twigs, garnished with the half-charred remains of a vine root. Then she set a match to the broom. At once it became a mass of flames, which settled down to a steadily glowing heap of twigs, from which rose a thread of blue smoke, erect in the still air of evening. An hour later, the embers had been reduced to hot ash and the *brasero* was ready. Rosalia lifted it by the handles and carried it into the house. Lurching perilously down the steep steps into the kitchen, she slotted it into the round hole in the base of the table. Then she stood back, pursing her lips with dissatisfaction. We lacked a tablecloth. The importance of the cloth only became apparent when, on subsequent days, we visited other families at this hour of the evening. There they sat round their little tables, with their knees tucked under a floor-length cloth, toasting their legs in the warmth emanating from the *brasero*. Knowingly or not, they were enjoying a centuries-old Arab method of central heating, inherited intact. But while the lower halves of their bodies were thus still rooted in the culture of Islam, the upper halves were committed to the twentieth century: every pair of eyes was directed at the television set.

14 April

Next morning it was as though the paths of sleep had led us to a different country. The sky was grey and the air was heavy with moisture. As we peered over our patio wall, the village appeared to have been transformed into a Kashmiri hill-station. Long scarves of mist trailed through the valley below us and wrapped the flanks of the mountain opposite. Voices had a slightly muffled quality, and a damp earthy smell prickled our nostrils.

Inside, the claustrophobic nature of our house's architecture impinged on us for the first time. The low ceilings weighed on our heads. The troglodytic walls loomed closer and took on the clamminess of a grotto. Lacking even a single window, and with the weather too chill for us to open the front door, the little sitting-room was as inhospitable as a subterranean ossuary. We turned on all the lights, chafed our hands in front of a gas heater, and wondered whether to light a log fire. But we lacked logs, and also the will to go searching for them on the dank hillsides.

With a crash Rosalia threw open the door, dislodging a sprinkling of plaster fragments from the crumbling frame. She would show us, she said, how to cook the octopus. We couldn't recall having told her we'd bought an octopus. She strode ahead of us into the kitchen, and rummaged through the refrigerator until she found the slimy little corpse. Taking it to the sink she deftly skinned it, and whittled at it with a knife, removing inedible portions. And now, she said, we must hang it up on the washing-line. We eyed her narrowly. Had our Spanish let us down again? We followed her sceptically as she walked through the house to the patio, where she hung the octopus on the line, between a couple of pairs of underpants. The sun would tenderize it, she said. But there was no sun, we cried, putting our finger on what appeared to be a major flaw in this project. There would be later, she replied with a finality that suggested that she would ordain it personally.

Later in the morning, at about noon, there was a voice at the door. It was Angel. He apologized for not having visited us before: was everything well in the house? We gave him a glass of Consuela's wine. His nostrils wrinkled imperceptibly as he tasted it. He would give us some wine, he said, some good wine. Did we have a spare bottle? If so, we could go along with him to his *bodega* now, and collect it.

Every house in the village, as we were coming to realize, was a unit incorporating a wine shed and a mule-stall. From outside, the simple white façades gave no clue to the interiors, and each of the heavy wooden doors was as likely to open into a stable as into a living-room. Angel's *bodega* was at the back of his house. He led us through his Stygian little sitting-room (windowless, like ours), and entered the *bodega* with the possessive purposefulness of a don entering his study. It was a tall, narrow lean-to, half lit by one small window high up near the roof. As in all the older rooms of the village, decades of whitewashing

91

had coated the surfaces with a layer as impalpable and contour-softening as liquescent ice cream. Along the left-hand side of the room, and filling it from end to end, was a row of enormous barrels. They varied slightly in size and condition: some had cracks in the end, sealed with wax. They were evidently of some age, and the oak was as dark and dense as a Jacobean dresser. Angel confirmed that one could no longer buy them. These survivors, scattered through the village in two dozen similar cellars, were relics of an earlier era of the cooper's craft: apt custodians, year by year, of the life-blood of the valley. Dalmácija was a miniature St Emilion. People came from miles around to buy its wine.

Angel scrambled up on to one of the barrels like a bareback rider. Removing the brick which sealed the square aperture in the top, he reached down into the depths with a scoop fashioned from a length of bamboo. The scoop exactly filled a glass. Angel held it up to the light, fished out a couple of mosquitoes with a stubby forefinger, and passed it to us, followed by another. We sipped the wine cautiously. This one, he explained, was a blend of muscatel and other varieties. All the village's wine was white – or rather of various tones of honey-colour – and all had the pervasive tang of the muscat, the grape of the Greeks. It was an acquired taste. We acquired it with no difficulty at all. But when, at the end of our visit, we took a bottle back to England, it tasted vile. Dalmácija's wine was part of its indigenous persona, as essentially rooted on that hillside as the wild flowers. It could not be transplanted.

Angel moved on to another barrel. This wine was drier. Where had its grapes come from? we asked. He gestured broadly in all directions. He had plots of land scattered everywhere, as did most of the villagers. Grapes from different sectors of the terrain had different characteristics, according to the soil, sun, vine variety and time of picking. Over the years he had developed, through progressive experimentation hardening into tradition, a number of mixtures to give him his various blends.

But the next one was not a blend. It came from the end barrel, and Angel approached it with the reverence of a high priest entering the holy of holies. The wine was darker, the colour of amber. It was pure muscatel. It filled the mouth, and appeared to be doing interesting things to the central nervous system. How strong was it? we asked. About seventeen degrees, he said. Nearly the strength of sherry, we said, impressed. It was the wrong thing to say. These villagers despised the more famous vinification that took place over the mountains. We put no chemicals in *our* wine, said Angel, with the nearest this kindly man could get to a sneer. This was pure, healthy wine, he continued, like a Victorian patent-medicine purveyor extolling some new elixir: nobody felt bad after drinking it.

Encouraged by this testimonial, we had another glass. How old was it? we asked. Very old. Three years. None of the other wines was more than a year old. Why not — didn't they keep? Well, no . . . and with a smile Angel made a gesture of raising a glass to his lips. It was the human factor that made Dalmácija wines short-lived.

Which wine would we like to take away with us, he asked. This one, we said, gesturing a little unsteadily with the glass of muscatel; it pleased us very much; it was of the best. 'Ooh!' said Angel. He had a way of saying 'Ooh!', to express approval or enthusiasm. His lips pursed, the bushy eyebrows shot up, and the eyes — always warm — positively caught fire. 'Ooh!' he would say, whenever we praised something tangible, like wine or home-cured ham, or something abstract, like the tranquillity of village life or the value of friendship. 'Ooh!': it was a monosyllable which seemed to come from his heart, from the most truthful centre of his being. We hardly knew Angel — we had only met him a few times since the initial purchase of his house – and by the normal rules of friendship we had little enough in common, whether in age or in language or in the tenor of our lives, yet if friendship is a kind of love (love without its wings, according to Byron), Angel was a good friend.

As he rinsed our bottle under the tap and filled it with the muscatel, his wife appeared in the doorway of the *bodega*. Ana had the same warmth of face and manner as Angel, but his gentleness was replaced, in her case, by a brisk animation. She talked faster than I have heard anyone speak any language before or since. As the Andalusian accent already sheds a number of consonants and elides the contiguous vowels that result, Ana's speeches came at us in a continuous stream, like a high-pressure hose. In lieu of comprehension we nodded and smiled, hoping that the conversation would require no head-shaking or frowning. On this occasion what we had thus assented to was, it soon transpired, some *tapas* to go with the glasses of wine: a big plate laden with slices of bread topped with Serrano ham.

While we ate, and continued our endorsement of the muscatel, Angel led us out to the little patio at the back of the house. On the way we passed his bathroom. This had been the first bathroom in the village, installed soon after we bought our house: a place of pride and pilgrimage. It had been kept locked, and distinguished visitors were occasionally taken on conducted tours of it. Now it was evidently regarded as of more casual value. Through the open door we could see a couple of sacks of almonds, and a chicken wandered in and out.

The patio was shaded by a vine, now in first leaf. Beyond it was a wine press, one of only two in the village. We looked forward to seeing it in action in October, when, Angel told us, it would be working flat out for a month. Below the patio was a tiny garden, barely five yards square, containing some newly planted fruit trees. This, he said, was a *chirimoyo*. We looked blank, and his description was no help. Later we discovered a *chirimoyo* to be a custard apple – a favourite fruit of the Arabs. Moving on down the slope Angel stopped by a little cherry tree. He had grafted the scion on to an almond stock. His finger caressed the graft where the two life forces had joined, as though in benediction. For a short moment he was a Pan, transpiring fertility into his creation.

It was three o'clock when we finally left Angel and Ana, and the sun was shining, as Rosalia had promised. In addition to the wine in the bottle, we were carrying a good deal of it internally. Back in our own little patio we sat down on the step, then lolled, then lay. The bright light beat down, the octopus and clothes hung motionless above us on the washing-line, and a great drowsiness swept over us. We closed our eyes.

Two hours later we awoke with a curious sensation. We felt fine. This was not at all what we had been expecting. Clearly Angel's promises about the local wine were true. No other brew, surely, would have allowed us to marinate on a stone step through the heat of the day and awake fresh at the end of it. We arose with new ambition, unpegged the octopus from the line and took him inside. Surely he must be tenderized by now. Rosalia, in the course of her cocktail-hour visit, recommended simmering him in wine and saffron, but we were in no mood for an extended cooking process. Instead, we chopped him up and grilled him over the open fire in the sitting-room. The result was delicious. Tender it was not. The texture was that of heavy-duty polythene, and our jaws ached for days.

15 April
We had been given the name of a builder in Álamos. We needed him for the rebuilding of the *bodega*. It was, at the moment, a ruin. The gaunt peeling room was empty except for the large manger at one end, and the masonry trestles on which the barrels used to stand. Daylight could be seen through chinks in

the roof, and half a dozen of the massive earthenware tiles were poking through the ruined wattle like loose teeth in rotten gums. Since the roof needed renewal in any case, our intention was to rebuild it as a flat terrace, accessible through a new door to be cut in the exterior wall upstairs: and to convert the *bodega* into a downstairs bedroom.

This seemed too major a task for Luis, our local builder. Luis was an amiable hypochondriac and a drunk. Thin as a bamboo, with a bright eye, a jaunty walk and a pocketful of pills for whatever happened to be his latest ailment, he had done an excellent job in helping the plumber to install the kitchen sink and the bathroom; but we were not sure he would be capable of any architectural niceties. He was better – despite the claimed disintegration of his heart, liver, right ear and respiratory system – at the more rugged manual tasks. It was he, served by a surly youth as his peon, who had reduced the alleyway below our house to an approximation of one of the more disputed corners of the Somme, while installing our main drain. For the villagers, it had been a traumatic introduction to plumbing: any visitor to the shop or the cemetery had had to teeter over Matterhorns of rubble. The destination of the sewer, as for all other waste matter, was the nearest hillside. Here it emptied itself with typical insouciance, and soon prompted the burgeoning of a lush green oasis, visible far down the valley. While digging the last few yards of the trench, Luis's pick had turned up an unmistakable stone axe. We'd pounced on it with squeaks of excitement, but Luis had taken it calmly: there were plenty of things like that to be found in the village, he said. We took the axe back to England to be dated by the British Museum. Neolithic, about 3,500 BC, was the verdict.

That had been last year. Luis's reputation in the village had dipped a little since then. Following increased inroads into the beer supply at the bar, he had embarked on various whitewashing projects which had left more whitewash on the ground than on the walls. And he had taken to climbing into our rear patio and availing himself of our newly installed shower, on the grounds that it was his responsibility – as installer – to test the product in use. While there, he also felt obliged to test my razor, after-shave and deodorant, and apparently Georgina's hairspray. As for the First Aid pack which we had bought in anticipation of future visits by our children, this was seriously depleted: Luis had evidently suffered a multiple crisis requiring antiseptic spray, several yards of bandages and a bottle of diarrhoea pills.

Rosalia claimed to have caught Luis on top of the wall one night, reeking of after-shave, and to have had an altercation with him during which he threatened her with a machete. This seemed unlikely. It would have required more courage than most men possess, and did not square with Luis's sunny nature. But it helped to explain why Rosalia extolled the virtues of a man called José, in Álamos. Apart from being a cousin, like everyone else, he was a *buen hombre*, a *maestro*, a king among builders. And he could be guaranteed not to purloin my after-shave.

There was, as it transpired, a further motive for Rosalia's encouraging our visit to Álamos that day. Could we please buy her some goat? It was on sale in the market. A kilo would do her nicely.

We parked the car in the road below Álamos, and walked up a rutted track beside a small almond ware-house, built a few years before but still unwhitewashed. Although meticulous about the annual or even bi-annual whitewashing of the old houses, Andalusians are more casual about the recent additions, and every village is pockmarked with cubes of bare brick among the prevailing white. Most of them get whitewashed in due course. These things take time.

The alleyway was generously strewn with mule droppings, and the central rut was moist with the evidence of an imperfect or non-existent drainage system. Álamos was a grubbier village than Dalmácija: but being bigger it had more architectural variety. Ahead of us the alley threaded a deep tunnel under a tall, narrow building with an arcaded loggia on top; and behind the wall on our left waved the palm and banana fronds of a small garden. The smell of the dung hung heavy between the narrow walls. It was going to be a warm day.

The market was an unusual little building: circular, with a Chinese-hat-shaped tiled roof, and a series of small stalls opening outwards round the perimeter. Only three of the stalls were open. One was selling some rather flaccid-looking vegetables, and another was a fishmonger's, purveying two sizes of sardine and a pile of glistening gravelly clams. The third was the butcher's. It was manned, if that's the word, by a gristly old lady with a weather-beaten face, her black dress largely eclipsed by a voluminous plastic apron. She eyed us incuriously as we approached. Small portions of meat hung along the front of the stall like a fringe, and in answer to our request for goat she unhooked a couple of them, visually indistinguishable from the rest, and set about them with a ferocious cleaver. The resulting debris was tossed into two pieces of newspaper, one for Rosalia and one for us, and pushed unceremoniously across the counter. This lady had clearly not been on the same gift-wrapping course as the rest of the population.

Our next stop was the post office, a few yards down the hill. Rosalia had gleefully given us a formidable document, brought by the postman, which apparently summoned us for non-payment of rates. This came as a shock. We had thought we were beyond the reach of bureaucracy, up in these hills. Clutching the dread proscription, we knocked on the post office door. There was no answer. Evidently the institution operated in the same way as Consuela's shop: its hours were dependent on the routine of the administrator.

A man passed by and saw us belabouring the door. The lady was not there, he explained superfluously, but he knew where she was. Or where she might be. He would lead us thither. This was kind of him, as the streets of Álamos proved to be steep, and all of them led upwards. We followed him past a fountain and up a corkscrew ascent. The houses, clustered together to provide mutual support against the tug of gravity, had evidently been erected wherever a pick could clear a platform of rock, and the alley followed the former goat track between them. The walls were largely blank at street level, punctuated only by the occasional curtained doorway, or by gated orifices leading into gloomy undercrofts. We looked hopefully into these for a glimpse of wine barrels, as at Dalmácija, but they were tenanted by mules, or cluttered with firewood, hessian sacks and chicken-coops.

At first-floor level jutted small balconies with wrought-iron railings. Every inch of their horizontal space was crammed with flower-pots, or with boxes and rusty cans pressed into service as planters, and more flower-pots were lashed to the rim of the railings. All the containers were planted with geraniums, carnations and various succulents, and little light could have penetrated to the rooms behind. In this close-packed warren of human habitation few villagers had flowerbeds on terra firma, so they had moved their horticulture aloft and their hanging gardens decked the walls above us like celebratory hangings at a procession, drawing our eyes from the breakneck cobbles beneath our feet to the bright ribbon of firmament that shone between the earthenware eaves above.

Breathing heavily, we finally reached a broader street which was almost level, where our guide suddenly vanished through one of the curtained doorways. A moment later he reappeared, shaking his head. The post-office lady was not there, but he knew exactly where she was. This confidence was not dented by the fact that the quarry proved not to be at the town hall, nor at a trio of private houses, nor the tiny hardware stall on the corner, nor visible in the square by the church. By now we seemed to have covered the entire ground-plan of Álamos, which was more extensive than we had supposed, and our guide's patience must have been wearing thin. But his courtesy was undiminished as he parted yet another curtain over the door of yet another shop. This time, evidently, we were lucky. He introduced us to a stout lady waiting at the counter, and departed with a smile and a touch of his hat.

Our elusive civil servant evidently had a long shopping list. We waited while her purchases were weighed out seriatim on a pair of brass scales like Consuela's, and stuffed into two baskets the size of mule panniers. The full inventory could have fed the Eighth Army for a week. At last she pushed a bundle of lacerated peseta notes across the counter, and creaked sideways through the doorway into the sunshine outside. Back at the post office we explained our mission and showed her the document. She shook her head decisively. This was not a matter for her. We must go to the Office of Rural Domestic Something-or-other in Valdez.

We digested this information in silence: then, in an attempt to retrieve something from the ruin of the morning, we asked her for some stamps. She looked at us compassionately. Clearly we were new to the region. Stamps were not to be purchased at the post office but at the tobacconist's. Where was the tobacconist? At the top of the village. We decided to forgo the purchase of stamps. Did she know where José the builder lived? To our relief it was quite close by. We trudged along a couple of alleyways to his house and knocked on the door. It was opened, eventually, by his wife. No, José was not there, he was working. Perhaps we could return in the evening.

By now the day was half gone, and we had nothing to show for it except two soggy and increasingly redolent packages of goat. When we reached the car it was no longer in the shade but in full sunshine. Opening the door was like peering into the fire-box of the Orient Express.

I returned to Álamos that evening to renew the search for José. The warmth had gone out of the day, and I shivered a little in my sweater. The twilight softened the outlines of the seedy little village, and outside all the houses the women had lit their *braseros*. In the absolute stillness of the air the thin plumes of grey smoke formed an insubstantial colonnade, a row of slender pillars that rose to the level of the eaves, where the fumes dispersed and drifted and regathered, and finally returned to fill my nostrils.

José's wife admitted me to his house. No, he was not yet back. He was working on a big new warehouse on the far side of the village, which had to be completed before the almond season. Would I like a glass of wine? She sat me down in a hallway in the centre of the house. In the dim light it looked like the lobby of a rural bank, in miniature: a glimmer of polished floor, a thicket of potted plants silhouetted against some kind of patio which opened behind. I had been sipping my wine a while in silence before a creak and a flicker of movement betrayed the presence of an old man seated in the shadows at the far end of the room. I bade him good evening, and announced my mission. I had bought a house in Dalmácija, I said, and wanted José to help me with some building work. A house in Dalmácija? In Dalmácija! It was as though I had announced a construction project in Irkutsk instead of two kilometres up the road. In Dalmácija! He was evidently speculating inwardly on whether his son was capable of travelling that far to work.

José's wife reappeared to refill my glass and apologize for her husband's non-appearance. Would I like some *tapas*? I declined, explaining that I was hoping to eat supper shortly. The darkness intensified, and the barely visible bulk of the old man, silent in his chair, took on the immobility of a crusader on a monument. On the wall beside me a face glowed like an icon. It was a photograph of José – I assumed – in sailor's uniform. His wife, meantime, had vanished again. The session was turning into a vigil.

I drained the glass and stood up, shattering the silence with the grating of my chair on the paving. This brought the wife again, with renewed apologies and a proposal. José was going up to Dalmácija tomorrow to see a friend: could he call in on me? Of course, I replied: at what hour? In the evening, she said. At what hour? In the evening. I briefly clasped the cold, saurian hand of the old man and returned to the car.

Later, in front of the comparative warmth of our sitting-room fire, we discussed the village of Álamos with Rosalia and Jesus. It was dirty, we said. Yes, agreed Rosalia, and the people were unfriendly. This seemed a hard judgement – after all, one man had guided us all over Álamos that morning – but Rosalia pressed the point. They fought with knives in Álamos, she said. And we should lock our doors, added Jesus, if people from Álamos ever came up here, for a *fiesta*, for instance. But how, we asked, could the people of two villages so close together be so different? Jesus held out his hand. Look at those two fingers, he said. They're touching each other – but they're different.

16 April

We were hardly clothed and in our right minds the next morning when there was a rattle at the bead curtains, and a man came in. He was elderly, but long-striding and upright, with a gallant bearing and a bright, direct stare. *¡Guapa!* he had cried when he had first met Georgina a couple of years ago: a good-looker! His name was Aurelio, and today, after some enquiries as to how we were settling into the village, he came to the point: would we like some lemons?

We followed him down the slope, past the church to a shed at the bottom, where he unlocked the big new steel doors. Inside, the walls were bare brick, unwhitewashed. He apologized for the unfinished state: the place was paying for itself, year by year: maybe next year . . . All along one wall were string-mesh sacks of lemons, glistening in the gloom. Aurelio half raised one of them, painstakingly attached a cord around the middle, and inserted the hook of an ancient weighing machine. Then, quivering with effort, he raised hook and sack with one hand, and slid the weight along the machine's metal arm with the other: sixteen kilograms. He seemed disappointed and tried another: eighteen kilograms. He looked along the rows of yellow sacks and picked a plump one: nineteen kilograms. It doesn't want to go to twenty, he said regretfully.

There were no free samples for us here. All these lemons were packed up, ready for collection by lorry. He had only brought us in here as a sideshow: the main event was still to come, a visit to the lemon grove. We waited, intrigued, while he relocked the door of the shed, and led us down on to the road. We had not seen any lemon trees hereabouts.

We crossed the road and scrambled down the bank on the other side. Two men were hacking at the ground with mattocks, removing every trace of the brilliantly flowering bugloss, marigold and Cape sorrel that grew thicker than buttercups in a Thames water-meadow along the old terraces beneath the dark almond trunks. Why did they have to do it? I asked. To strengthen the almond trees, they said: the weeds consumed vitamins from the soil. But wouldn't the summer sun kill all the wild flowers in a month anyway? They shrugged. The work was necessary. Besides, they took home the grubbed-out weeds for their mules.

As we followed Aurelio along one of the terraces I mused on the disappearance from northern Europe of the mattock, the archetypal peasant agricultural tool since the Stone Age. Across the more impoverished regions of the world it is still the universal implement, and the rhythmic rise and fall of the heavy metal incisor into the earth . . . clunk, clunk, clunk . . . is the most characteristic activity of rural labour, whether of an Andean Indian scarifying his hillside, or a Sumatran farmer regulating the irrigation of his paddy-fields, or a Chinese labour force building a dam. But in England we have opted for the spade, although I did once find a rusty mattock-head in my grandfather's shed.

Aurelio stopped ahead, where the path plunged down from the rim of the terrace into the neck of a gully. We followed him through this miniature pass, and found that beyond it the gully opened out into two broad terraces, carved out from the side of the little valley. They were filled with lemon trees. We were only fifty yards below the village but this orchard was so secret, so neatly inserted into the landscape, that we had never suspected its existence.

There were a hundred trees here, said Aurelio: he had planted them thirty years before, after levelling the terraces and building the rock-faced retaining walls, using only his hands and a mattock. He had dug two cisterns for irrigation, which drew on the underground moisture of the gully bottom. The water never failed, he said. It was led along the terraces and from level to level by a series of trenches and pipes. All through the year he had to check them, and keep them clear of earth and weeds and leaves.

We walked among the trees in deep, blossom-scented shade, crunching underfoot the layer of last year's almond husks which had been spread for compost. In a peasant economy, nothing is wasted. Aurelio urged me up one of the trees: the largest lemons, he said, were at the top. Some of them, indeed, were as huge as grapefruit, cadmium-yellow, faintly flushed with green, glowing in the dappled half-light between the branches. The trees fruited throughout the year, said Aurelio, bearing blossom and fruit together: but now was the best time. Did they command a good price? we asked. No, not very much, he said, less than almonds and raisins. But this was all the land he now had. He was too old to work the vineyards any more.

Back in the village, our pockets bulging with lemons, we thanked Aurelio and tried to take our leave. But his generosity was not yet done. Would we like some vinegar? We walked along one of the alleys below the church to his *bodega*, a small white room with three barrels at one end. He swilled out a brandy bottle with some murky fluid from a plastic jug on the window ledge, and unhooked from a nail in the wall a dipper, made not of the usual bamboo but of an anchovy tin with a handle soldered to it. Reaching through the top of the left-hand barrel he scooped out the vinegar (a failure in vinification, perhaps? – we didn't ask) and filled the bottle. Then he rinsed out the scoop, and from the second barrel poured us each a glass of wine. Whether through hospitality or instinct, even strangers here assume – unerringly – that Georgina is a wine-drinker. No other woman in the village drinks wine, that we have seen. The various *bodegas* are like a network of pubs or clubs, where the men gather when they are not working in the fields. The women stick to lemonade or coffee.

It was now ten in the morning as we sipped our wine, but wine-bibbing in these parts knows no hours. As we drank, we looked around the room. There was a plastic curtain on a rod across the centre, and an up-ended plastic armchair. Aurelio told us that he lived with his daughter-in-law in a house at the top of the village, but when that filled up with almonds at the end of the summer, he would move down here. The almonds had to be where the women were: the dehusking was done by hand and took all day for many weeks. At that time of the year he would sit here in his *bodega* and read. Read? Few of the villagers appeared to be literate, and we had seen no books. Television was the evening pastime. Yes, said Aurelio, he enjoyed reading. Especially history. Those Arab terraces on the hillside, and the castle, he knew all about them. And the prickly pears: did we know they had been imported from the Indies by Columbus as food for the cochineal insect? The insect was used to produce purple dye. Purple was worth much money in those days . . . a big export from the region. As he sat erect on a primitive stool his eyes softened, like a cinematographic dissolve signalling a flashback, and his mind appeared to flicker away from the rigours of the present to a more prosperous and flamboyant past. And what about this village? we asked. How long had it been here? For a moment Aurelio's learning faltered. He waved his arm in a vaguely expansive gesture. For ever, he said.

It was far down the afternoon before José the builder arrived. Business here tends to be conducted early or late, even in the less torrid parts of the year. José was a man of medium build, with a rolling gait and an air of contained efficiency. He would, I thought, be hard to remember in future years, because of the equilibrium of all his characteristics. His shyness controlled his personal mannerisms, and he said little except when addressed. But his large leathery hand had a firm clasp, and his face was open and friendly. At once we trusted him. This was the man to tackle our architectural problems.

It became clear that he was going to tackle them by instinct, by a kind of osmotic comprehension. Although I pursued him like an acolyte with diagrams on several sheets of paper, over which I had laboured for hours with, I fancied, an impressive degree of dexterity, he shrugged them aside. After a brief review of what had been accomplished to date – clearly to a lower standard than that of his own home – we moved on to the rest of the house. First, the main roof upstairs. It had looked robust enough to us, or we would not have bought the house, but José's lips pursed as his eyes flickered over the beams. He shook one, and a pound or two of mixed solids cascaded on to my pillow, accompanied by an indignant beetle. Three beams would need to be replaced, he said. They must be rough round ones, we said anxiously: everything *tipico*. Yes, yes, he appreciated that. He had some old beams in his yard. He would donate them to us.

We retraced our steps down the narrow stairs – very *tipico*, commented José, as he hit his head on the low overhang – and made our way into the *bodega*, where the bulk of the work was to be done. José eyed the roof with the detachment of a surgeon surveying a gangrenous limb. We explained that it was to be replaced with a flat terrace. Concrete beams, he asked, infilled with *bovedillas*? I knew all about *bovedillas*. By now I dreamed in builders' jargon. *Bovedillas* would be a possibility, I said, but how about a more *tipico* roof of beams and canes, as in the rest of the house? Beams and canes would be *tipico*, José agreed, with the air of a man being asked to erect a thatched cottage in Piccadilly: but for a flat roof they might leak. We could have a leaky *tipico* roof, or we could have concrete beams and *bovedillas*. We settled for the *bovedillas*. Plus a relining of the uphill wall, to try and prevent the effluence of the next-door farmyard from seeping under the beds.

We then quickly agreed the built-in cupboard, which would go from *here* to *here*; and the double-arched window opening into a new light-well at the end; and the replacement of the stable door leading into the patio; and the removal of the manger, creating space for a store cupboard extending from *here* to *here.* Then, moving outside, we looked up at the non-existent roof terrace and the non-existent door leading out of our bedroom, and planned the pillars to support the vine trellis *there* and *there*: and at the far end a barbecue, about *so* big, with masonry shelves on either side, *so* and *so*, and my hand inscribed a deft architect's drawing in mid-air. And the terrace would be paved with earthenware tiles. And cast-iron railings. Yes, understood: he would show us where to buy them and we could specify the pattern we needed.

The briefing was finished. José had taken not a single note. It was like Eisenhower planning the Normandy landings in his head. Only the man's air of competence dissuaded us from discharging him on the spot, and re-engaging Luis, aftershave and all. But there were notes for us to take. José produced a retracting tape from his pocket, and proceeded to run it over the dimensions involved. We would need so many *bloques*, he told us, and so many *medios-bloques:* this many *sacos de cemento*, and that many *vigas de cemento*, of such-and-such a length. And of course the *bovedillas*: thus many would suffice. And so many square metres of tiles. My pen scribbled furiously on the back of an envelope. Where would I find all these articles? I asked. José specified a large builder's merchant in Valdez, for most of them. And transport? Who would bring them up here for us? There was a man in Álamos with a lorry, he said. He, too, was called José. But it would be easy to identify him. We must simply ask for Chico de Álamos: the Child of Álamos. Everyone called him that. Why? José smiled for the first time. Everyone called him that, he repeated.

17 April

We didn't feel capable of tackling José the builder's shopping list on our own. We decided to enlist the help of José the plumber. The various Josés were beginning to assemble themselves into a Welsh-style cast list. We had already met a couple in the village, and José the lorryman – mentioned last night by José the builder – was yet to come.

It was José the plumber who had helped Luis install our bathroom and kitchen. He lived in Valdez, down in the plain, and his fear of the mountain roads up to Dalmácija had delayed the plumbing of the house by several months – eventually years – but in the process he had become our friend. He was the only local Spaniard who could comprehend our interest in antique objects (including the house). The ambition of all local inhabitants, rural and urban, was to buy brightly veneered modern furniture as soon as they could afford it, and throw out the old. Cement floors were thought preferable to earthenware tiles, plastic dolls and framed photographs of Granada were superior ornaments to the traditional pottery dishes and jugs. But José realized that we had reactionary tastes, and had catered to them the year before by selling us our brass bedstead, and a massive old double ox-yoke which we had hung on the wall of our sitting-room. It bore a few traces of russet paint, much faded by time, and the underside had a glossy patina achieved by years of rhythmic frotting from the great patient shoulders beneath.

José had built himself a new house. It stood in a dust-bowl on the edge of Valdez, a waste area between the lowermost shopping street and the bull-ring. A makeshift automotive repair shop and a small electrical warehouse were his only neighbours, and on our arrival the area was deserted apart from two girls playing hopscotch in the dust. But we had evidently timed our visit right: José's wizened grey van was standing outside. It looked like a long-term out-patient of the mechanic next door.

Our ringing of the doorbell brought a squawk from above. José's wife Paquita, leaning over the balcony, shouted to us to come upstairs. The ground floor of the house was taken up with a garage and workshop, with the living quarters over them: a twentieth-century version of our villagers living over their mules and their wine.

The staircase was formidable and immaculate: brightly patterned tiles on the steps, a large brass chandelier over the half-landing, and an aggressive-looking aspidistra in a pot in the corner. At the top, a smiling Paquita sat us down in the kitchen to await the great man. It was a well-equipped room, but tiny. All Andalusian rooms are tiny. Most of the rooms in the Alhambra at Granada and the Alcázar at Seville are of modest size, even the state reception rooms. Only the Great Mosque is huge. As in the rest of medieval Europe, God has been assigned more space than man.

After a wait nicely calculated to sharpen anticipation without abrading patience, José appeared to greet us, dapper in a freshly laundered shirt and well pressed trousers. He was a tiny man with hooded eyes and the fragility of one recovering from long illness. He had an air of dignified reserve, which forever teetered on the brink of self-importance. Only later did we discover that this manner was largely assumed, and constituted a shallow disguise: on a subsequent visit, when we brought our young children, his underlying warmth was instantly revealed: down on his knees, he dandled the little boys, clucking like a broody hen, his sombre eyes incandescent with vicarious paternity.

But now it was José the entrepreneur we saw, the man of affairs, with his finger on all the requisite sources of supply. We needed floor tiles? And railings? And a door? He would take us to the places that sold them. Yes, today: it would be a pleasure, and no inconvenience. Could we please excuse him while he prepared himself. He disappeared for a further ten minutes and returned wearing a hat. We rose to go. First, he said, there was something he wanted to show us. He led us down a short corridor and opened the door at the end. We realized he was showing us his bathroom.

¡Estupendo! we said, as he flushed the loo to give us the full *son et lumière* treatment. Over the next couple of minutes we worked through our diminishing stock of approbationary adjectives as he showed us the two bedrooms, the balcony, the hot-water system, and the sitting-room. The latter was austere and unwelcoming. The leather armchairs were like escapees from a London club, although their effect was somewhat diminished by the crocheted doily on the central table which smacked more of an Eastbourne boarding-house. Over the massive stone fireplace (which showed no trace of ash) hung a shotgun which, similarly, showed no signs of recent use. The ratio of rust to surviving metal was higher than anything I'd seen outside a scrapyard, but to its owner the gun evidently connoted José the Collector, or possibly José the Sportsman: aspects of his persona which he judged to be of interest to us. Through the medium of this decaying fowling-piece, and of the sombre armchairs which faced it, this cement cube of a house in its dusty suburban no-man's-land was to be perceived as the residence of a man of parts.

The conducted tour continued downstairs. After our experiences of the last few days it came almost as a shock to us to see no sacks of almonds nor barrels of wine: instead there were lavatory cisterns, bundles of elbow-joints, taps, ballcocks, and the multifarious paraphernalia of José's trade. From the workshop we passed into the garden, a little kibbutz reclaimed from the rubble-strewn wilderness around it. There were rows of vegetables and flowers. José passed down the ranks of tomatoes like the Queen at Trooping the Colour, pausing at the end to pluck a carnation from a plant beside the path. He gave it to Georgina with a gesture not so much of gallantry as of munificence. At the far end of the garden was a cluster of rabbit hutches, and here, as later with our children, we glimpsed José's essential responsiveness: crouching in the dust, he tickled the furry noses through the wire and apostrophized them lovingly. Then he rose briskly, brushed down his trousers and led us out of the gate, locking it carefully behind him.

Back on the main street we followed him at a great pace up the hill, surprised that a brick-works was to be found in these parts. At the next corner he disappeared abruptly into a bar, where he ordered drinks for Georgina and me: nothing for himself: his kidneys, he said. He had, for a small man, an impressively resonant voice, and his request for a beer and a wine rang with the authority of Caesar ordering his legions across the Rubicon. While Georgina and I drank, he conversed forcefully with the other inhabitants of the bar, all of whom he knew. Several pairs of eyes swivelled in our direction as he explained our errands, and I wished I'd worn a more dashing shirt. We were evidently on show. This was the reason for the visit to the bar.

Having finished our drinks we were ordered back down the hill to our car. José was a nervous passenger, wincing whenever a pedestrian crossed the road within fifty yards of us, and keeping his eyes tightly closed at intersections. In his calmer moments he directed us out of town, on the road towards the mountains. After half a mile he instructed us to turn off, and we bumped down a track towards a group of shacks enclosed within a yard.

Inside the gates, the first sight to greet us was of a half-nude man up to his waist in liquid clay. He was immersed in a large rectangular sunken pit. His task, evidently, was to trudge to and fro, kneading and homogenizing the imprisoning medium, in a muddy and lugubrious travesty of a vintner treading grapes. As the sun beat down on his grime-encrusted shoulders, his slow lurching repetitive endeavours had the despairing intensity of a Dantean penance: a degrading juxtaposition of human and mineral clay: an abasement of man to the role of a mere pestle in this scene of premechanical industry.

Across the yard could be seen the next stage of this crude production line. Another man was trundling a wheelbarrow filled with clay from the pit, and dabbing it out with a shovel into a precise row of liquescent molehills. He was followed by a third man, clad only in a pair of shorts as abbreviated and shapeless as a loin-cloth, who crouched alongside each little pile, wielding an instrument like a giant's pastry-cutter. With it, having first levelled and smoothed the clay with a baton, he stamped out a neat flat square. Behind him lay several rows of them in the sun, still the dark grey colour of the original mud. A few yards away, near the entrance were stacks of the finished product. A week's slow cooking in the kiln had transformed them from grey to pink, like lobsters. It was these crude tiles, rough and mottled and dusty, which were to pave our roof terrace.

José ignored the sweating peons in the yard and strode into one of the sheds. It was a low building, open at the sides and filled with rows of shelving accessible via long central aisles. These aisles, lit only by chinks in the roof and by the few frets of sunshine that could penetrate the enclosing shelves, recalled the monastic gloom of some ancient library, and the artefacts stacked with massive regularity along either side had the same fulvous tones of calf and vellum. They were tiles: the long, curved, tapering, weighty roof-tiles that for centuries have crowned the dwellings of southern Europe, and have in turn provided, in their rough earthenware pores, a habitation for hosts of wind-borne lichens and mosses.

José's newly washed shirt shone in the half-light like a surplice in a crypt: but the man to whom he was now talking was so indistinguishable from the stacks of his wares that he might have been moulded from the same material. He was smaller still than José – an unglazed garden gnome, even to the pyramidal stocking cap on his head. Cap and face and whatever

113

garments he was wearing were deeply encrusted with dust, which had solidified along the contours and recesses of his physiognomy like an armadillo's hide. One was surprised when his earthenware face split to speak. But this happened seldom. It was José who did the talking: having ascertained from us the square meterage of paving tiles required, he briskly translated this into a number of units, and placed our order for us, explaining that they would be collected by Chico de Álamos. Yes, he knew him: and to whom were the tiles to be delivered? To the foreigners at Dalmácija. Dalmácija? Where was Dalmácija? Above Álamos, José explained. The village of Álamos evidently constituted the ultimate limit of civilization up our valley.

Our next stop was also on the edge of town, but in a contrary direction. It was a tall black zeppelin-hangar of a building, echoing with noise. Every element of it except the earthen floor was of metal: walls, roof, gates, and all the contents. We picked our way between a ferrous forest of bed-heads, ploughshares and gear boxes; intestinal tracts of rusty piping lay in unapproachable corners; *chevaux de frise* of part-assembled grillwork barred our way; concussed panels of auto bodies bestrewed the floor like discarded carapaces. The master of this realm was a six-foot, leather-aproned Vulcan, blackened with fire and iron filings, huge-headed in a welding mask. His cross-examination of our requirements was incisive. How many sectors of railing? Of what length apiece? He gestured in the direction of some latter-day curlicues on one of the grilles, but we opted for simple knops midway on the uprights: an approximation of all the older balcony rails in town. The deal was finalized in minutes and we climbed back into the car, picking razor-edged fragments of sprue from our sweaters.

Back in the centre of town we stopped outside a double-gated entrance whose redolence signalled a cleaner order of craftsmanship than at our two earlier ports of call and a graduation from the mineral to the vegetable kingdom. The gates were open, and inside a stone corridor led upwards at a slight incline. Along each wall, like headstones at a mortician's, were propped a continuous row of doors, of varying dimensions, coffered or plain, solid or half-glazed, with shutters or bars or neither, some studded with convex bosses in the traditional style, others aggressively late-twentieth-century in their moulded decoration: all in bare fragrant wood. Sawdust floured the floor, and misted the air, and lay lightly along every horizontal surface. At the top of the incline the passageway opened into a spacious warehouse, busy with the buzz of saws and sanders, and filled with a honey-coloured array of chests and bookcases and tables and window frames. Here too our order for the patio door was attentively received, professionally assessed and discussed, and readied for collection by the ubiquitous Chico de Álamos. We hoped his truck was a large one.

Our day was done. We offered José a drink, as an inadequate gesture of thanks, but again he declined, his delicately fingered hand flickering instinctively towards his kidneys. When were we coming again? In the summer? And we were bringing our children? We must certainly meet. On impulse we invited him and his family to have supper with us during that visit, up at Dalmácija. He looked pleased, but hesitant: partly, we surmised, because of the intervening eleven kilometres which evidently constituted his own personal nightmare: but perhaps also through surprise – Spaniards do not often entertain at home, they prefer to dine out. Having pondered the invitation for a moment, he accepted. We shook hands on it, and parted.

That evening, during the brief pre-Rosalia minutes in front of the fire, we reflected on the experiences of the day. It was not the first time we had renovated a house, but here, unlike in England, we were procuring our materials and components at source. Back home, these purchases would have reached us through the filtration of many middlemen. The workmanship would have been similar: in some instances better, and in others worse: but the journey through the retail system would have obscured the birth of the goods and thus, to our minds, some of their character. Here, we were assembling around us artefacts which had been made nearby – almost on the spot – and thereby steeping ourselves that much more deeply in this little corner of Spain.

18 April
This morning, a little before midday, there was a sudden commotion outside the house. Female voices were raised, and I could hear the movement of feet. A quarrel? An accident? I looked out. A group of women was eddying to and fro in the little square below us. Tied to the acacia tree, and nibbling speculatively at Rosalia's geraniums, stood a mule, laden with a wooden crate on either side of its crupper. The crates were full of lettuces and tomatoes. The vegetable-man was making one of his irregular visits to the village.

A few women had pocket handkerchief-sized bean patches in the gully below the village, but mainly they relied on Consuela, or on the market and shops in Álamos. Álamos was a steep two kilometres away, so buying these mule-borne vegetables avoided the necessity for a sweaty walk. Consuela was also buying, perhaps to hold stock against the morrow, perhaps because she assumed that some of the more distant homes would be unaware of the vegetable-man's visit and therefore dependent on her shop.

Every individual purchase was evidently a major investment project. Prices were disputed down to the last peseta: lettuces were inspected with the thoroughness of a police body-search: tomatoes were so aggressively fingered that one expected to see them puréed on the spot. In this aspect of personal survival, village life was a matriarchal society. The vegetable-man, head and shoulders above his customers, was like a lone swimmer in the swirling tide of black dresses, a solitary male engulfed by females, outnumbered, outshouted, on the defensive in every negotiation. The scene filled the little space between the white walls, while the valley opened up behind to form the backdrop. Gertrude Bone wrote in 1942 that 'on the tawny earth of southern Spain black has all the value of a colour. Nowhere, perhaps, does one appreciate the black sombrero of the men and the mantilla and black dress of the women as in this southern province. A legacy from the veiled Moorish women, or of convent habit, it is wonderfully right, out of doors in the sunlight.' Sombreros and mantillas have disappeared over the intervening years, but in this village the predominant colours are still black for the women, white for the walls, and scarlet for the geraniums.

Georgina bought a lettuce at a price hammered out for us by a negotiating team of Marta (our uphill neighbour) and two other unknown crones. Clutching our trophy, we strolled up to the little platform in front of the church door. The church was unlocked, and we walked in. It consisted of a single whitewashed room filled with benches. A large wooden crucifix hung above the altar, and there were smaller images on the side walls: otherwise the place was bare. The only touch of decoration came from the roof, where the tie-beams that straddled the room were linked, in pairs, by carved Mudejar lattice-work. Nobody knew how old the church was: perhaps seventeenth century.

Three young women were bustling around the church as we looked in. Two were the sisters who lived in the house below Rosalia, one shy and exuberantly blonde, the other petite and sprightly with sharp currant eyes. The third girl was Rosalia's daughter. This was a surprise, as she had left the village to marry a Guardia Civil in a nearby town: what was she doing here? She

117

was here for Easter. So, she said, was her brother Pedro, who had driven all the way from his army post in North Africa for the occasion. Indeed, throughout the week we had seen unfamiliar faces in the streets. The village was filling up. Family bonds stretching far across Spain were being given a central tug by the year's most potent religious festival, and the *emigrés* – many long-departed – were drawn back to their place of birth.

The girls were sweeping the floors and arranging flowers on the altar. They were amused to see us: what were two heathens doing in the church? We tried, not for the first time, to draw a distinction between Protestantism and heathenism, but they remained unconvinced. Did we, then, celebrate Easter in England with processions as they did here? Well, no, but . . . Or saints' days, then? We had no saints' *days*, or rather there were some saints' days, but we didn't celebrate them . . . our holidays were mostly occasions like bank holidays. We worshipped banks? There was much merry laughter: we were evidently making no converts. Defeated, we left the church and took our lettuce home.

For lunch, as the day was fine, we carried a small table out into the little patio at the back. It was like lunching at the bottom of a well, since the house and patio walls stood high around the narrow patch of paving, but enough sunshine permeated the tangle of jasmine to warm our backs and illuminate the pages of our books. The afternoon floated by. Most of the men were out in the fields, and anyone still in the village was indoors, eating or dozing in front of the radio. The thick house walls, almost unpenetrated by windows, sealed in every trace of sound, and the silence was absolute.

By early evening the heart of the village was beating faster. Mules were being unsaddled, and the women were piling twigs on their *braseros*, ready for firing. We too had work to do. Putting on sweaters and more socially acceptable trousers, we strolled down to the car and drove to Álamos. We needed to meet José the lorryman and arrange for the transport of our building materials.

'Just ask for Chico de Álamos,' had been our instruction, and indeed the sobriquet had the efficacy of a password as we penetrated the outworks of the village and moved inwards. *¿El Chico de Álamos?* – and the directing hands would point upwards, indicating a flight of steps, a higher level to be attained. As we neared the summit of the cone of houses, in the thickening twilight, our search began to assume the centripetal momentum of a Conradian pilgrimage, and Chico de Álamos, he who bore the name of the village in his own nickname and resided up here at its apex, achieved in our minds the significance of a shaman . . . the Child, a symbol of rejuvenation . . . the Lorryman, a manipulator who controlled his citizens' contacts with the outer world . . .

His shrine, when we found it, was a curtain-covered doorway like any other. But the room inside was small even in this country of small rooms: and in it sat one of the smallest men I had ever seen. José was strongly built, barrel-chested and vigorous; but his height, standing, was that of another man sitting. He was about forty years of age and extremely friendly. As we explained our business he sat us down and called out into the street through the curtain for the provision of refreshments. Evidently his house contained none. While waiting for their arrival, he questioned us eagerly. Were we German? Ah, English. He had an English friend. Perhaps we knew him: John Richards (he had some trouble in pronouncing the surname, as did we in understanding it), from Plymouth? No, we didn't know Mr Richards: we lived in London. This was accepted as a sufficient excuse for non-acquaintance.

The curtain parted and a woman entered, carrying two beers and a bottle of Málaga wine. José introduced her as his wife. She was, in Sylvia Townsend

119

Warner's phrase, a large smooth creature like a bed-room ewer. Beside her, José was an egg-cup. The discrepancy between their sizes was so immense that the same thought – as we later confessed – occurred to both Georgina and me instantly: how did this pair ever manage to copulate? The act would, surely, present severe technical problems and a degree of personal hazard for José.

However, the man appeared to be unscathed as he poured the drinks and jotted down the details of our purchases on a professionally styled business pad with a large fountain pen. We looked round the room. It showed the same dissonance of dimensions as between José and his spouse. The room itself was minuscule, hardly bigger than a cupboard, with no windows – only the street door and an archway leading into a kitchen which was, at a glance, smaller still. Yet the furniture was massive. Ninety per cent of the floor space was occupied by a table: as we sat around it on hard upright chairs, our backs were against the walls. In a near corner, jammed between the table and the entrance door, was a big colour television set. The far end of the room was filled, wall to wall, with a dresser veneered in a high-gloss plastic finish. Its glass-fronted shelves were crowded with brightly glazed coffee pots, gilt-rimmed liqueur glasses, inlaid cigarette boxes, a donkey carrying a thermometer, a crucifix, an ash-tray from Torremolinos, two flamenco dolls, a copper vase filled with plastic flowers, a corkscrew with a plastic-pelted bull for a handle, and some kind of official citation with José's name on it. On a lower shelf, masking some of these exhibits, was a big, sleek transistor radio. The overall effect suggested that the maturing of José's career had encouraged the acquisition of possessions commensurate more with his status than with his stature, but not a move to larger premises. Perhaps the little man felt more secure in his tiny whitewashed crevice.

Had we paid for our building materials? he asked. No, we said. Then he would pay for them, said José. And how would we pay him? Next time, he said with a shrug. We must come and visit him again when we returned in the summer. He waved an empty beer bottle at his wife, but we declined another drink, shook hands and departed.

It was cold that night, and in addition to the *brasero* and the open fire in our sitting-room hearth we lit a portable gas heater. Its steady hiss contributed a continuo accompaniment to the arpeggios of the wind in the alleyway outside. Rosalia alternately warmed her rheumatic leg at the fire and her hands at the heater: yet in her own house she had neither, only her *brasero*. All these old dwellings had open fireplaces, but none was used except, in many cases, for the siting of simple two-burner gas cookers whose fumes escaped up the chimney.

Rosalia knew all about our visit to Chico de Álamos, of course. When would he deliver the stuff? she asked. In the next couple of days, we said. And who would then provide the *caballeria*? she enquired. The *caballeria*? Cavalry? I had a wild vision of a troop of lancers escorting Chico's lorry up the valley. Rosalia explained. Our goods would be dumped at the bottom of the village: it would then be necessary to bring them up to the house on horse-back, or rather mule-back. We should ask Emilio, the mayor. We had not yet met him, as his house lay on the edge of the village, on the far side. He was a *buen hombre*, said Jesus, very strong, very hard-working. He had worked in Switzerland for four years, to send home money for his family. A number of the men here had done that. It was hard to earn enough from the raisins and almonds: most husbands supplemented their incomes by working for the government on the roads. Jesus did so himself. But when? we asked: wasn't working the fields a full-time job? He smiled, embarrassed at the predicament of his

121

life and how to explain it to foreigners: he pushed back his hat, revealing a Plimsoll-line of white forehead above the weather-beaten brows. Yes, he said, there was much work here on the land, but less in the winter. Then he could take time off, and work for someone else. He had no holidays. He had once taken his children to the sea, seven years ago, when they were young.

19 April
Good Friday. By now the events of the weekend had been outlined for us. There would be a procession in the village today and another on Easter Sunday. There were also processions tonight in Valdez and on the coast at Teles Pires. The latter, we decided, would attract too multinational an audience. So we would attend the one at Valdez tonight – a fine spectacle according to Rosalia – and the one in our own village on Sunday.

The previous night's wind had dropped, and the day was clear and still. Soon it was warmer outside the house than in. Our sweaters came off, then our socks and shoes. We began to fret in the confines of our little rear patio, where the world outside was only visible when we stood on tiptoe. We took our books to the terrace outside the front door. Below us, in an angle formed by a buttress of the church, Remedios sat sewing, as immobile in the sun as a bee on a buddleia. After a few minutes I began to unbutton my shirt and to ponder another move. We decided to drive to the beach. We would spend the day there, and visit the Valdez festivities on the way back.

At that time of year the main beach at Teles Pires was almost empty. When we arrived, there were no more than a few dozen families lying on towels or on long chairs provided by the restaurant. A handful of hardy children were splashing in the water. The bright triangular sails of two wet-suited wind-surfers shone fifty yards offshore, but there was too little wind for them, and they stood there motionless. The scene was a montage of colourful details: what Philip Larkin calls the miniature gaiety of seasides.

The restaurant, too, was sparsely peopled. We picked a table in the sun beside a dispirited oleander, growing reluctantly with its feet in the sand, far from its preferred habitat in the bed of a stream. Gin came and went, and grilled prawns, and wine and coffee and brandy. After a long read the hard chairs began to impinge on our sacroiliacs, and we went for a walk along the beach, past ranks of gaily painted fishing boats to a lighthouse at the end. Shorewards, behind the tall cliffs of the apartment blocks, the encircling mountains filled the northern sky. Somewhere up there, enfolded in a groove of the foothills, lay Dalmácija.

Since all the shops were shut for Good Friday, there was nothing to do except read some more and walk some more and drink some more, until the sky thickened and the Sierras darkened from lavender to heliotrope. It was, in Homer's recurring phrase, the time of the lighting of the lamps: time to go to Valdez for the procession.

The little town was packed. We picked our way through the crowds on foot, following the general drift of humanity up to the big baroque-fronted church of San Juan where the procession was due to begin. As we neared the assembly point every side-turning and alleyway, every alcove between the buttresses of the church, was crammed with the participants in their various costumes, pullulating with anticipation, smoking hurried cigarettes, checking their accoutrements, examining themselves in hand-mirrors: people of all ages from six to sixty, in party dress or religious garb or military uniform. Apprehensive faces glimmered in the shadows between the street lamps. Shouts of command echoed off the narrow walls. Elaborately painted wooden figures stood half revealed on top of their floats, parked ready for action under makeshift tented shelters like shrines. Shouldering our way through this feverish scene was like blundering backstage at some spectacularly costumed opera.

Every street – every person – was imbued with the significance of the day. In this most Catholic of nations, Easter is the most sacred time, and each year the collective devotion crystallizes in every town and village into the processions of Holy Week. Seville, of course, is the doyen of these celebrations, though Málaga claims to be more spectacular still. The occasion is part religious service, part theatre, and presents, above all on Good Friday, the same blend of ritual and colour and death that the Spaniards have reassembled – from different materials – in every staging of a bullfight.

The distant throb of a drum signalled that our march had begun. Georgina and I found a part of the route where we could penetrate as far as the edge of the street. We stood and waited. The first participants to arrive struck a secular note: a detachment of army Pioneers, sauntering past with picks and shovels and other reassuringly rural instruments slung across their shoulders, and forage caps pushed low over pimply foreheads. Not a man seemed to be over twenty years old, and only when they recognized friends in the crowd did their faces show any trace of emotion.

The sight of the next group caused an uneasy tightening of the stomach. Seven foot tall, dwarfing the onlookers, they strode towards us in the long robes and high pointed hoods that have become more familiar as the garb of the Ku-Klux-Klan. 'Thus do rascals appropriate the robes of the just and contaminate them,' a Sevillano once said to James Michener. In fact the costumes are based on those formerly worn by heretics condemned by the Inquisition, and are the insignia of the *confradias*, or confraternities, each connected with a different parish church. There are fifty-two *confradias* in Seville, says Michener: here in Valdez we saw at least a dozen versions of the heretics' robes by the end of the evening.

This first group was in white with embroidered vestments. Some carried banners slung from silver crosses, others huge trumpet-shaped censers, also in silver. Behind the total anonymity of their robes and pointed caps, their identities were an intriguing enigma . . . sex, age, physique, let alone social status, were all in doubt. Here a pair of glasses glinting through the eye-holes, there a rotund belly, here a well-turned ankle, or there a diminutive size and an occasional hop and skip, were partial indicators. Only the Gandalf-like master of ceremonies was clearly defined. Tall, bulky, and waving a crozier like a conductor's baton, he strode to and fro from the front of his posse to the rear, accelerating or retarding the speed of progress, all in mime (there is no mouthpiece in a heretic's hood), and leaving no doubt as to his gender and personality. An alderman, surely, in real life, or a managing director. Certainly one of society's organizers.

There was plenty of time for him to patrol his beat. The procession spent more time standing than moving, and the chinks between the components were filled with townspeople crossing the street or walking down it, mingling with the participants and conversing with them. Chattering children eddied around the stationary phalanxes of soldiers and confraternities like surf around a beached fleet. The cortège advanced a few steps, stopped, and advanced again. The next contingent was a group of embryo nuns – ten-year-old girls, wide-eyed and preternaturally solemn in their austere robes; then came the sinister leather hats of a Guardia Civil band; and then the first of the floats.

The floats in Spanish Easter processions follow a long tradition. The oldest figures on some of them date back to the seventeenth century, but over the years most of them have been renewed, especially during the nineteenth century when there was a period of vivid refurbishment, and glass tears and drops of blood replaced plaster and paint. The twentieth century has brought a further elaboration of costumes and jewellery, and the wonders of electric light have permitted a further heightening of effect. Each creation weighs up to half a ton.

Whatever the excess of detail, the overall impact of these huge images in the half-lit setting of a narrow southern street was colossal. The first float in our procession came lurching round a bend to the beat of a single drum, hugely ominous, almost terrifying. The rhythmic tramp of the bearers gave it a slow rocking motion, which was transmitted upwards to the tall figure of Christ crucified. The Saviour was at first-storey height, turned to one side as though inspecting the contents of every house through the open windows, and the vibrations of His progress gave Him the air of conversing with the watchers who crowded every balcony. At His feet knelt the Madonna, richly dressed. The two figures were illuminated by a floodlight concealed in the framework of the float, and the rest of the design was filled out with flowers, ribbons, and a number of red-glazed lamps like giant strawberries.

It was borne by four rows of bearers. The two exterior rows consisted each of twenty-one men: whether the two central rows continued uninterrupted beneath the catafalque was hard to tell, short of turning the whole thing upside-down like a gargantuan centipede and counting its legs. The mood of the bearers reflected a mixture of relaxation and dedication, the Mediterranean part of their nature conflicting with the purely Spanish. Almost all were chewing gum, and many were smoking: yet the labour of their progress conveyed a powerful discipline and solemnity. At a toll from the bell of the leading man, shouldering a central beam with a carved ram's head like the prow of an Athenian galley, the float stopped and was lowered on to its legs while the bearers stepped out from under it and rubbed their shoulders. At another clang they picked it up again: a third clang, and their lurching gait continued. At some of the longer pauses, the bearers sauntered into the roadside bars to refresh themselves with beer.

There were several such floats, and dozens of contingents of army and police, and hundreds of heretics' robes in white and gold and crimson. All along the route the onlookers were standing in multiple ranks, or sitting on chairs brought out of their houses, or holding blazing flares from upstairs windows. The bars were thronged with consumers of beer and wine and hot chocolate. The occasional tourist – Valdez, being off the coast road, is little frequented – scuttled from viewpoint to viewpoint as the long glittering dragon-tail of the procession snaked in extensive zigzags through the little town. When we walked down to the main viewing stand outside the monastery at the bottom, three hours after our arrival, the head of the cortège had still not arrived, and the lollipop sellers were doing brisk business from their handcarts in the middle of the road. Up the hill, the glow of the approaching flares cast a sepia haze over the white walls and tiled roofs, and a drum throbbed like a heart-beat. Tonight, under the clear spring sky, this rough-and-tumble settlement of Arab streets and modern flats, of markets and stalls and artisans' workshops, had fused into a single sentient organism, united by the intensity of the event. On Monday it would be its normal self again. By then, all the embroidered robes and silver censers and carved crucifixes would be stored away, to await the year to come.

20 April
We are never alone in this house. There are inhabitants here which have been in residence much longer than we. I met one of them this morning, as I reached for some clothes in a cupboard: a gecko, which flickered up the wall and disappeared into a chink between the canes of the roof. He was a ghostly off-white, as though

he had spent all his life deprived of light. I was pleased to see him, as geckoes eat flies, which were in fairly plentiful supply even now in the spring.

My attitudes to symbiosis and ecological recycling had changed over the previous few days. Take the ants. I had found a thriving nest of them in one of the cracks between the earthenware tiles of the kitchen floor. My first reaction when I spotted them was to reach for a kettle of boiling water: I had recollections, I suppose, of my boyhood in the tropics where table legs stood in saucers of paraffin to prevent creepy-crawlies from overrunning the food on the table. But at the last minute I gave these Spanish ants a stay of execution. They didn't assault the table. And next morning I noticed that the breadcrumbs we had spilt on the floor, which I had been too lazy to sweep up, had been neatly removed. The ants were an ecological vacuum-cleaner.

The village operated a similar system on a larger scale. There was no garbage collection. The villagers had been offered one, at the cost of about £1 per family per month, but had refused it. They preferred the old system. The old system consisted of throwing all the rubbish over the side of the hill. Any hill. This was hard to justify aesthetically, but the villagers had no sense of aesthetics, despite living in such a beautiful place; or at any rate a very mixed sense. They loved flowers, but invariably planted them in rusty buckets or discarded oil tins. This was only partly a question of cost-saving – earthenware pots were cheap enough: it was simply that they saw the flowers but didn't see the oil tins. Similarly, they didn't see the rubbish, which by now flecked the slopes below the village like spume around a Hebridean rock.

Until recently this informal system of garbage disposal must have worked well enough. Such villagers live – or certainly used to live – largely on fresh food: bread, rice, fruit, vegetables, fish, the occasional chicken. The uneaten residue of such food, when dumped in the various gullies, would not have lasted long, nor did it nowadays. Cats, birds, rats and mice, and a host of insects soon disposed of it: and anything that even they left was rapidly dried and composted by the sun. The non-biodegradable exceptions to this natural recycling, such as beer bottles, were returnable items, worth money at any shop and therefore seldom discarded. (Even bleach bottles were returnable and stacks of empty ones stood in the corner of every store.) But the symmetry of all this had been changed by the arrival of plastic. Cans were still in scant use, and soon rusted to a discreet brown: but plastic bags, washing-up-liquid bottles and yoghurt pots littered the surrounding hillsides, unperishable and unlovely.

Georgina and I, being more squeamish about such matters, first tried to adapt ourselves to the local situation, and subsequently to circumnavigate it. After a couple of days our garbage bag was full. Lacking the heart to dump it in the nearest olive-grove we decided to compromise, in the best British tradition. We would dump it on the *other side* of the village. At dead of night, with cat-like tread, we carried our load through the alleyway behind the church and down the cobbled track to Angel's house, beyond which was a large and precipitous gully. Cans rattled guiltily inside the plastic sack as we scuttled along. A dog began to bark. Would Angel throw open his door and surprise us on our squalid errand? How could we justify fouling his doorstep rather than ours? We reached the gully and heaved the sack out into the night, like a burial party at the Château d'If. There was a pause before the refuse hit the hillside and rolled into the cactus. Having thus got rid of the evidence, we strolled nonchalantly home, with the air of two star-gazing romantics taking an evening walk. On subsequent days we packed the garbage into the car along with our beach paraphernalia, and dumped it in a dustbin on the coast. This made for smelly driving conditions, but clear consciences.

Today was cloudy, with a wind, and we were busy with indoor tasks. Georgina, washing sheets in the bath, found that we were short of washing-line. I was dispatched to Consuela's house to buy some more. She had some, of course, hanging on a nail between a straw hat and a pair of whitewash brushes. How many metres did I want? She took the hank of cord and trundled to the doorstep, where she got down on her knees like a pilgrim at a shrine. I hadn't realized that selling washing-line was such a solemn business. But no – the threshold was her measure: from one door post to a spidery crack in a certain earthenware tile was exactly a metre. She measured out the length I needed, and then tried to sell me some saffron (for cooking octopus), a copper bowl (for our mantelpiece), a bar of chocolate (a treat for Georgina), and a broom made from a bundle of palm leaves lashed to what looked like a recycled fence pole.

It was half an hour before I emerged, with my washing line securely wrapped and trussed like a Twentieth Dynasty mummified baby. Two small girls were outside the shop, playing with something at the end of a piece of string. It was a gigantic moth, a Great Peacock, with a wing-span of five inches. They called it a *paloma*, the Spanish for dove. The string was tied in a kind of child's harness round its thorax. I'd never seen a moth being taken for a walk before. It didn't seem to mind much.

Something went wrong with our *brasero* that night. We brought it indoors before the burning twigs were fully reduced to ash. In a couple of minutes our kitchen was transformed to a smoke-house, with Georgina and me playing the role of the hams. The sound of our coughing brought Rosalia even earlier than usual, and our predicament raised her to a high good humour. Her laugh is high and soft, almost melodious, but with a predatory edge to it, like an owl's call. We heard a good deal of it that night, as she took the offending *brasero* outdoors again. Was our house in London always full of smoke, hoo, hoo, hoo? Clearly she thought we had bungled a simple everyday chore.

As we tried to explain our reliance on central heating, Jesus's clear blue eyes widened in puzzlement. Finally he shook his head. Life was different in Spain, he said, with the air of a man stumbling on some cosmic truth. And indeed the differences that were emerging daily were of as much interest to them as to us. Rosalia, in her relationship with us, was part mother, part child. She would stand with her arm around Georgina, smiling possessively as she organized her day for her, but simultaneously studying her clothes and earrings. What were these made of? What did they cost? What sort of make-up did she use? Why was she so thin – didn't we eat as well in England? Was meat very expensive there? Similarly she was fascinated by gadgets: an egg-timer, an automatic gas-lighter, even a nutcracker. (Like the other villagers, she used a hammer to crack her almonds.) The most impressive performance was provided on this occasion by our garlic-crusher. Rosalia watched, eyes glistening, as the pale odorous worms of purée curled out through the little grille, and asked if she could borrow it. We said we'd bring her one on our next visit. Rosalia is the personification of honesty, but chattels that are borrowed tend to stay borrowed. Over the years to come we were practically to furnish her house for her with our various loans: spade, hammer, alarm clock, paraffin lamp, various cooking utensils, a cushion for her poor back, a pot for her arum lily, a mirror for her aged mother. Perhaps this represented a latter-day evolution of the Arab spirit of hospitality: whatever the guest admires is pressed on him as a gift. Rosalia found much to admire among our motley possessions.

21 April
Easter Sunday began, for us, at midnight. We were awakened by a shot. Then came another, closer, and

another. By now we were thoroughly alarmed. Were they still fighting the Civil War out there? Had the village decided to purge its foreigners? The next shot sounded in the alleyway outside, and Georgina and I clung together, quaking with apprehension. But there were no more explosions. In the morning all was explained. It is an Andalusian tradition to rouse Christ from His tomb in this way on Easter Day.

All through the morning the little alleyways, normally deserted in the middle of the day, began to fill with people: some unfamiliar, and all garbed with unusual elegance. Two or three sharply urban suits and dresses were on show, with sunglasses and jewellery to match. Rosalia and a handful of other matrons were still in black, but the young ladies of the village had donned bright finery, as though evolving from the pupa stage of their development into the butterfly colours of spring. Tiny boys in sailor suits were manipulated by proud mothers sweating excitedly through their unaccustomed make-up, and pert little girls scuttled to and fro in costumes as crisp as icing sugar.

The church bell began to toll, with more tinny a note than one expects from a belfry, like a guardsman singing in falsetto: and the populace drifted towards the doors of the church. Now for the first time we could assess their numbers: about eighty, including the visitors. As the sun tilted towards afternoon they stood around in groups that intermingled and percolated with the simmering nervousness of a cocktail party. Women adjusted and readjusted their earrings, and Aurelio the lemon man, resplendent in a tweed suit the match of any Madrileno's, flashed us a smile in which friendliness was overlaid with preoccupation. Everyone was waiting for the *Cura*. Dalmácija was too small to have a priest of its own, and on such occasions as this it needed to borrow one from the outside world. Until he arrived, nothing could happen.

Finally a small van could be seen approaching up the valley. It disappeared below the buildings, and the sewing-machine whine of its engine stopped. A couple of minutes later the *Cura* appeared, dark-suited, climbing the hill without much sign of Easter joy. He was a severe young man, and dusted off his trousers with an air of reproach. The presence of the villagers was barely acknowledged as he threaded his way through them and entered the church to make his preparations.

Soon afterwards the women and children went in, and Georgina and I with them. Most of the men stayed outside on the platform in front of the double doors, talking and laughing as though gathered in a bar. Inside the mood was similar. The congregation behaved exactly as Spaniards do in a restaurant. Children raced up and down the aisle while their parents conversed animatedly with friends in the row in front or behind. The service consisted largely of a monologue by the *Cura*, an amalgam of prayers, lessons and a sermon, interspersed by occasional responses from the women. He stuck manfully to his task, gesturing forcefully as though trying to nail his message into a soft and shifting surface. Midway through he lost his temper, when the prattle and laughter of the men outside the open doors rose to swamp his sermon into inaudibility: at a sharp word of command the doors were shut and the service continued in the gloom. After half an hour it ended with a general embrace among the women and a shaking of hands among the few attendant males. Then we streamed out into the sunshine.

We were followed out by Christ, standing in glory on a wooden platform carried by four men – a miniature version of Friday night's massive floats. He was robed in white, with the rays of His halo projecting aggressively above His head like an Apache war-bonnet. Around His feet were garlands of flowers, carnations and roses and lilies, which must have come up from

133

the coast and been kept fresh for this moment. As He emerged from the double doors two young men discharged their shotguns in a *feu de joie* that left the tiled platform littered with scarlet cartridges like flower petals beneath the congregation's feet.

Gingerly the bearers threaded the figure through the narrow alleyway behind the church, lowering Him as though in a curtsey to clear an overhead electricity cable. Outside our house the cortège took shape. In front of the Christ walked the women in dignified devotion, many of them barefoot. Behind came the men, smoking and chatting and comfortably shod. In and out ran the children, brandishing hand-held fireworks. As they passed, the figure of Jesus, silhouetted against the sky on his rooftop, raised a revolver and fired it into the air. The sound reverberated off the church tower like a slap.

The procession continued down the alleyway past Consuela's shop and round the corner by the cemetery gates. Here it slowed a little. The broad figure of Rosalia was at the front, and now she began to pick her way with some deliberation. As we approached we saw why. Down this stretch of path was where Luis had dumped the rubble from the refurbishment of our kitchen, and Rosalia, barefoot, was compelled to stumble through sharp-edged brick-ends and fragments of tile. We dropped rapidly to the rear of the procession, away from her basilisk eye.

Down on the road, and at two or three other points of the circuit, the children discharged their fireworks. Each time this happened the procession stopped and the bearers stood there, proud of their load, while green and yellow smoke drifted across the path and temporarily veiled the Christ. Then, when the hissing of the flares had stopped and the air had cleared, they picked up their burden again and continued on their way, along the road below the village and up the steep track on the further side, making a complete circle around the little cluster of houses.

At the top of the village, where the girdling track looked down on the cubist configuration of russet roofs and across the valley to the mountain behind, there was an interruption of a different kind. One of the men, a stranger in a well-cut suit, stepped suddenly on to a bank above the procession and burst into song. His voice was high, and the fractured melody sounded out clearly in the mountain air, a threnody of rising and falling and vibrating notes, driven from his lungs in gusts of passion that contrasted strangely with his city garb. The song was a *saeta*, a lament traditional to Spain's holy ceremonies, wrung spontaneously from a spectator overcome with holy fervour. The walkers stopped suddenly, like a freeze-frame in a film, and listened respectfully until the last words died away. Then the shuffling feet continued along the dusty path and down the headlong alleyway by our house: the Christ ducked again under the electric cable and re-entered His church.

The *Cura* had taken no part in the walk – he was a busy man – but very few of the villagers had missed it. Only here and there, at a window or leaning against a wall, could be seen the figures of those too old or too infirm to have joined the march.

22 April

The next morning was cold and overcast and we sat long over our breakfast, hunched on the hard kitchen chairs. Even Rosalia remained in her house, deterred by the chill, or possibly tending her feet after their contretemps yesterday with our brickbats.

But by noon the mist had cleared. The new brightness of the air, the clarity of the light on every sprouting vine and sap-green almond tree, drew us out of the village and into the countryside. We packed picnic materials into the car and drove slowly up the valley, away from the usual route down to the coast. Behind us, as we zigzagged upwards, Dalmácija looked hardly recognizable, although still close: it was like walking around a sculpture to gain a different perspective, or catching a glimpse of a familiar face in a mirror, with the features reversed. From this direction the sun illuminated the opposite side of the village from that of our house, picking out buildings that we could barely identify, changing the proportions of the church, reshaping the whole accreted swallow's nest of houses and setting it against a nearer and brighter backdrop of hillside. It was thrilling – like seeing the place for the first time. We were glad we lived there.

The village slid out of sight behind a hanging grove of almonds as the track rounded a spur, on the top of which stood a long, low house with the remains of raisin racks ranged along the slope in front of it. Between the racks grew clumps of white iris – *Iris florentina*, on which the fleur de lis is based – and thickets of neglected roses burgeoned beside the ruined pillars of the former vine arbour. The house was magnificently situated, with views down the valley up which we had come, and over into the next ravine and, beyond, to the jagged mountain skyline that pointed the way to Granada. The place was empty, and we hankered after it in a yearning, greedy, impractical kind of way. It was precisely the house we had dreamed of and searched for during our original quest five years ago, before we settled for the house at Dalmácija. Later we discovered, with a kind of inevitability, that it belonged to Consuela.

The track continued to climb as it meandered around the corrugations of the hillsides. At this height the cultivation began to recede, and the vines and almonds were replaced by expanses of flowering scrub. After a few more minutes we reached a pass. In front of us the track spilled abruptly into a big valley, far wider and greener and more populated than the one behind us. It was closed at its upper end by a tall massif of rock, which continued round to the left behind our own village, and ahead rolled away up the coast in varying Cézanne-like planes of mountainside that softened with distance and broke up into a machicolation of peaks. A town was built high against the mountain wall, confronting us from across the valley. Lower down, and smaller, were two other towns, or villages, and all the land between was studded with white *cortijos* of varying sizes: some were substantial two-storey affairs, surrounded by three, six, even ten raisin racks: others were the more usual two- or three-room shacks, perched on steep hillsides or on knuckles of rock and probably only utilized during times of harvest. Vines and almonds grew everywhere, and down on the narrow valley bottom were bright green gardens of beans or tomatoes. The place was rich and well-watered: an embryo Nepal tucked into a recess of the Sierra de Almijara.

We had driven up this valley when we were first house-hunting, and had been offered a couple of houses in the town at the top. It was an attractive, bustling community, and the surrounding scenery was very grand, but now we were glad we had not settled there. The area was becoming popular with foreigners, who were buying up the little *cortijos* at inflated prices and converting them into retirement homes. Despite the fact that we were doing essentially the same thing ourselves, we resented this, and avoided contact with foreigners, especially those of our own nationality. Temperamentally we were like the mid-Victorian traveller Alexander Kinglake who, while crossing the Sinai Desert, a five-day struggle through an unpeopled wilderness, suddenly saw a lone figure coming the other way. It was another Englishman. Kinglake passed him at a safe fifty-yard interval, pausing only to raise his hat.

On this occasion we decided to drive no further. A track led up the hillside from the col. We turned the car along it and drove up to a ridge, where we stopped. On the spine of the ridge a circular, level platform marked an old threshing floor, located to catch the breezes blowing up from the coast and thus to disperse the chaff more efficiently. Now grasses and small wiry herbs grew between the stone slabs: but the paving was still intact amid the encroaching scrub, and offered a spectacular site for our picnic. Around us, the hillsides showed why this relic was no longer in use. There was no corn planted. The land had been progressively drying out for years – since the Bronze Age, according to Brenan. Down the slopes where the land was cultivated the peasants had been installing new vineyards and fresh young almond saplings – crops more tolerant of drought than grain. Up here, the stony ground was thickly mantled with cistus shrubs which turned their large papery blooms to the sun, lavender-pink with bright yellow anthers, or white with a crimson blotch at the centre. The flowers were odourless, but the furry leaves and gummy twigs exuded an aromatic sweat in the midday warmth. Between these larger thickets grew the smaller flowers: harebells and bugloss and that aggressive imported weed the Bermuda buttercup, a species of wood-sorrel whose cadmium-yellow flowers gild the Andalusian roadsides when the sun is out, and fold themselves to invisibility when the evening comes. Here and there, on little patches of grass between the shrubs and the boulders, we found clusters of *Orchis papilionacea*, the pink butterfly orchid, and a few clumps of the wild lupin, *angustifolius.* Hungry as we were, we spent a quarter of an hour wandering along the goat paths and scrambling among the ledges and screes, assimilating this wealth of flora, before we settled down to pour the wine and slice the sausage.

A few minutes later, out of the corner of my eye, I saw the rocks behind us begin to move. I looked with new respect at Consuela's wine, checking the level in the bottle, but the animation of the hillside was quickly rationalized: a flock of goats was passing along the slope. They streamed past us as we lay on our rug . . . fawn and grey, fulvous and white, black and beige, umber and raw sienna . . . all the earth colours of an artist's palette. Long horns twirled with a devilish insouciance from several heads: bullet-shaped udders trailed perilously among the spiky shrubs: flecked amber eyes scrutinized us with more curiosity than those of the goatherd, a rangy saturnine youth who barely acknowledged our greeting as he passed us by. The scene had a colourful fluidity. Picnicking among cows in Northern Europe is like straying inside a Victorian primitive painting or a seventeenth-century Dutch landscape; but these goats belonged to an older world, a pre-Christian era: they were Homeric goats, Old Testament goats, the goats of Esau. Our eyes followed them far down the valley, until they merged into the crevices of the landscape and disappeared as a swarm of ants vanishes among stems of grass.

Clouds were blowing up from the west, striating the hillsides with sliding lavender shadows. We got up, stretched, and looked around at the panorama encircling us. The Sierras had moved closer while we ate, and now stood massed behind the intervening ridge across the valley like a dense blue wave piling against a dyke. In the other direction, where the little track wound down towards the coast, the bright afternoon sky had sucked up the silver sea from its narrow V-cleft at the bottom of the valley, erasing the ultimate horizon. All was silence, except for the faint soughing of the breeze among the cistus. After a few minutes of Cortez-like immobility, we roused ourselves and repacked the car and drove back to Dalmácija.

Before walking up through the village to our house we looked around for signs of the arrival of our building materials. Chico de Álamos had promised to deliver them today, the first day after the Easter weekend. We were leaving for England in a couple of days' time, and wanted to see some evidence of activity before our departure. Otherwise, we felt sure, Spanish inertia would maintain the status quo until our next return. Modernizing an Andalusian house was like stirring a spoon through very thick molasses: one had to keep the spoon moving, or the whole thing would solidify.

Already the molasses showed signs of hardening. There were no builder's materials to be seen. I resolved to go Chico-hunting, to try to expedite matters. This fortnight was proving no holiday, but a perpetual-motion machine.

The streets of Álamos were slippery with evening mist, which melded with the smoke of the *braseros* to form a soft and scented blanket around me as I climbed to Chico's house. The little cubby-hole was empty, but as I peered nervously through the curtain into the kitchen the entrance behind me darkened, and the last of the daylight was snuffed out by the immense figure of his wife. Was José at home? I asked. She shook her head: the movement sent a vibration through her frame like an earth tremor through the Massif Central. When would he be back? It was not possible to say, she replied: sometimes his work finished early, sometimes late. He had promised to bring some materials for me, I said, hearing my voice go shrill with indignation. If he had promised my materials, she said, then he would surely bring them. But when? When it was possible: José had much work but he would bring my materials when it was possible. He could not bring them before then. She would tell him I had come seeking him. Would I like some beer or a glass of wine? I declined, and departed feeling small in more senses than one.

On my way home I called on Emilio to discuss the *caballeria*, the bringing up of my building materials. His house stood beside a track above the village, separate from the main cluster of houses. He had built it himself. For two years we had been searching for a builder to complete our house, and had ended by engaging one from Álamos. Yet everyone here built his own house, or added a room or two. Emilio's was in the new style: tall and slab-sided with a flat roof, modern windows and a metal door. Nobody nowadays built the low narrow-windowed houses topped with banks of earthenware tiles. And nobody bought wooden doors and shutters any more.

Emilio's wife Concepcion sat me down in the spanking new sitting-room. Emilio was washing, she said. He had only recently returned from work on the roads for the Council. As she spoke there was a footstep outside, and he walked in. I had not met him before, partly because of the comparative remoteness of his house, and partly because of the long hours he worked. He was a short man, aged about forty, with a slight physique: it was not until the next day that I had evidence of his strength. His dark eyes assessed me with a look in which civility was blended with truculence, and above them his brows ran level across his lean face in a line which paralleled the hard, thin fissure of his lips. He was the one man in the village of whom I was immediately afraid – and that was before I discovered how much he drank. For the last few years he had been mayor, and looking down at him I was reminded of Julius Caesar, who said he would rather be first in the country's smallest village than second in Rome.

I shook his hand, which was as hard and rough as a brick, and explained my problem. If Chico de Álamos delivered my materials tomorrow, could he, Emilio, carry them up to my house, so that José the builder could get going on the construction work? When was I returning to England, asked Emilio. The day after tomorrow, I said. A short visit, he commented. Yes, I said: I had to go back to work. Work! He smiled, as though at the mention of an old friend. What sort of work did I do? I worked in an office, I explained. He eyed me without comment, and offered me a drink. When I accepted, he beckoned me to follow him.

We stepped out of the front door on to a raised terrace overlooking the village. Below us the street lights, five of them, shone in the indigo darkness like Cassiopeia. We walked down a short slope to his *bodega*. Like the rest of the house it was modern. Lacking the thick rubble walls of the older dwellings down the hill, it had the lean and bloodless austerity of a garage. Along one wall was a row of five barrels. They, at least, were old: but in the opposite corner stood a washing machine, which, after what we had seen of peasant life, seemed as incongruous as a computer in Anne Hathaway's cottage.

Emilio reached down into one of the barrels with a plastic jug and poured two glasses of wine. It was thin and hard, like the man himself. He knocked his glass back without ceremony, and waited for me to do the same. He refilled them, and this time took a little longer to swallow his wine: about thirty seconds. Easing the metallic liquid down my throat, I gestured towards the washing machine: were they very expensive in Spain? He nodded proudly. But he was paying for it little by little, over many years. It was to make the payments that he was working on the roads. This was the only washing machine in the village. He thought there were no others in the next village either. But if a man worked hard, he could have such things. Come, he would show me the rest of the house.

Stepping over the crawling figure of Emilio's youngest son, half-naked despite the chill, we strolled around the house. The plain, rectilinear rooms with their high ceilings and polished floors were as functional as a hospital ward. The furniture, conversely, was plastic-veneered neo-baroque. I told myself that this house was more practical, comfortable, and undeniably more impressive than the squat, round-edged, womb-like hovels of the rest of the village, including mine.

As we retraced our steps through the sitting-room Emilio stopped in front of a placard hanging on the wall. It was a poster for the local Communist party. Was I a Communist? he asked. I hesitated. I felt I wanted to be on this man's side in the next civil war. But there was no help for it: no, I said. Then I was a capitalist? I was about to demur, but he grabbed my hand and looked at it: yes, he said, I was a capitalist. I could think of no answer to this. Luckily none was needed: Emilio was already leading the way back to the *bodega*. I protested that Georgina was awaiting me, and dinner was doubtless ready by now, but with an impatient gesture he consigned women and food to a limbo of inconsequentiality. He reached down again into the wine barrel.

Several glasses later, he returned to the subject of my builder's materials. If, tomorrow, he saw they had been delivered on his return for his midday meal, he could bring them up to me in the early afternoon, during the siesta time. Would I be asleep then? No, I said, although sleep suddenly seemed an attractive notion. I got to my feet – I appeared to have been sitting on the concrete floor – and held out my hand to bid Emilio farewell. I missed his by several inches, but the gesture evidently sufficed. I departed down the track towards home. It was a rougher track than I remembered – surely Paco hadn't dumped our rubble up here as well? – and I stumbled several times. Once I fell. Dangerous places after dark, these Spanish villages. I must warn Georgina about this track, I thought, if I could ever find her: it seemed a very long way back to our house. I paused and leant against a wall, to reorient myself. A dog barked at me, silly animal, but all else was quiet, except for a persistent trickle of water, amplified by a resonant echo. I was leaning against the village cistern. Inside, the water ran off the mountain and into the big tank that supplied the fountains. The sound of the splashing was soothing, intricate, a varied composition of notes and grace-notes, and I decided to settle down and listen to it for a while. The Arabs had designed their palaces around the sound

143

of falling water, and I . . . well, I, in forty-eight hours, would be far from Andalusia, and then any sound of falling water would be the sound of rain.

23 April

Rosalia had a lachrymose air when she brought us our bread next morning. Ah, Jorgina, she said, subjecting Georgina to the full intensity of her large hazel eyes. Georgina and I looked at each other with alarm: had there been some bereavement? Tomorrow, said Rosalia, tomorrow you're going. She rolled her eyes again, but this time I detected a thespian glint behind the gloom. She was playing the scene for all it was worth, and enjoying it. She waddled over to Georgina and embraced her round the shoulders. There was a crepitation of buckling ribs and Georgina gasped, which Rosalia took to be a whimper of sorrow. Tomorrow, she repeated, we'd be back in England, and this house would be empty. It was fortunate for us that we had her to look after it. There was much work for her, caring for a house like this, but she was our friend.

Perhaps I'll stay behind, said Georgina. Hugo could go back to England, she continued, and she would stay here in Spain. Could Rosalia find some man to look after her while Hugo was away? Rosalia quaked with mirth. *¿Como no?* There were plenty of men in the village: which one would Jorgina like? There was Aurelio? Too old. Rosalia's son Pedro? Too young. Luis the barman? Too fat. Luis the builder? Too drunk. Emilio the mayor? Too strong – he'd crush her. By now Rosalia was bubbling like a great black kettle and wiping her eyes with the corner of her apron. Ah! Jorgina, she said, this time with genuine fondness: what pleasure we would have if you stayed with us in Spain.

She settled back in a chair, rubbing her rheumatic leg, and began the daily inquisition, like a governess

144

checking on the movements of her charges before sending them out to play. What would Georgina and I be doing today? Well, we said, Emilio would be delivering the building materials, if they arrived. Yes, yes, she knew all about that. (How? I'd only returned from Emilio at midnight.) And the building work? she asked: José would do that while we were in England? Yes, that was our hope: and we explained to her the projected design of the new roof terrace above the *bodega* . . . the door entering it from above . . . the vine arbour . . . the barbecue. And what would we do up there? We hesitated over our reply. Spanish peasants have an imperfect conception of leisure, through unfamiliarity. We'd take the sun, we said, and read. She nodded, a sign that she had heard rather than understood: these villagers avoided the sun when they could, and few could read. And we'd cook on the barbecue, we added, and we'd talk, and admire the view.

At this point a thought struck us. Our house stood at the edge of the village, with a taller house above and Consuela's shop below, but with open country beside it at the far end. From our projected roof terrace we would be able to look down the length of the little valley over the roofs below, to the mountain with the castle on it: and laterally we would have a view over the olive trees next to the house, across to the upper curve of the valley and the ridge that encircled the village. Unlike the rest of the community, where new houses were beginning to sprout, ugly sharp-edged cubes with flat roofs, our little corner was immune. Consuela would not rebuild, surely, and the remainder of our outlook was rural. But what if someone built in the vacant olive grove? The house . . . or suburb, or skyscraper complex, as we now began to see it . . . would be right next to our roof terrace, beetling over it, thick with vocal children and transistor radios and washing-lines. Serried ranks of inquisitive neighbours would crowd their balconies to scrutinize our flabby forms as we sun-bathed, and peer into our fry-pans as we cooked, and enfoliate us with lolly-wrappers. The possibility was intolerable. We'd have to sell the house.

We asked Rosalia who owned the olive grove. A man in Álamos, she said, a cousin of Jesus's: why did we want to know? We told her about our worries. She shrugged. Nobody would build a house there, she said: it would overlook the cemetery. It was bad luck to build houses overlooking cemeteries.

Georgina and I were unconvinced. After Rosalia had taken herself away to prepare Jesus's lunch for him (a broth of chick-peas, onions, garlic, tomatoes, and a sliver or two of sausage, she told us, eyes gleaming with purposeful anticipation), we pushed open the ramshackle gate of our patio and stepped across the intervening mule-track into the olive grove. It sloped away from our house, down to the white-walled cemetery a couple of dozen yards below. At the far end the plot narrowed and sloped more sharply from right to left: at this point it was divided longitudinally into four ruined terraces, before tumbling suddenly into the little valley below. Along the terraces, and scattered across the flatter slope at the top end, were a dozen olive trees and three almonds. In one of the open gaps a tethered mule was lunching off the wild flowers. Along the upper rim of the plot, where it sloped steeply up to meet a row of raisin racks on the shoulder of the hillside, a long thicket of prickly pears formed a natural boundary, together with a palisade of agaves which brandished their sword-shaped leaves against the sky.

At the moment, the land's main crop was garbage. It was one of the more flourishing rubbish dumps on the village's perimeter. But as Georgina and I picked our way among the sardine cans and old shoes, the discarded mop heads and the multiplicity of plastic bags, a vision began to sprout and burgeon which transfigured all such ephemeral squalor. In our minds, as though encased in a thought-balloon, leapt a plan for the Hanging Gardens of Dalmácija, a cascading paradise of exotic trees and shrubs leading from one fragrant bower to another . . . plunging vistas culminating in discreet groups of statuary . . . a pool fed by a musical trickle from a lion's-head fountain. A jacaranda tree would go *there*, visible over the thickets of oleander encircling the terrace *here*, where we would sit in long chairs, sipping long drinks, and looking down past the big acacia by the cemetery gates to where the road led away down the valley.

Surely Jesus's cousin would sell us this land. The trees looked neglected, the terraces were tumbling down, and the place was hard of access, encircled by the cemetery and the prickly pears and the plunging slope. Perhaps we could even clinch the sale before our departure tomorrow, offer the man a good price in cash, emphasize that we were doing him a favour by relieving him of the responsibility of this remote, meagre garbage-ridden plot. As we discussed the matter thus, it seemed inconceivable that the man would not agree on the spot. We'd go and see him tonight.

Our ecstatic musings were interrupted by a shout from below. Our building materials had arrived. Chico de Álamos had dumped them by the road at the bottom of the village. We began to gird ourselves for action. Emilio would see the goods lying there and would deliver them up to us after lunch: that is, if I had remembered the arrangements correctly through the vinous haze of the previous evening.

I had. There was a knock on the door a couple of hours later. There stood Emilio, leading a mule equipped with large leather panniers. I followed them down to the road, where the supplies from the builders' merchants were stacked: bricks, cement, sand, concrete beams (of varying lengths: our *bodega* was wedge-shaped) and of course the *bovedillas*, big elaborately honey-combed earthenware biscuits which slotted between the beams like components of a child's construction kit.

Emilio walked first to the sacks of cement, the only perishable items. He dropped the mule's leading rope and the animal stood motionless: then he took one end of a sack of cement and signalled me to take the other. We carried it to the mule. It was at this point that I realized that mules were much taller than I had appreciated. The pannier, mounted high on the animal's ribs, was level with my shoulders. I could raise my end of the cement sack waist-high with relative ease, but the final upward heave, the equivalent of the weightlifter's snatch, was quite beyond me. Emilio watched my feeble antics for a moment or two, and then, perhaps fearful of a rupture or a coronary, told me to put the sack down. He took a double-ended grip on it himself, straightened his back, and with little apparent effort he flipped it into the pannier, where he roped it in place. Then, for a moment, there was a useful role for me. I stood there, like a book-end, supporting the first pannier while Emilio loaded the one on the other side to balance the weight. He then picked up a third sack. He was a small man, and this sack had to be lifted into place on the mule's spine, between the other two, high over Emilio's head. Declining my offer of help with a decisiveness based on previous experience, he raised the load half-way, then, straining upward on tiptoe, bundled it on to the apex of the pyramid. As he roped it he glanced at me with an expression of . . . was it pride, or contempt, or an unspoken battle-cry of *à bas les capitalistes*? The glance was unnecessary. I already realized I would fail to make the grade of peon, class III, on any Spanish labour force.

So I left him to it for the rest of the afternoon. Up and down the steep track plodded the mule, bringing up the components in endless instalments: first the cement, which Emilio carefully encased in sheets of plastic, then the bricks, packed into the panniers as though into giant hods, then the sand, carried loose and shovelled out into a pile below the wall of the house. At one point, when we came to the *bovedillas*, I re-entered the fray:

but though light they were awkwardly large, and I could only carry two, one under each arm. It was a long walk for so little result, and I soon desisted. If I had known then how much Emilio would charge for this half-day's work, plus another half-day for the remaining items, I might have worked harder myself.

At dusk there was a more important task for me. At last even I could be positively useful. The concrete beams were too long to be mule-borne. Bundling an old shirt into a pad to protect my collar-bone, I shouldered one end of the first beam and set off up the hill, following Emilio who set a brisk pace at the other end. Every fifty yards a different muscle sent out a distress signal. Shoulder, arm, calf, thigh, back . . . long before we reached the top I was a complete *Gray's Anatomy* of tortured bone and sinew. I tried taking the front end of the next beam, in an attempt to slow the pace: but Emilio, in a forceful equivalent of rear-wheel drive, projected me upwards even faster than before, lurching and weaving between the rocks, scrabbling with my feet to avoid falling on my face under the weight of several kilos of reinforced concrete.

And this was only the second beam. As darkness fell, and our plodding multiplied up and down the rapidly steepening hillside, I became convinced that we had grossly over-ordered. Our *bodega* was surely never of this length. These beams would have roofed Long Chamber at Eton, with some to spare. Moreover Emilio had begun with the shorter beams, perhaps apprehensive that I would decline the job if he had started me off with a long one. Thus as the hours lengthened, so did the beams. By the time the last and biggest was stacked below our house, I had long lost interest in architecture. I offered Emilio a glass of wine, but to my relief he declined and took his leave. I grabbed the bottle myself.

It was some time during the second or third glass that Georgina gently reminded me of the projected visit to

Salvador, Jesus's cousin in Álamos. If we were to become Spanish landowners before our departure tomorrow, now was the time to effect it. To me in my present condition, supine on the sofa, chafing any limbs I could reach without bending too far, a trip to Álamos seemed about as impracticable as supper in the Karakorams: but by the fourth glass it became clear that the infusion of local wine was having an effect. Just as the pure unpressed juice of Hungarian grapes, dripping from silken bags into silver ewers and fermented to form the ineffable Essence of Tokay, was revered by emperors and tsars as the potion that extended life . . . even so Consuela's muscatel was coursing through my veins like ichor, opening up unimagined possibilities. Even a visit to Álamos.

On attempting to stand up, I discovered that the wine had restored life, but not movement. It was only by leaning heavily on Georgina that I could change from my Builder's Mate clothes into my Estate Agent clothes. She then folded me into the little car and drove me down the hill. We had been told that Salvador's house was on the road at the bottom of Álamos, opposite the bar which contained the only telephone for several miles around. We found the place easily enough, and knocked on the door. It was answered by a young woman who ushered us into the front parlour and went to fetch her husband.

It says much for Spanish manners that an inhabitant of a small hill village, opening her door at night to two strange foreigners – one of them apparently a cripple – should behave so spontaneously and graciously. Georgina and I were invited to sit at the table, and were offered a drink. Gin and Coca Cola: we were moving in more sophisticated circles down here in Álamos. Salvador, when he appeared, was a wiry man in his thirties. He looked as hard as tungsten, and his facial colouring was very dark: the effect was intimidating until, later, he smiled: then at once his face glowed with an irresistible incandescence, and his eyes softened from their initial sardonic glint to a flash of amusement and friendliness.

The friendliness was not, however, immediately in evidence as we explained the reason for our visit. We lived in Dalmácija, we said. Yes, said Salvador, he knew about us. Our house, we continued, was next to the cemetery. Yes, he had heard that. We had been told that the land above the cemetery was his. Yes, that was true. How was it, we asked in our attempt at chattiness, that he owned land in Dalmácija? It was family land. He was a cousin of Jesus. Ah yes, Rosalia had told us. Did we like Dalmácija? Very much . . . but about that land of his. Yes? There were some trees on it, were there not? Fourteen olive trees and three almond trees. Did they give much fruit? He gathered the almonds, he said, but didn't bother about the olives. Sensing in my fuddled cerebellum that the moment had come, I leant across the table and struck like a drunken cobra: would Salvador then like to sell the land, since he gathered but little of the produce?

Sell the land? Salvador managed a convincing look of surprise. But to whom? To me, I said, beaming through the gin. We wanted to make a garden there. A garden? He looked almost as bemused as if I had announced plans for a rocket-launching pad. Spanish mountain villages have no gardens. Land is scant, and so is leisure. Every housewife has her flower-pots on balconies or beside the front door; or crams the ubiquitous geraniums, which need little water, into masonry troughs that run along the edge of the street: but to allot good ground to flowers instead of to almonds or olives or oranges, that would be spendthrift.

We persisted nevertheless. Would Salvador sell us the land? He shrugged. He would have to ask his wife. The wife was sitting three feet away, dandling a small boy on her lap. Her darting eyes and the contrastingly slow liquidity of her movements combined to give an impression of mischievous sexuality contained within an absolute self-possession. She had not contributed to the conversation, nor did she now. There was a pause. How long would it take Salvador to ask his wife? I enquired cautiously. He didn't as much as glance in her direction: a week, he said. We should discuss the matter again next week. But . . . I hesitated to superimpose our English time-scale on a Spanish one . . . but we were leaving tomorrow. Then we must see him again on our next visit, said Salvador: and, for the first time, he smiled.

Whether the smile indicated amusement at our head-long life-rhythm, or whether it opened the door to a new friendship, it had a liberating and assuaging effect on our anxiety. Suddenly the imagined urgency of the matter evaporated. The land would still be there when we returned in the summer. Salvador would still be here. Self-imposed schedules, a time-regulated men-tality, an attempt to accelerate the spontaneous flow of Andalusian existence . . . such philosophies now seemed like foolishness. We smiled too, and rose, and shook Salvador by the hand. *Hasta el verano*, we said. Until the summer.

24 April
We woke to a bright day, with a high wind. Dust devils were spiralling in the alley outside our front door. Most of them, we soon discovered, emanated from our pile of sand which Emilio had carried up on his mule. The narrow space outside the shop had been transformed into a builder's yard, and Consuela's customers were compelled to tackle an assault course of tangled masonry in order to reach her doorway. When we arrived to buy some lemons to take back to England, we found Remedios perched on a concrete beam like a nestling learning to fly. I took her dry little hand to help her down. Were we going today? She clung tightly and peered anxiously into my face. Yes, alas, I

said, we were going today, at midday. She would come and see us before then, she said.

Rosalia had already inaugurated the count-down at breakfast time. Settling into the rocking chair, oblivious of Georgina's frantic need to start packing, she proceeded to disinter the feeble drolleries of yesterday, interspersed with more commercial matters. Was Georgina going to stay behind? Hoo, hoo. Did she want Rosalia to find a man for her? Hoo, hoo. And what would Hugo be up to in England on his own? Hoo, hoo. Hadn't he said only yesterday that he preferred large blonde ladies? Hoo, hoo. But if we were both going today, she continued, who was going to wash the sheets? Georgina frowned, as though seeking abstruse solutions to this problem: well, how about . . . and then, evidently, an idea smote her with Pentecostal brilliance . . . how about Rosalia herself? Rosalia shook her head decisively. She was too busy. Working in the fields. Cooking for her family. Cleaning her house. Looking after our house and watering our geraniums. No, she would have no time for our washing. But perhaps, just conceivably, she knew someone who would. Who? we asked eagerly. Nobody we knew, replied Rosalia hastily, but a good reliable woman who could do such work for us: the only trouble was, we would have to pay the woman for the labour. How much? we asked. Rosalia, with only a flicker of hesitation, named a sum approximately three times higher than we would expect to pay at a London laundrette. Expensive, we said. Rosalia shrugged: this woman, this admirable neighbour of hers, was also very busy. She herself, of course, was a friend of ours, and would not take money for looking after our house, but this other woman was a different matter. One couldn't expect *her* to work for nothing, could we? And she sat back in the rocking chair, oscillating like a metronome, watching us benignly. At what hour, exactly, were we leaving? At midday? We must have much packing to do, she said, eyeing the gaping suitcases with relish.

Georgina and I poured ourselves more coffee. Rosalia declined a cup, as usual, but showed no signs of departure. This woman, said Georgina, this friend of Rosalia's, could she do cleaning as well? Perhaps we could pay her a sum which could include doing the laundry when we left and also sweeping and dusting the house before our next arrival? Rosalia thought for a moment, then nodded and named another sum, which Georgina and I digested, assessed on an annual basis, and reduced, putting forward a counter-bid. Rosalia proposed splitting the difference. We agreed.

Would it be necessary, we asked, to consult Rosalia's friend, to see if this sum was acceptable? No, said Rosalia, she could speak for her. She rose to leave, promising to return several times before our departure.

It was pinchingly cold as we bustled about the mournful business of packing up the house. The dim, glacial sitting-room was a repository for the damp and chill of the previous months, but the bright rectangle of cobalt sky that gleamed through the front door was an oriflamme leading our thoughts forward to the great heat that would await us on our next visit. As we filled our suitcases, we juggled our minds between retrospection of the last two weeks and anticipation of the London that awaited us later in the same day. Despite the closeness in time, how little overlap there seemed to be between this place and that: only we ourselves, strutting and fretting on two such different stages. Yet we too, no doubt, would be changed.

The cobalt rectangle darkened, and Angel came in. His bushy eyebrows rose at the sight of the widely scattered piles of miscellany awaiting stowage in our luggage. How sad that we were going, he said: our visit had been so short. Too short, I agreed: but I must return to my office, I said, as portentously as a knight-errant compelled by the force of his vow to leave some earthly paradise. However, said Georgina, we would return in the summer with our children. With our children! Angel's eyes brightened with pleasure. Two boys! He would take pleasure in seeing our two boys: he himself had fathered only girls. And now, since he could see we were busy, he would go. We must visit him on our return, for a glass of wine: it would be hot . . . thirsty weather. Meantime, here was a bottle to take with us to London, wherewith to remember him. He embraced Georgina, a long, slow embrace, murmuring a diminutive of her name, then stepped quickly out through the door. I stood for a moment, holding the old anise bottle he had used for his wine, listening to the receding tap of his stick down the alleyway.

At once Rosalia reappeared, as though she had been watching for Angel's departure, which doubtless was the case. She gave Georgina a plastic bag tightly knotted at the top, bulging knobbily through its sides. Almonds, she said, for our children. She then had the grace to leave us, for once, to our activities, although her scavenging curiosity compelled a quick spate of questions before her departure: how long would our flight to England take? How far was our home from the airport? How many people would be on the plane?

At last the suitcases were filled and locked, the accumulated garbage from the last two days tipped into a sack for disposal down on the coast, and the back door roped shut against the boisterous spring gales. Small eye-catching gadgets were concealed at the bottom of a spare suitcase, as a precaution against their being borrowed by Rosalia, and our dirty laundry heaped in the middle of the floor for collection by her mythical friend. The fridge was switched off. It was time to go and say good-bye to Consuela.

We found her seated behind a table in the inner sanctum of her house, tearing at a sandwich of bread and salami with a disconcertingly male ferocity. But her great face softened and puckered when we held out our hands to say farewell. Wobbling to her feet, she bade us stay there while she went out for a minute. In her absence we looked around the little room. It was a modernized, and hence more immaculate, version of our own. The earthenware floor had been relaid with polished composition tiles. The canes of the ceiling had been plastered over. The fireplace had a glazed brick surround and contained a cooker. Only the row of brass pans on the mantelpiece and the brazier under the table maintained a deliberate link with tradition. Consuela returned, a little breathless, with a bag of raisins in one hand – for the children, she said – and a bottle of olive oil in the other. The bottle was stoppered with a cork evidently derived from some other container, and was leaking. Shaking hands with Consuela and embracing her had the effect of returning some of her oil to her, as a light basting on her wrist and upper arm.

Returning home with our gifts, holding the bottle well away from the body and leaning against the wind, we found Remedios awaiting us outside our front door. Crouched in the lee of the entrance, she looked as shrivelled as one of Consuela's raisins, but her eyes were bright with excitement. When were we going? She was afraid she had missed us. When would we return? Was it true we were bringing our children with us? She had a present for them, she said, and held out a plastic bag. In it was a box of marzipan biscuits. Remedios had no land to yield her wine or raisins or almonds, nor, in consequence, can she have had much money: but she had spent her widow's pittance to buy our children, whom she had never seen, a box of biscuits. For the children, she repeated as I embraced her. After the fleshy resilience of Consuela's shoulders, her little frame was a mere husk. *¡Vaya con Dios!* she said as she left us: the old Spanish farewell, 'Go with God.'

Ten minutes later we were on our way. Rosalia was in attendance as we closed the battered blue door and formally handed her the key. We took a last look at the newly planted bougainvillea beside the steps, and she,

I felt, was looking at us in a similarly possessive way, as new assets of a moderately decorative nature which if sufficiently tended would brighten her life a little. She embraced Georgina tenderly and the warmth of her smile flickered only for as long as it took for her to palm the bundle of notes for her friend, count them and fold them into her bosom. Then she turned to accompany us down the hill, bringing up the rear like an outrider.

Stumbling down the unpaved slope under the weight of the suitcases, I was glad of the pauses along the way, as the inhabitants turned out to bid us good-bye. Below Rosalia's house stood the two girls we had met in the church, framed in the narrow cul-de-sac that led to their mother's house. Pots of ferns and carnations hung beside them as they waved to us, themselves adding to the efflorescence of colour, the only grown females in the village not to be clad in black. Further down, Luis the barman sat on the terrace outside his bar, massively motionless. The circular Coca Cola sign on the wall behind him framed his head like a halo, and his smile had, indeed, the distancing solemnity of an icon. We had hardly seen him during the last fortnight, but we shouted a greeting as we passed. Behind us, down the hill, the trail of olive oil was as definitive as Ariadne's thread.

At the bottom, the wife of José the builder was filling a bucket at the fountain. We sent greetings to him: without his previous work we could not have spent this fortnight here. Two little girls watched us as we loaded the suitcases into the car. A woman, unknown to us, stepped out on to the geranium-festooned terrace above the fountain to say farewell. Rosalia gave Georgina a last embrace. Georgina wept. *¡Hasta el verano!* We slammed the car doors and drove away. A dozen figures, dotted here and there up the village cliff-face, watched us go. We drove around the first three or four twists of the road, and stopped at the bend whence, we knew, could be seen the last – or first – view of Dalmácija.

We walked off the dusty road on to the endless ribbon of convolvulus, bugloss and poppy which ran along its rim. These flowers would not be here when we next returned. Much would be changed in the precious, secret landscape of this valley – but not Dalmácija itself. From this distance, as we gazed back on it, the village looked small enough to pick up in two hands, a double palmful of white sand which had been dropped on the hillside, casually, so that some individual grains had escaped from the main cone and lodged among the rocks where gravity had carried them. Behind the village, the slope, soft with almond trees, rose to a sky where dark clouds threatened to extinguish the shining whiteness of the houses. Around us the silence was complete. Where would we find such silence in the next three months? We returned to the car and drove slowly round the bend, still looking back, until the side of the valley swung across behind us, and Dalmácija disappeared from sight.

4

SUMMER

Here is no water but only rock
Rock and no water and the sandy road
The road winding above among the mountains . . .

T. S. Eliot

16 July

It seemed as though Dalmácija had been moved five
hundred miles further south since the spring. The
flowers were gone, and with them most of the foliage
of ground and tree. Only a faint hazy bloom of dull
green from the olives and almonds mantled the fierce
red earth. Andalusia had reverted to the austerity
of colour and outline which had first attracted us:
the extremity of its style and beauty offered us the
maximum contrast to the soft and soggy England we
had left behind. In two and a half hours we had
been translated to a country as thrillingly different as
if we had crossed the world.

The temperature, for one thing, was nearly 30 degrees
higher than in London. It was mid-afternoon when we
reached the village, and the sun beat on our backs as
we staggered up the slope with our luggage. Every few
steps we paused, both to rest and to delight ourselves
again in the higgledy-piggledy white houses around us,
but the sweat trickled into our eyes and blurred the
view. No-one was about. We reached our front door
unaccosted, turned the key and entered. Inside, the

low-ceilinged sepulchral little room with its round-edged recesses, and the muted glow of old Arab rugs on the floor, completed our feeling of transference to another world and another time.

Dumping the suitcases, we sped upstairs to inspect our new roof terrace, if any. Yes, there was now a glazed door at the end of our bedroom, and yes, it opened on to a flat roof where once the *bodega*'s tiles had been. We stepped out. At once it was apparent that this was where our future life here would be centred, at least in summer. The tiny rooms inside the house, however *tipico*, were constraining: but up here the whole vívid countryside was around us. Below the terrace, across the alley, were the jumbled roofs of Consuela's shop and the buildings abutting it. Straight ahead, at the end of the terrace, a large olive tree thrust up a thicket of silver-grey. Below it on one side could be seen the white gateway to the cemetery. Above and sweeping round to the right was the slope of hillside which bounded the valley on this side, studded with the green specks of the vines and the shadowless tracery of the almond trees. Above the terrace, and running its full length, was a high protective wall, behind which could be heard the guttural clucking of chickens belonging to our uphill neighbour, Marta.

We walked to the far end to inspect the barbecue. It was exactly as we had specified it to José via sign-language. He had also built three pillars and linked them with rough beams, along which lay the shoots of our own vine. We had planted it down in the patio when we first bought the house, and it had rocketed skyward at great speed – an inch a day in the growing season – hitherto without any support to discipline it. Someone, presumably Jesus, had tied its tendrils to the beams to form a pattern indicative of the shade it would eventually throw, but as yet it was inadequate for the task, and the sun beat fiercely on us. We would need to roof the terrace with split-cane matting before we could use it. A little loggia right below us, next to Consuela's shop, was shaded in this way. She would tell us where to obtain the canes.

A delicious thought had occurred to us . . . it had germinated early, on the plane, or perhaps even back in England . . . that this terrace, in addition to its other merits, might have a key social advantage. It might be Rosalia-proof. Up here, at the far end of the house, protected by the narrow and precipitous stairway, we would surely be able to sip gin and tonic in peace and peruse Proust uninterrupted. It was a foolish thought: the kind that gives optimism a bad name. We had spent barely five minutes leaning on the railings in the sunshine, before the familiar voice rang out in the distance. *¡Arriba!* we replied: we're upstairs! Now came the test. Would she come round the outside of the house and parlay with us from below, from a position of weakness, like an envoy outside the castle walls? Not she. From the inner recesses of the house came a heavy creaking and vibration as of some powerful piece of machinery, and Rosalia appeared on the terrace, more florid in complexion than usual, but smiling. She embraced Georgina, and shook my hand with a grip that left my fingers numb. Where were our children? she asked. We had decided not to bring them after all, we explained, until the house was fully furnished and equipped.

She bade us welcome, told Georgina she was looking too thin, and questioned us closely on the weather in England, price of our air-tickets, and food served on the flight. Extricating ourselves with difficulty from these matters, we asked her about José's building programme: was it all finished down below? We had only seen the terrace so far. Yes, it was finished, she said, and it had meant much work for her. Or rather for her friend, she amended quickly. So much cleaning up afterwards. Many hours. But look at the result, we quickly interjected before the conversation could take a financial turn: was this not a fine terrace? It was well made, Rosalia agreed, but we would not be able to use it during the day. It would be too hot. No problem, we replied: we would buy some shading material tomorrow, like those split canes down there on Consuela's loggia. Rosalia shook her head contemptuously. Those canes would never do. They would be too heavy for a wide area like ours. She, Rosalia, would tell us where to buy the right kind.

The building work in the rest of the house was indeed finished, and once again it was exactly as specified, despite the absence of any written plans. The *bodega* was now a separate bedroom. A new door led into the patio: or rather an old door, which we had seen lying in the street in Álamos on our previous visit, and had brought home on the roof of the car. Outside, the jasmine was still in flower. The exuberant branches sprawled across in front of the door to the bathroom, and the fragrance reached into the house.

Remedios came to see us. She seemed to have shrunk further, and I had to bend from the waist like a Ruritanian grandee in order to reach her little hand. She was sorry our children had not come. She had some presents for them. Would they be coming soon? There were too few children in this village.

We had other visitors during the evening as we unpacked, and met further acquaintances in Consuela's shop when we went to stock up on food. Everybody seemed pleased to see us. No doubt we were a diversion for them, a harmless curiosity in their midst, but at least we felt that our behaviour on our previous visit must have been tolerable. We were accepted, now, as part-time villagers . . . seasonal visitors, like the swifts. A feeling of happiness surrounded us, as characteristic and insistent as the heat.

We perched on two hard chairs up on the terrace, and watched the light go out of the day. The sun had gone down behind the hillside, leaving a round-edged carob tree and half a dozen olives protruding blackly from the line of the crest: but the temperature was still close to 80 degrees, and runnels of moisture slid down the sides of our ice-crammed glasses. Far across the valley a tower of the Moorish castle glowed like a candle-end in the reflected radiance of the evening sky. The first of the owls mewed, and close below us a tiny bat bustled down the alleyway as though on an errand, turned above the cemetery gates, and repeated the same journey again and again. Georgina and I recharged our glasses. Oh, this was going to be a famous stamping-ground in our lives, this terrace! What days of hallucinatory heat we would be spending up here in the years to come! What long velvet evenings of food and drink and talk! Friends would visit us from the world over, to sun themselves and carouse and muse. Our boys would read Robert Louis Stevenson and Rider Haggard under the shade of the arbour, and cheat at chess. It would be a place of rare pleasure-taking. A place to sing and tell old tales and laugh at gilded butterflies . . .

17 July

We drove down to Valdez early, before the full heat of the day was upon us, in search of *cañizos* – the split-cane roofing for the terrace. Following Rosalia's directions we passed through the town and out on to the road that led up the broad river valley towards the mountains. We turned off it after a mile, and bumped across the valley on a dirt road, crossing the gravelly dried-up gullies of the river-bed on a series of hazardous bridges. Along these gullies sprouted thickets of ten-foot reeds, the raw material of the canes we were about to buy. Between them, arcaded stretches of low Arab aqueducts served the land that lay above river-level. The terrain was flat and dusty, with an occasional farmhouse standing on a protruding knoll like an island.

On one of these high sand-banks we saw what appeared at first glance to be a Huron village. The teepees, on closer examination, proved to be conical stacks of reeds. We drove up onto the little plateau and found a low building from which emanated a continuous mechanical clattering. A couple of young men, floured with pale dust like whitebait ready for the pan, were carrying bundles of reeds from the stacks into the building, and we followed them. Inside, the din was intense and the visibility almost nil. The air – or rather the internal space, since there was little air – was filled with floating particles of cane-chaff. The effect was of fragrance made solid. It was like inhaling hay. Georgina and I groped and spluttered our way to the source of both the noise and the dust: a kind of loom which seized on the canes fed into it at one end, stripped them, cut them to size and wove them into a continuous length connected by wire. Beyond this infernal contraption, in a brighter space beside an open doorway, stood rolls of the finished product in varying widths, like bamboo carpeting. Pre-equipped with the measurements of our arbour, we purchased three rolls of the required dimensions, and bundled them into and onto the car. Then, dusting the chaff from our clothes, except where sweat had congealed it to a batter, we walked to the edge of the plateau for a view over the plain. Compared with the uplands of Dalmácija this scenery was drab stuff: no vines and few trees, only an intermittently cultivated flatland of sandy mounds and hollows like a badly stuffed mattress. But behind it rose the castle and two massive church towers of Valdez, and behind that again the circling ramparts of the Sierras, lowering to the cleft that offered the only link, in these parts, between the coastal strip and the inland plain. Thence the mountains continued to the west, until hidden from our view by the foothills: while to the south the river-bed opened out to reveal the sea, barely visible behind a palisade of skyscrapers. Heat and dust had combined to strip this scene of all its colour. The sky shimmered like grey silk, and the various tones of plain and hill shone with an exhausted pallor.

Feeling somewhat exhausted ourselves after wrestling with our rotund bundles of cane, we stopped in a Valdez bar for cold beer. The first couple of swallows tasted of chaff but revived us wonderfully. One end of the room was piled with bags of charcoal, and we bought two for our barbecue. Then, realizing we lacked a grill, we found one in a hardware shop. Finally we procured some deck-chairs. Their plastic webbing was of a bird-scaring brightness, and looked too flimsy to sustain a Rosalia, but they were the only models available.

On our way back through Álamos we stopped and went in search of José the builder, to thank him for the work and to pay him. For once, he was at home. He shrugged off our thanks with his usual downward droop of the eyes. Then, over a glass of wine, he asked us how we were settling into the house. Did we need any more furniture? If so, he had a table for us. A gift. We accepted it with gratitude. It would do well for the terrace. We promised to collect it the next day, since our car was already laden like a trans-Sahara camion.

Back in Dalmácija we strung wire between the horizontal beams of the roof arbour and laid the *cañizos* on top, tying them down against the occasional gales. The canes threw an elegantly hatched shadow against the white wall behind, long parallel lines of indigo with dazzling slots of reflected sunshine between. I vaguely wondered if we would be tanning our skins in stripes, like zebras. Certainly the protection was only partial, and we marinated in an all-pervading heat as we lolled on our iridescent deck-chairs under our newly created shade.

Over the rooftops the sky was full of swifts and martins. The two species were distinct. The swifts inhabited the hunch-backed, lichened tiles of the church roof, into which at dusk they would hurtle at full tilt, furling their wings at the split-second of entry, like a dagger slamming into its sheath: and in flight, they would circle, scimitar-winged, in high, powerful sweeps interrupted by sudden jerks to intercept their prey, calling to each other in shrieks so shrill as barely to fall within the compass of human hearing. The martins were more parochial. They lived in lay premises – a ruined house next to the cemetery which they shared with a colony of bees: and their flight was less celestial, a busy fluttering down the alleyways and round the white corners and over the terracotta gables, after which efforts they would gather chattering on an electricity cable under the big acacia by the cemetery gate. Sometimes there must have been a big hatch of aerial flies, like the advent of mayflies on a trout stream, and the sky would fill with swifts and martins together, hurtling specks gyrating with a force and delicacy that constitutes, surely, one of the most graceful examples of food-gathering in all nature. We wondered how there could be a single fly surviving in the village. Alas, there were many that visited us as we lay there. They were unwelcome, but we saw them, now, as a link in a chain of village symbiosis: man attracted the flies that attracted the birds.

Rosalia braved the stairs again this evening, bringing Jesus with her. While he crouched formally on an upright chair, with his large rough fist encasing a whisky glass, she responded to the opportunities of a larger stage than that offered by our little sitting-room below. Leaning over the railing, she harangued every arrival at Consuela's shop, with asides to Georgina and me on the domestic arrangements and personal habits of each. She fingered our barbecue grill with suspicion, apparently testing its breaking strength, and making us aware of the anomaly of our introduction of a primitive cooking method into a primitive community, while it meanwhile had progressed to bottled gas. Even the roof terrace itself was a rarity in this place. Rosalia and our other visitors professed to admire the movement of the air up there, and the view, yet they made no use of similar facilities themselves. The few loggias or flat roofs in the village were assigned to pot-plants and cats and washing-lines. The villagers never used them.

18 July
We drove down to Álamos to collect Jose's table. Since his house, like most in the village, was inaccessible except on foot, we had to park the car on the road at the bottom and carry the table down to it through a labyrinth of alleyways, stepping jerkily over the mule-dung. Long before we reached the bottom it was evident that he had given us a very stoutly made piece of furniture. A group of old men abandoned their usual place in the shade beside the road, laid aside their sticks, and helped us to hoist the table onto the car's roof-rack and rope it into position, legs up like a moribund sheep.

After handshakes all round, and a reluctant refusal to join the men in the nearest bar, we walked back up the hill. We had heard that one of the food shops sold rabbit. The proprietress – the wife of the mayor, as we later discovered – confirmed the fact. The rabbit would be ready for us in half an hour. Could we not take it now? we asked. Not now, she said, it was still alive.

As we worked our way through the leisurely ritual of buying onions, cheese, salami, vinegar and other staples, a fleshy grey-haired man came in to buy a handful of broad beans. We had not seen him before, but he greeted us expansively. We were the foreigners from Dalmácija, were we not? He had heard about us, and was glad to meet us. He held my hand so long that I had difficulty in retrieving it. Would we have a drink with him when we had finished? He owned a bar – right next door. A new one.

He was behind the counter when we went in. He introduced himself as Gil Nuñez. He poured us glasses of local wine, and offered us *tapas* – large sardines from a plate on the counter. When we assented, he took them to a small grill at the back of the bar, where he sprinkled them with herbs and garlic, gilded them with oil and set them to cook. He then came round to our side of the bar, chattering effusively and dimpled with smiles, and scrambled up on a stool, leaning affectionately on my shoulder for support and squeezing my arm. He reached up to a hook on the ceiling and brought down two *morcillas*, soft purple home-made sausages. We eyed them apprehensively. We had a well-developed liking for most Spanish food, but when Rosalia had given us a *morcilla*, back in the spring, most of it had found its way to the garbage bin. Unlike the various *salchichones* and *salchichas*, all of which, like the ham, needed well-knit jaw muscles for their consumption, *morcillas* were pulpy. They had a predigested texture which, combined with their disconcerting colour and a flavour suggestive of raw flesh, put them low on our list of preferred local cuisine.

But these *morcillas* were less flabby, and well seasoned. While we sliced them on to crusts of bread, and manipulated the hot, fragrant sardines, our host told us about himself. For the previous ten years he had been running a bar in Madrid. Before that he had been in South America: in Brazil, Argentina, Chile, Uruguay. A sailor? No . . . and he stooped with the gesture of a Raleigh laying a cloak in a puddle . . . a bullfighter. Or a bullfighter's assistant, he added, with a deprecating shrug. A hazardous life, we said. Had he suffered injury? No. Well, nothing serious, he said, flicking a plump buttock. Why had he come to live in such a small village as Álamos? He was born here, he said.

He stood us a round of drinks, and asked if we wanted to eat a meal. He was about to prepare a paella, he said, and flourished the huge black pan at us: rabbit and shrimp and a plateful of vegetables which he proceeded to chop while talking to us. The beans from the next-door shop were there. The prospect was enticing, but we declined, shook his hand, and turned to go. Wait, he said, he had something to show us. He hurried over to a satchel hanging from a nail on the wall, an incongruously elegant satchel of leather. From it he took a yellowed and fragmented newspaper clipping. It was from a South American paper. Near the bottom, under a small cross-heading, and commanding less than two column inches, was a laconic account of a bullfight on the previous day. Whatever the date had been, and wherever the place, the *torero*'s name had been Gil Nuñez.

Before leaving Álamos we went in search of Salvador, the owner of the land next to our house. We were increasingly eager to make the purchase. Surely he would have managed to consult his wife in the three months since our last meeting: that would not be rushing things, even by Spanish standards. Filled with optimism we knocked on his door. But there was no reply. The house was locked and silent.

Back on our roof terrace we lay full length on our bright new chairs, our feet and lower legs in the sun and the rest of us in the shade of the *cañizos*. José's table was still on the car at the bottom of the village: the idea of carrying it up the hill in the heat of the day was unappealing. As for the problem of getting it onto the roof terrace, that too was beyond the scope of heat-fuddled brains. Surely the thing would not fit up the narrow stairway. We would have to manhandle it over the patio wall, and up the side of the house and over the railings. Or lower it from a helicopter . . .

Below us as we lay there was a scene which, though modest, was composed of elements so delightfully arranged as to inspire all artistic visitors, over the succeeding years, to reach for their pencils or paints. Opposite us was Consuela's shop, a small building whose roof ran away from us to merge with those of the buildings behind. All these roofs were lean-to's: they sloped only one way from their gables, but all in different directions and at different angles. The topmost row of tiles in each case was whitewashed: the rest, richly russet, flowed down the slopes in a succession of rounded ridges with deep furrows between, creating shadows which, like mountains or the sea, changed their definition according to the time of the day and the position of the sun. Next to the shop, behind a wall, was a tiny yard roofed with *cañizos*, on which a cat lay asleep. Overlooking the yard was Consuela's roof-garden. It was a raised platform about the size of a double bed, reached by an exterior flight of steps. Like the yard it was roofed with canes, lashed together into three rafts of slightly varying sizes and colours, arranged irregularly, thereby contributing to the sweet disorder which was characteristic of the whole. In the shadow of the canes were a couple of dozen flowering plants in buckets, rusty cans and truncated plastic jars. They were carefully watered every day by Consuela's elderly mother or by her half-sister Isabel, both of whom lived with her. She herself was too busy for such duties. Apart from these ministrations the garden was never visited, nor could it be seen by anyone but ourselves from our position above.

Beside the roof garden an alleyway ran away down the slope, side-stepping the corner of another building with a deep-set entrance at the head of a flight of earthenware-tiled steps. In the angle of the steps grew a thicket of scarlet geraniums. Across the alley lay shadows, thrown by the houses. They changed colour hour by hour, as did the whitewashed walls of the buildings themselves, which ranged in tone from grey and blue to a whiteness too brilliant for the eye, according to whether they were in sun or shade or indirectly lit by reflections from the walls opposite. The alley ended at the rim of the village, where the land fell away sharply. Beyond, in the cleft between the buildings,

170

we could see the approach road winding up the valley, and over the roofs rose the mountain where we had picknicked in the castle ruins. It too changed its form during the day. At noon, with the sun behind it, the silhouette was flat, without a third dimension: but in the morning and evening the muscles of its broad shoulders stood out clearly, scarred from top to bottom with intricate terracing, and the intervening ridges glowed in a multiplicity of colours from tawny red at dawn to roseate lavender at dusk.

All this formed the background to the miniature scenes of village life which were regularly enacted in the alley below us. The shop door was like the entrance of an ants' nest, the source of a two-way trickle of visitors, in and out. It was an intermittent trickle, drying up completely through the central hours of the day and dependent on demand at other times. Whenever it was open a low hum of conversation would emanate from within, as though from the saloon bar of a small Cotswold pub in high summer.

Towards dusk came another spectacle, the return of the workers from the hillsides. First, the eye would be caught by a movement on the opposing slope. Passing down one of the diagonal tracks could be seen a little procession: a couple of mules, a couple of human figures, and two or three attendant dogs. From time to time they would disappear behind a fold of the hill, to reappear lower and closer. Finally the steps of the mules could be heard round the corner behind the shop and passing the cemetery gates. Then they were plodding up the alley below us. Leaning on our railings, uneasily aware of our role as *flâneurs* and *voyeurs*, we would wave to the men. They, too weary to give us more than a brief *¡Hola!*, passed on into the little square, to water the mules and disperse to their homes.

The first of them to return was always Luis, the rotund bartender who had officiated over our purchase of the house. Like everyone else in the village, he owned various plots of land, which he needed to cultivate during the day while the bar stayed closed. He evidently toiled alone: his return in the evening was a solitary one, a memorable pairing of man and mule. On the final climb up to the village, Luis would hang on to the mule's tail. Despite his bulk, this arrangement seemed not to disconcert the animal. The two of them would turn off by the cemetery, before reaching the shop, and we would glimpse them as they crossed the end of the transverse alley, still attached to each other in distinctive silhouette, like an elephant water-skiing.

Later, Luis would reappear on foot in the same alley, up which he would walk, very slowly, to Consuela's door. He was a bachelor, and he had come to an arrangement with Consuela, his cousin, that she would feed him every night. We soon found that we could set a watch by his arrival. The regularity was reassuring. The pattern of these little happenings through the day, changing in detail but never in essence, formed a ritual which enacted for us the rhythm of life in this place. Coming from a society of frantic change, we found such reiterations important. Not merely were they survivals of an existence which had endured for centuries, but their very repetitiveness gave evidence of a continuing life-force. They were like heart-beats. No single event could achieve such strength. *Einmal ist keinmal.*

19 July
Today we made a discovery which would change our lives. Strolling up to the track at the top of the village, we saw a car parked there. How had it got there? It was only twenty paces above our house. If we could drive up to this spot, we would avoid the climb on foot from the road at the bottom which now faced us every time we ventured abroad. It was a climb which, when compounded by a load of heavy shopping, would tax a sherpa. How we would manage it in our tottering senility had been a serious worry to us.

But now we realized that the track which ran on from the end of the road, where it stopped below the village, was penetrable by car. After a hundred yards there was a turn-off which climbed up beside the village and joined the track along the top. It was, in fact, the route that the Easter procession had taken, but at that time it had not seemed passable to cars. Nor was it, by any normal standards. It was reminiscent of the way up to the castle. But for a small car with high clearance it seemed a prospect worth undertaking. I decided to try it forthwith, and walked down to the road to collect the car.

There was a small crowd of women at the bottom of the village. The fish-man had arrived. He drove up from the coast about a couple of times a week in a small van. Like the bread-man he gave notice of his arrival by sounding his horn when still half-way down the valley, and maintaining this fanfare until the hillsides echoed. In the back of the van were buckets of squid and clams and baby anchovies. The village women eyed and sniffed and prodded this slippery merchandise, which was weighed out for them on a set of portable scales and dispensed in thin plastic bags through which the fish shone silver as they were borne away. Rosalia was there. I wanted to buy some clams, which were favourites of ours, but she would have none of it. The anchovies were a better bargain, she said. Taking my anchovies I climbed into the car. Where was I going, she asked sharply, and where was Jorgina? I explained that I was driving the car up to the top of the village. I had discovered, I said with pride, that I could park it near our house. Much more convenient. But of course, said Rosalia; she and Jesus had always wondered why we insisted on parking at the bottom and climbing the hill. They had often discussed it together.

When I got back to the house – now a short downhill stroll from our new parking place – I found Emilio there. We had not seen him since his transportation of our building materials. With him was a young man we had not previously met, called Aurelio. Every male in this village was called José or Aurelio or Luis, with a sprinkling of Salvadors, plus our friend Angel. The surnames were all Perez or Torres or Moreno. The paucity of names was due to the fact that everyone was related to everyone else. This in-breeding appeared to have no ill effects, but its physical patterns were often visible. At gatherings like the Easter procession three or four facial types would constantly recur through the crowd, and on several occasions over the years Georgina or I would greet an acquaintance in the street, only to find that it was, in fact, a sister or cousin. It was the female physiognomies that more often confused us: but their names were more disparate than the men's, ranging from the religious through the classical to the coy: Maria, Concepcion, Consuela, Constanza, Mari-Luz.

Young Aurelio had a complexion as dark as a stoker's. His eyes flashed above smudgy stubble with a disconcerting frankness. The openness of the villagers' manner towards us had always been one of their most impressive and endearing features. It was compounded of dignity and friendliness, with no trace of reserve nor, conversely, of over-curiosity. But in Aurelio's case it bordered on insolence. Perhaps I was reacting to his satanic darkness. Certainly he was civil enough. He had come to introduce himself, and to invite us to his house. It was a modern one, on the far side of the village. On our new-found driveway, in fact. Would we like to come and visit him one evening? Were we interested in music? He had a cousin who played the guitar. This was a most alluring prospect. We had heard none of the traditional *cante jondo* since arriving in Spain. I nodded vigorously, trying not to look at his teeth, which shone voraciously behind steak-coloured lips.

Emilio was another man of whom I was definitely nervous, but I turned to him with something approaching relief. How was his wife Concepcion? She, we knew, had kidney trouble. For two years she had worn a sack under her skirt, and needed to make regular trips to Málaga, forty kilometres away. She was unfailingly courageous. To every enquiry into her condition, she would reply with a smile and the invariable Spanish euphemism *'regular'*, which roughly corresponds to the deprecatory English 'can't grumble'.

Emilio said that Concepcion was awaiting a kidney transplant. It was a long time to wait: kidneys were scarce. Besides, it had to be a female one. Surely the gender of the donor was not important, we said. It had to be female, he repeated. He didn't want to give Concepcion a man's kidney. It would affect her – make her less feminine. Suddenly medical science, so incongruous a subject of small-talk on this remote hillside, was overlaid with primitive belief.

We offered our guests a drink. Each made a dismissive gesture with down-turned eyes, as though we had proposed some unseemly and possibly perverted activity. This, we knew by now, was Spanish for 'yes'. But they did not linger over their wine. They had work to do, as always. Besides, their social obligations were discharged. Emilio had come to introduce us to Aurelio. Aurelio had come to invite us to his house.

Shortly after their departure Rosalia arrived. Immediately after, in fact, giving the usual uneasy impression that our front door was under constant surveillance, or else wired for sound. She was carrying a bowl. Soup, she said. For us. We eyed it apprehensively. It was like no soup we had ever seen. It was cold, and had grapes floating in it. It was concocted, we learnt, of crushed almonds and milk and various spices. We took it and thanked her, in what we hoped was a terminal way, but she stood her ground. Drink it, she said, like a school matron. Georgina fetched two spoons, and standing in our sitting-room we finished the soup. The prospect of leaving some in the bowl was tempting, but out of the question. We didn't ask her for the recipe.

Meanwhile she had passed through into the kitchen. Where were the anchovies I had bought? she asked, riffling through the contents of our fridge. Taking the fish she put them in a bowl she selected from a pile on the shelf, then covered them with a thick sprinkling of salt and put them back in the fridge. After two hours, she said, the salt must be washed off. How were we going to cook them? she asked. On the barbecue, we said. Everything was now cooked on the barbecue, except breakfast. It was our new toy. The anchovies would be better fried, said Rosalia. She would return and fry them for us.

When she did so, she was with Jesus, who sat talking with me while Rosalia lectured Georgina on fish cuisine. At one point I asked him, fatuously, when he was planning a holiday in England. But he didn't take it as a joke. His eyes fixed on me with a glinting intensity, and he breathed the word ¡Ojalá! Ojalá is used for expressing a wish. It is an ancient word, an Arabic imprecation to Allah, and the guttural pronunciation of the 'j' gives it a grunting force, as of an oath or a specially potent plea. It has always seemed to me most apt for wishes of a forlorn and despairing kind – for retrospective wishes, for instance, which are always the most anguished. ¡Ojalá! If only Mozart and Schubert had lived a further ten years apiece!

20 July
Another abortive attempt to find Salvador. Again there was no reply to my battering on his door. The man must have been spending long hours in the fields, or in bed with his wife. His sinewy body had looked well fitted to either activity. But I was determined to track him down. The failure to settle the matter of the land was beginning to weigh on me.

The possibility that Salvador might actually refuse to sell it to us was unthinkable. That would be virtually to negate a reality – the garden was beginning to take shape in my mind. By now I was possessed of a lavishly illustrated book on tropical plants. Admittedly the map at the front showed only the area between the Tropics of Cancer and Capricorn, circling the belly of the world a great many leagues from Spain, but I ignored this, as I did any deflating comments such as the information that one of the commonest tropical plants was the potato. Instead, inflamed to an almost lascivious passion by the colour photographs and accompanying texts, I drew up an international cast-list of exotica extensive enough to overcrowd Kew Gardens. Increasingly I saw the gritty slope next to our house, with its thriving crop of plastic bags and rusty tins, as a kind of reverse cornucopia: instead of the riches of nature pouring out, flowers and fruits would pour in, converging on this narrow plot from all over the world.

From Madagascar, I read, originated the scarlet-flowered flamboyant tree which I remembered from my childhood in Ceylon. I had no idea whether it would grow in Spain, or where to buy one, but these were mere details. The delicate blue jacaranda I knew to be a possibility – it grew in the next village, although it originated in tropical America and the Antilles. The ice-cream scented frangipani, which this severe book told me was a dogbane, was native to the West Indies but was subsequently planted near temples and in cemeteries in Ceylon, India and South-East Asia. From Brazil came the coral tree, which had edible fruit. The yucca came from Mexico and Guatemala, the hibiscus from China (unless I fancied the fringed version from East Africa) and the bottlebrush tree, *Callistemon citrinus*, from Australia. The sky-blue plumbago came from South Africa, as did the bird-of-paradise flower, *Strelitzia reginae*, which was named after George III's wife Charlotte von Mecklenburg-Strelitz. The book did not say why. The Yesterday-today-and-tomorrow shrub, whose flowers changed colour with age, was native to Central and South America, and apparently cured snake-bite, which might be useful: I wasn't sure if St Patrick had visited Andalusia. Conversely the night-scented Moon-tree from Peru was poisonous and narcotic, and no Spaniard would touch it. This one I would clearly have to plant myself.

Passing on to palm trees, I knew the Moors had imported the date palm, but it was evident from the book that I needn't stop there. The coconut palm seemed unsuitable, and probably unwilling, but I could consider importing a royal palm from Cuba, a spindle palm from the Mascarene Islands (wherever they might be), of which the fruits were suitable for pig fodder, a sealing-wax palm from Sumatra, or a pigmy date palm from Assam. Or perhaps I should consider the Manila palm which came from South-East Asia (but was botanically named after a nineteenth-century Chelsea nurseryman) or the Chinese fan palm from Malaya (but botanically named after the Laird of Liviston in West Lothian). The latter – the palm not the Laird – could easily be confused, I read, with the Washingtonia, which hailed not from Washington but from California and Northern Mexico. I was confused all right, and that was before I went on to pore over the respective merits of the queen palm, the petticoat palm, the ruffled fan palm, the sentry palm, the wine palm. According to the book, the wine palm produced sago, brushes, brooms and baskets. Ah, and wine.

As for fruit trees, the orange originated in China; however, the seedless mandarin which I planned to plant as an ornamental standard, popped up as a fluke species in Oran, Algeria. The mango came from Burma and the Himalayan foothills, but I was going to have trouble here from Georgina, who had hostile memories of the fruit falling on her head as a small child in

West Africa. Luckily she had no objection to papayas – the essential preliminary to a tropical breakfast – which originated in Central America and contained, the book said, the protein-splitting enzyme papain, used as a meat-tenderizer and digestion aid, which sounded promising for our old age. Additionally, the plot of land was already fringed along one side by prickly pears, which were imported from Mexico, and by the spiky agave (ludicrously classed as a daffodil), cultivated 8,000 years ago by the Mexicans for the production of rope. Also for fermenting the powerfully motivating first-cousin to tequila – pulque. I made a mental note to learn the recipe.

My tropical plant book was not the only source of inspiration. A few weeks previously we had visited a nursery garden in Surrey on other business, and had been side-tracked into a long discussion on tropicana with the local guru on the subject, a knowledgeable stripling who looked too young to have crossed the Channel, let alone to have become an expert on the plants of the world. He proceeded to recommend, inter alia, an Australian mint bush with heliotrope flowers and aromatic leaves, a lobster's-claw shrub from New Zealand, a strawberry guava, and a fruit-salad tree – *Feijoa Sellowiana* – with edible fuchsia-like flowers and fruit which tasted, he said, of a mixture of pineapple, strawberry and banana. Unfortunately no fruit was available for sampling. It was a day of torrential rain, and our interview with this amiable youth took place under a green golf umbrella in an ankle-deep puddle. How would the *Feijoa* stand up to drought? we asked, peering at the lad through the curtain of water that ran off the rim of the umbrella. He was sure it could stand quite a bit of drought, he said, raising his voice above the relentless roar of the rain.

Now, sitting on the roof terrace in 90 degree heat, I mused a while on such matters, before peering over the railings to check on events below. The shop was shut, but outside Consuela's house Isabel was hard at work. Although she was Consuela's half-sister, her physical appearance was very different. She was small-boned and slim by Spanish standards, with a sweet and delicate face, and her voice was similarly slight and fragile: it was high-pitched, and each word seemed to be produced with difficulty, which made any conversation with her seem something precious. With us she was shyly courteous and interested in all our affairs, and the charm of her nature made us wonder why, at the age of about forty, she was unmarried and reduced to circumstances which, though comfortable enough, were menial: the Cinderella of the household. Had she had no *novios*, no boy friends? We questioned Rosalia on the matter. Yes, she said, Isabel had nearly got married, many years before, when she was young. A man from Málaga. A rich man. But the wedding had never happened: it was impossible to know why not. Looking down on the thin, busy figure below I was reminded of the five saddest words in Shakespeare: Aguecheek's murmur of 'I was adored once, too'.

Isabel had a small brush in her hand and a bucket beside her. Despite the noon sun she was devotedly touching up invisible defects in the whitewash on Consuela's wall. She then carefully dusted it down like a Victorian tweenie polishing a tall-boy, and finished by sweeping the alley on hands and knees. I asked her why she was working so hard. Because of San Anton, she said.

This was the season of *fiestas*. Almost every town and village had one at this time of year – it was the reason we had picked this month to return. Here in Dalmácija the big event was the *feria* of San Anton, the patron saint of the village. It was going to take place next week, and the festivities would last two days. There would be bands, and dancing, and various sporting events, and a procession. The procession was the reason for Isabel's activities. It would pass Consuela's house, she

180

said. There would be visitors to the village for the *feria*. Everything must look good.

I absorbed the significance of this remark, and bestirred myself to walk down and take a look at our own exterior wall. If Isabel was worried about the acceptability of hers, what in heaven's name would the passing procession think of ours? Far from being the searing white of the rest of the village, our house was the colour of a dirty sheet, the worst bit being the lower part of the patio wall where a generation or two of effluent had seeped through from the former chicken-yard. Surely Georgina and I could refurbish this bit, at least, before the *feria*. We had a few days' grace. We'd ask Rosalia about whitewash: where to buy it and how to apply it.

But there was no sign of Rosalia that night. We lit the barbecue apprehensively, expecting her to arrive at the moment the charcoal glow reached its apogee. We poured gin and tonic, which normally triggered her appearance like rubbing the genie's lamp. Nothing happened. We put the chicken on the grill. Then, indeed, there was an immediate cry of greeting from below. But it was not Rosalia. It was Emilio and Aurelio. They stood swaying in the doorway, muttering some complaint, but the words emerged so congealed, so thick with wine and indignation, that I could make no sense of them. So I shepherded them upstairs and poured them each a whisky, in the hope that straight alcohol would clear the vocal chords.

And indeed the trouble now became clear. What had happened to us tonight? asked Aurelio. Yesterday evening we had promised to visit his house. He had been awaiting us. His cousin had been awaiting us, with his guitar. His wife had been awaiting us, with food specially prepared. Emilio had evidently been awaiting us too, and goodness knows who else. I tried to apologize and explain. We hadn't known the invitation was for *tonight*. We hadn't understood. We felt the mistake very much.

I made this little speech with some difficulty, as Emilio was leaning on me, with one arm on my shoulder, as though about to suggest a waltz. Nobody respected the poor, he said. He then repeated it, in case I hadn't understood it the first time, as indeed I hadn't: nobody . . . respects . . . the . . . poor. But he wasn't poor, I said. I knew he prided himself on the money he earned. No, he wasn't poor, he said, and sat down on one of the deck-chairs. Deceived, in his current state, by the depth of it, he subsided backwards and lay there with limbs flailing, like an inverted woodlouse. I pulled him upright. He sat there for a moment, savouring verticality, then teetered to his feet. He preferred standing, he said.

Across the terrace, Aurelio had cornered Georgina against the railings like a boxer crowding the ropes. He had been awaiting us since six o'clock, he said. With his cousin. And his wife. And Emilio. We had promised. No, said Georgina, it was a misunderstanding. A *misunderstanding* – and she reached hastily for the dictionary on the table to check the word, or possibly to introduce a large solid object between herself and Aurelio, who was launching his grievance at her so physically that his unshaven chin almost touched her brow. He was at the sharp and dangerous divide between self-pity and wrath. I waved the whisky bottle at him like a toreador signalling to the bull with his cloak. Emilio intercepted it. Nobody respected the poor, he said. We had promised to come, said Aurelio. It was a misunderstanding, said Georgina, now word-perfect. Smoke began to rise from the chicken. This had the makings of a long evening.

And so it was. Midnight had passed before we succeeded in buying off our visitors with a promise – a cross-my-heart and *seguro-seguro* promise – to visit Aurelio's house the next evening. By this time the whisky was gone, the chicken charred beyond redemption, and Georgina and I reduced to husks. Social pressures in Spain were more demanding than we were used to in London.

21 July
It was good bread today, said Rosalia. The bread was baked from the same flour by the same man in the same oven year-round, but it varied daily. Normally Georgina and I welcomed this lack of sameness, but today, after the rigours of the night before, we were indifferent to the finer points of bakery. Rosalia put the loaves down on the kitchen table. She always brought the same number, but every evening she asked us how many we wanted for the next day. The query was an excuse for a visit.

But last night, she said, she had been unable to ask us. She had walked over to our house but it was evident we had company. She'd heard noise from the roof terrace. Much noise. Had we passed the evening well? she asked slyly. I felt unable to get my tongue around an explanation – I had forgotten the word for misunderstanding – and in any case I knew there was something else we wanted to discuss with her. I reached deep into the whisky-sodden cellars of my mind. Ah yes, whitewashing.

She nodded approvingly when we told her of our plan to whitewash our patio wall. The nod carried a clear implication of 'and about time, too'. What we needed, she said, was some *cal*. A sackful of it would do, whatever it was. We could buy it in Valdez. She told us where. After breakfast – the bread was indeed excellent, topped with Sierra Nevada honey – we set off to procure it. Better get this task over and done with, especially with the *feria* imminent. Perhaps whitewash took a long time to dry, or needed several coats.

We soon found the place Rosalia had described, a gateway in a side-street on the edge of town, leading to a ramshackle yard full of firewood and paving tiles. Just inside the entrance was a low building, deep-browed like a hovel in a Rembrandt drawing, with thick stone walls and no windows. Within we could dimly see a dragon's hoard of large pale irregularly shaped blocks which seemed to glimmer through the darkness. Quicklime. Familiar with its reputation as an exterminator and, conversely, as a vitalizer (up to the beginning of this century children were held over quicklime to cure their whooping cough), we were now about to discover its virtues as a decorator. We purchased a sack of it and drove back up to the village.

From Consuela we bought, on Rosalia's instructions, a bucket and a large wooden-handled brush with tufted nylon bristles of bright blue and pink. She also lent us some plastic sheets to spread on the ground, and a 50-gallon oil-drum. The latter she extricated from her store-room behind the shop and spun effortlessly up the alley to our back door, like a child rolling a hoop. A swing of her broad shoulders, and it was up the steps and in our patio. We were ready to go to work. First we half-filled the oil-drum with water, as specified. Then we dropped in the *cal*.

The effect was cataclysmic. The quicklime's fearful pent-up energy was instantly released in a maelstrom of activity. The water seethed and gurgled, and the oil-drum leapt up and down on the paving like a Brobdingnagian jumping-bean. Stupefied by the infernal forces we had unleashed, Georgina and I cowered at a safe distance until the hissing white broth had subsided and cooled. Then we went to work.

At first we tried smearing the stuff on to the wall like paint, but this was like painting with water. Nothing stuck to the brush. After a few minutes we still had a full bucket of whitewash and a few scratch-marks on the wall. The sun was nearing its zenith, and our duties to San Anton began to seem less pressing. Then there was a soft footfall in the alley behind us and up came Isabel, almost on tiptoe with diffidence. We were doing things the wrong way, she murmured. She would show us. We should not smear the *cal* but flick it, like so. She cocked her slender wrist, and a fine spray of whitewash was transferred to the wall as delicately as with an atomiser. I took the brush from her, loaded it, and flicked. There was an explosion like a wet dog shaking itself. Whitewash flew into my eye and pattered on to the plastic sheet at our feet. Isabel and Georgina sprang back a pace. I flicked again, and again. I was getting a taste for whitewashing. I kept at it for a while longer, then stood back to assess the effect. This was frankly disappointing. Every inch of my clothes was, by now, encrusted as stiff and white as the cerements of a corpse, while the wall remained its grey knobbly self. But I was doing better than I knew. Fresh whitewash is grey-blue until it dries. After a few minutes in the sun the newly treated sector of our wall shone dazzling white. We admired it through screwed-up eyes.

But there was much to do, and we had picked the wrong time of day to do it. As I painted I was seared on both sides, by the midday sun on my back, and by the radiation from the shimmering stones so close in front of me. I continued until the wall started to go out of focus. Then, cravenly, I passed the brush to Georgina, and went to gulp down some water. When I emerged an hour later she was still at it, but by now was visibly tottering on her feet. I persuaded her indoors. The patio wall remained two-toned. We decided to assign all future whitewashing to someone else.

By the evening we were both still feeling weak, but our social duties called. We had promised to visit Aurelio's house, and we could not fail him a second time. No more misunderstandings. As dusk fell we staggered to our feet and set out along the perimeter track. His house was the newest in the village and the largest. He had been working on it for a couple of years, whenever he had the time and the money.

185

Now, apparently, the latter had run out. The house remained half-finished. There were a couple of other similarly incomplete houses in the village: nobody here could amass enough capital to build an entire house in one go. In Aurelio's case it was paradoxically the top half which was finished. The roof was of brilliant orange tiles and the upper story was whitewashed: but the ground floor, like a contrasting dado, was of bare brick. In the middle of it was an opening, a kind of stable door, from which shone a light. We went in.

We found ourselves in a dim, cavernous expanse covering all the ground-space of the house. Concrete pillars rose to an unplastered ceiling. The walls, too, were of rough, naked brick. In one corner was a large canopied fireplace, so incongruous in this austere warehouse that it reminded me of those fireplaces one sees high on the walls of ruined castles, isolated above the vanished floors of solars or great halls. Nearby was an immense and ultra-modern cooker the size of a bar-billiards table. It was the only furniture in the place, apart from a small round table and four chairs. Two men were seated there, who rose as we entered.

At first both were unrecognizable. Then we saw that one was Aurelio – but a transformed Aurelio, wearing a razor-creased three-piece suit of dove-grey. The waistcoat was buttoned so tightly across his chest as to maintain him stiffly upright, in an attitude of stilted courtliness. His face was recently shaved, and his black hair sleeked back. He looked like a movie Mafioso as he introduced us to his companion. This, an altogether more homely figure in short-sleeved shirt and baggy slacks, proved to be the mayor of Álamos. Aurelio seemed to specialize in mayors, I thought, remembering last night's extended contretemps with Emilio. There was no sign of the guitar-playing cousin.

We all sat down at the table, under a dangling light-bulb which was the sole illumination. Away in the shadows, barely visible at the extremities of this gigantic cave, lay a collection of rural and mechanical impedimenta: logs, a wheelbarrow, a tree in a bucket of water, butane cylinders, sacks of fertilizer. As we composed ourselves for conversation, there was a sudden muffled thumping in the outer darkness. It approached us – as ominously as Blind Pugh – and into the dusty circle of light stepped a mule with hobbled forelegs. Aurelio ushered it away, and went to get some wine.

He reappeared with his wife, who carried a plate of bread and another loaded with three kinds of home-made sausage, the dreaded *morcillas.* In our queasy state, Georgina and I eyed them without enthusiasm. They were fresh, said Aurelio's wife, meaning to reassure us. The pig had been killed last week. She was curing the hams upstairs. The *morcillas* were in varying shades of blood-red. Georgina and I each took a small slice of the least virulently coloured, and covertly looked around for a hungry dog.

The mayor of Álamos, we were told, had jurisdiction over Dalmácija, and was its representative in securing government funds for improvement. He told us of plans to install the village's first telephone. Also to pave the approach road and extend it over the hill into the next valley. We listened to these forecasts with mixed feelings. We had fallen in love with Dalmácija because of its timelessness: now it began to look as though we had arrived in an era of change. A paved road! From our roof terrace could be seen a path winding up the side of the valley towards Álamos: until a few years ago this had been the only approach to the village, which could thus only be reached by mule. Now cars could come here – including ours – and lorries bearing loads of building materials. It was no wonder that the new houses looked different: the old ones had been built of rocks from the surrounding hillsides. This house of Aurelio's where we were sitting now was, literally, the shape of things to come.

His wife offered to show us around. We accepted quickly, leaving the half-eaten *morcillas* on the table. At the rear of the warehouse where we'd been sitting a bare concrete staircase led upstairs. Half-way up, on a small landing, a wooden stump projected from the wall like a gallows. From it hung two shapeless packages. They were hams, wrapped in muslin against the flies. Beside them, on the floor, lay the instruments of their making: two massive stones, which had been used for flattening them into shape, and a pile of khaki-coloured salt. The hams would hang here for four months, we were told, ripening in the relative coolness of this dark corner dug out of the rising hillside behind the house.

Upstairs the house was finished, but looked as uninhabited as the ground floor. There was virtually no furniture, except for a bed in a bedroom and two chairs in front of a television set. Acres of highly polished floor reflected the intermittent light-bulbs. The bathroom fittings were worth the entire purchase price of our house. But there was a homelier touch in the kitchen-to-be. From wall to wall, at head height, stretched a pair of iron bars round which were looped dozens of circlets of *morcillas*, graded by colour. Aurelio's wife fiddled proudly with them, spacing them more symmetrically along the bars, like a housewife plumping up the cushions on a sofa, while Aurelio expatiated on the significance of the various stub-ends of pipe or electric wiring that protruded from the walls . . . this was for the sink, that for the cooker, that for the fridge. Behind him an open doorway gave on to a balcony which stretched the length of the house. It overlooked the village, at the perfect distance for appreciating the cluster of dwellings *in toto*. We wondered to how much use this balcony would be put in the years to come. There were no chairs on it. Aurelio and his wife evidently preferred to sit in the warehouse below, although up here the night air moved perceptibly against our faces. In front of us the white buildings glowed in the darkness, while in the southern sky the Square of Pegasus shone as precise as a signal. But the villagers, we knew, were no star-gazers. The night sky which so delighted Georgina and me was, to them, as commonplace as a roof overhead.

22 July

Breakfast on the roof terrace as usual, and a marvellously clear still day. Across the valley the ruins of the castle stood out so distinctly that it seemed one could pick out every sprig of cistus between the tumbled stones: sounds, too, reached us with a heightened intensity in the mountain air. Half a mile away a man was loosening the earth around a vine, and the fall of every pebble sounded like an avalanche. We poured ourselves more coffee and settled back for a quiet morning after our exertions of the day before. And there were more exertions to come: tonight there was to be a *feria* at Álamos.

As I lay on my chair I looked at the earthenware tiles beneath me, now warming in the morning sun. Despite their common ingredient they possessed individual characters, like wines from different vineyards. Some were pale, almost salmon-coloured. Others were made of darker clay and carried tones of brown and green. Others evidently contained traces of salt, which sweated out in whorls of white. One had a cat's foot precisely imprinted, like a predator's at an African water-hole. All changed colour after rain. With such pleasure to be derived from a plain floor, I thought, how could I ever fail to be enthralled by this place?

While Georgina and I lolled and sipped and read, the village was at work, achieving its morning tasks before the heat of the day came upon it. Today Emilio was restocking Consuela's shop. This was another Emilio, an elderly assistant, employee, lover/ex-lover who lived in Consuela's house. His mule stood half-way down the alley, motionless while he unloaded it. Its panniers were filled with boxes of lemonade, which he manhandled off the beast's back and into the store-room behind the shop. Then he led it back down the hill, evidently to a stack of goods which had been dumped by lorry at the bottom, as had happened to our building materials. A few minutes later he reappeared with a more multifarious load, which he brought to the front door of the shop. I lay back low in my chair, peeping at him over the edge of the terrace, apprehensive that I should appear to be spying on him while he worked. This part of his task took him longer, because of the number of small objects to be taken in . . . rolls of lavatory paper, bottles of olive oil, powdered milk, half a dozen forlorn-looking lettuces, flat boxes of lollipops. Thus, on four hooves, were imported the materials for the village's only regular commercial activity – the sole material contact, for some of the older women, with the outside world.

The *feria* at Álamos began at dusk. We drove down there and found the place transformed. The venue for the fair was a wide stretch of road at the bottom of the village. Evidently the possibility of a car needing to drive through and up to Dalmácija was considered negligible, for the celebrants and their equipment filled the street from side to side. Multi-coloured lightbulbs were strung overhead, and a flurry of flags, and along both sides were stalls selling plastic toys, sweetmeats and popcorn. At one end of this miniature promenade was a merry-go-round. The seats were garish Walt Disneyesque Bambis and donkeys, plus a motor-bike, a car and a hansom carriage. In the carriage sat two exquisite little girls, so poised, so immaculate and so highly painted that they seemed to be an integral part of the carousel. Their seven-year-old cheeks were rouged and their huge moist eyes mascaraed, and they were dressed in full Andalusian costume – long flounced dresses in ice-cream colours of pink and green, with flaring sleeves, and shawls, and highly polished pumps.

They sat carefully erect, unsmiling, daintily fingering the huge bright combs in their chignons as the carousel slowly bore them round. Georgina and I watched them fascinated, as they were swung back into the half-light on the far side, brief silhouettes against the white wall of a street-side house, reappearing in the glow of the streetlights and passing before us with a rhythmic up-and-down motion, like birds of paradise fluttering across a forest glade. Their speed of passage varied from circuit to circuit, for the carousel had no motor. It was propelled by the exertions of a stout and rubicund man who from time to time applied a mighty heave to the rim of the machine – an Atlas supporting the spinning globe on his shoulders – while still mustering the breath to solicit trade with cries that echoed down the street. The accompanying merry-go-round music came from a transistor radio standing beside him in the dust.

Everywhere strolled a chattering throng of all ages. Tiny girls in Andalusian dress – like the two figurines on the carousel – held hands with ancient crones in black. Young bloods lounged at the two or three bars erected for the occasion. The red and green and yellow bulbs illuminated the scene with the garish gloom of a faded mezzotint. Georgina and I picked our way through the crowd. We soon found we were instinctively following our noses. A broader area led down off the street and by the entrance to it was a stall selling kebabs. The succulent cubes of pork, sprinkled with herbs, sizzled over a pan of charcoal, broadcasting a fragrance which was immediately irresistible. We ordered two kebabs each, and two glasses of local wine. As we consumed them, a voice hailed us from across the alleyway. It was José the lorryman, seated outside a bar, drinking beer. We joined him, and asked why his wife was not with him. She was at home, he said. She was not much of a dancer, he added credibly. Where was the dancing? we asked. He gestured further down the alleyway. The open space ended in a wide concrete platform overhanging the ravine beyond. Round the edge, at some apparent risk of tumbling over into the oleanders far below, was a battery of gigantic loudspeakers. Amongst them a group of young men fiddled with festoons of trailing wires and tinkered with electric guitars. Intermittently a connection would be made, and an electronic clang would ring out, flushing the martins from their roosts and drowning the miniature music from the carousel.

During the quieter intervals we talked with José. His business was prospering. He had recently secured the concession for what sounded like a uniquely bilious collection of drinks: sweet wine from Málaga, carbonated apple juice, and some kind of ersatz milkshake. He would let us have some, he said. If he found that they sold well, and he made enough money, he would like to visit England one day. He had always wanted to visit England. He looked fondly at us. When acquaintances passed by he insisted that they join us so that he could introduce them to his English friends.

Suddenly all the guitars screeched together. The band was in action. Further conversation with José was impossible. Georgina warily considered the possibility of treading a measure with him, but he was evidently no more of a dancer than his wife. He had only come down here for a drink and a chat. For a few minutes we watched the crowd drift towards the dance-floor like a stream eddying between rocks to form a whirlpool below. Then we stood up and bellowed our farewell to José. As we drove back up to Dalmácija the sides of the valley echoed with hugely amplified rock music, and behind us the illuminations bathed the cool silver outlines of Álamos in a warmer radiance that glowed amid the surrounding darkness.

Hazy and hot at breakfast. These warnings of high temperatures to come were unwelcome, because this was to be the day of our party. We had been scattering invitations broadscale all week, including one to José the lorryman the night before. The reasons for the occasion went back to the spring.

Following our April holiday together, Georgina had returned for a short visit with a friend. One evening, when the two women were about to start cooking supper, there had been a knock at the door. It was one of the teenaged girls we had met in the church at Easter, and several times since then. There was to be a party, she said. Where? asked Georgina. Here, said the girl, in our house. A surprise. She and her friends would arrange everything. And forthwith appeared a gaggle of girls, in their newest dresses, bearing plates of cakes, bottles of wine, and a recorder equipped with tapes of dance music. Georgina rushed to contribute some *tapas* of bread and ham, and a bottle of whisky. The latter was for Emilio, who had soon appeared, attracted by the music, in grime-encrusted work clothes and wearing a hat which remained planted on his head throughout the proceedings.

The shrill metallic flamenco music rebounded off the walls of the little sitting-room as the bright figures of the girls flickered and gyrated in the half-light. There were no males, except Emilio. In between dances, the girls stuffed their already stocky bodies with cakes and ham. Nobody drank anything, again excepting Emilio, with some help from Georgina and her friend Henrietta. After a few whiskies Emilio decided to join the dancing. He selected Henrietta for the purpose. She was a tall girl, and the crown of Emilio's hat reached to her shoulders, giving him a good – indeed an exclusive – view of her chest. Perhaps for this reason, or possibly for support, he opted for a close style of dancing rather than a flamenco. Sweat poured from him, and the rich soil of

Andalusia which he had brought with him attached to his clothes was progressively transferred to Henrietta. After a few minutes she looked like a Hamburg mud-wrestler. She was also in some physical danger from Emilio's cigarette, which never left his mouth. At least there was no need for small talk. Georgina was also dancing, with a series of bright-eyed but leaden-footed girls. The temperature in the room had soared and the atmosphere thickened with the emanations from the glistening bodies, but the revels had continued inexorably until all the flamenco tapes had been played twice.

Now it was our turn to reciprocate. We had prepared for the occasion in advance. Our suitcases had been stuffed with fairy lights from the Christmas tree and wax flares on long canes and strings of the flags of all nations. Dance tapes had been selected and the menu planned. With memories of the oven-like conditions of the sitting-room, even in spring, we decided to hold the revels on the roof terrace. Extra chairs were imported for the older folk, and the lights and bunting were strung up, jaunty among the sparse leaves of the vine and the slats of the *cañizos.* Crates of lemonade were on hand for the females, and wine and beer for the men, and whisky for Emilio.

As the last carmine light drained out of the sky the guests began to arrive. The girls came in groups, through shyness. The men came as soon as they were cleaned up from their work on the mountainsides. Few women came, since they would neither drink nor dance: but Angel and Ana came together, and José the lorryman and his wife and daughters. One or two of the older girls brought boy-friends, strangers from another village, who stood in the shadows at the edge of the crowd, stiff with apprehension, until they could decently escape.

I seated José's wife in a large chair and hoped she would not dance. I wasn't sure that the specifications of the underlying beams were adequate. She clutched a lemonade contentedly but said little. José, however, was in a chatty vein: he had not been in our house before, but having brought the building materials up from Valdez he was interested to see how they had been disposed. While he talked, he kept a proud eye on the gyrations of his elder daughter who, to judge from the proportions of her limbs, was likely to take after her mother. At the head of the terrace sat Angel, hands propped on his stick, watching the proceedings from under bushy eyebrows with a paternal benevolence, as if he were responsible for the occasion, which in an extended sense he was. I slipped him a whisky while Ana's attention was diverted. How did it feel, I asked him, to be drinking six feet above the site of his former wine barrels? He looked down as though recreating the *bodega* beneath his feet. It had not always been a *bodega*, he said: before that it had been a bakery. During the Civil War his father had baked all the village bread. And before that again, a shoemaker had lived here. Clearly Dalmácija was more self-sufficient in those days when the only access was by mule-track. As for Angel himself, his connection with the house was fundamental. He had been born here, in the room that lay through the thick wall behind his back.

There was no sign of Emilio, nor of Rosalia. She tended to avoid large gatherings, preferring to dominate smaller groups. And no Rosalia meant no Jesus – he would not dare to come here without her. Consuela was also absent, presumably on duty, but to our surprise Isabel appeared and sat for a while, knees together, watching the dancing with the air of one who has been allowed out of an institution for a treat. As always, her expression looked older than her years, and sadder.

Above the chatter of the onlookers the music blared, and the girls danced together, darting the occasional glance at the boys, who remained apart. I danced what may or may not have been a rumba with the pretty blonde girl who lived next to Rosalia. She mostly kept her eyes lowered, perhaps bemused by my footwork, but when she looked up the effect was disconcerting. She appeared to have no boy-friend, which surprised me. Later I heard an explanation. She had been engaged to a boy in the next village, but he had been killed while working on the roads in Switzerland, trying to make enough money to marry her. A bulldozer had run over him. The village had been in mourning. That was last year, and the girl was still, it seemed, in a kind of social limbo. I wondered if she would now remain perennially isolated, deep-frozen, like Isabel.

The stars came out, effortlessly upstaging the fairy lights. An owl mewed. A soft warm breeze blew down the hill and ruffled the flags. José told us again about his ambitions to visit England, while his wife clutched her fifth bottle of lemonade. Aurelio backed into one of the flares, and his trouser seat had to be doused with wine. The girls danced, although the boys had fled. The adults watched and talked. To them, the occasion was a restful end to a hard day, an alternative to television: while for the young girls, conversely, it was an opportunity to escape and dance, and wear their church clothes to a gayer purpose. Both generations, this evening, seemed to be content. And so were we.

24 July

After the revels of the last two evenings, and with another *feria* due tomorrow in a neighbouring town, today was what the package-tour itineraries define as a day at leisure. All through the heat of the day we lay in our long chairs under the striped shade of the *cañizos*, reading and sipping *citrons pressés*, of which Georgina had prepared a pitcherful, freshly crushed from the sack of lemons that lay in our kitchen. We lunched off bread – at its best again today – and the Manchegan cheese which was made of the compounded milk of sheep, cows and goats. It was almost the only cheese available locally, and came in round black blocks of which the exterior wax was marked with a herring-bone pattern like Saxon masonry. The purchaser could choose from various grades of maturity. The newest was relatively soft and mild; the oldest was hard enough to turn a knife, and breathed a venerable tang, powerfully rich but smooth. A Madeira of a cheese. For a basic food, it was expensive, as was the indigenous ham. Although we had at first assumed that this was a peasant diet we were eating, we soon realized that peasants could seldom afford it. They breakfasted off bread dipped in olive oil, and their other meals were largely concoctions of broth bulked up with rice or various pulses. Meat in any quantity was beyond their pockets. When, in a subsequent year, some friends borrowed our house, Rosalia later reported on them with wonderment: they ate meat, she said, always meat, meat every day.

The sun was lowering, and we had edged our chairs further and further back, following the diminishing strip of shade, when we were roused by a scream. The drowsy silence then prevailing gave this sudden intrusion an extra stridency, and we were quickly out of our chairs and down the street, seeking the source. The cry had come from the other side of the village, beyond the church. Hurrying down towards Angel's house, we reached a side alley which was full of people. They were clustered round a corpse. The sudden sight of these figures silhouetted against the white walls, some crouching, some standing, all intent on the long dark body which lay in the middle of them, leaking runnels of blood which splayed ten or fifteen feet down the hill . . . this scene had a trenchant familiarity to any regular newspaper-reader. It looked like a photograph of a terrorist outrage. Georgina and I approached with a sense that we had strayed into a world of which we had previously had no direct experience. Then we saw that the body was that of a pig.

We hoped it was not the one we had chased out of our sitting-room two or three times in the spring. That had been a Beatrix Potter pigling, a sprightly young porker with much better manners than the numerous cats which plagued the house. But no, this one was larger, a full-grown hog, and to judge from the surrounding throng its death was a major event, signalling a time of plenty: like the fall of a buffalo, feathered with arrows, amid a hunting party of hungry Sioux. There was a buzz of anticipatory conversation as a young man crouched beside the body, singeing off the bristles. Then he stepped back into the doorway behind him and reappeared with a long knife.

The dismemberment so soon after the death provoked an illogical squeamishness in Georgina and me, and we turned away. Behind us, another witness to the scene, stood Angel. He embraced Georgina as though it had been months since their last meeting rather than the previous night. Would we like a *copa*, a glass of wine? We followed him into the shadowy *bodega*, and leant against a wine barrel while he slowly, awkwardly, scrambled up to reach the small square hole on top. With a pang, we realized he was getting old. He declined to pour a glass for himself, tapping his chest in explanation. The trouble was his *corazón* – that word which occurs in every Spanish love song. He was no longer allowed to drink. Last night's smuggled whisky had been against orders. His eyes sparkled conspiratorially as he recalled it.

Ducking below the cobwebs that hung from the crusted white beams, we carried our glasses out into the little lobby, where Ana greeted us with a plate of *tapas.* Mindful of the corpse outside, we avoided the sausage and opted for sardines. While we ate, Ana sprayed us with her usual torrent of words. Ears cocked like radar discs, we strained to decipher the message. It appeared to be related to San Anton. Her son-in-law, another José, was to be the master of ceremonies for the *feria*. They would be entertaining the band here, in this house. We must come.

It was dusk when we emerged, but a stain was still visible in the dust of the alleyway where the pig had lain. As we passed it we were hailed by a voice from the doorway behind. The young man who had wielded the knife appeared and beckoned us in. The door led into a small room filled with a large table. The scant remaining space was crowded with women. The light was dim and the air heavy with human breath and with an overlying, half-familiar pungency. It was the smell of a butcher's shop. On the table lay the remains of the pig reduced to component elements, small piles of flesh and bone and offal arranged in separate parcels like gifts around a Christmas tree. Compared with the live warmth of the faces in the electric light, the flesh glimmered in tones of grey and white, almost luminous. As we watched, each pile was weighed on a set of brass scales and assigned to one of the waiting women. Nothing was left behind. Every fragment of gristle, every shred of fibrous membrane, everything was carried away into the night, to enrich someone's broth over the days to come.

Outside, as we set off home, we were at once aware of an unfamiliar sound. Round the corner a man was playing a guitar. He sat on a chair in a little open-sided courtyard, below the level of the street. He was unfamiliar to us, and dressed like a townsman. As we stood and listened, a woman brought us, without a word, a couple of chairs. The man did not look in our direction, but bent over the guitar as though the music was visible and he was peering at the intricacies of the notes. It was not the stereotyped flamenco music he was playing, but long rippling cadences of sound, of a style unfamiliar to me. No-one else was listening, except the woman. The silence which earlier in the day had accentuated the urgency of the pig's cry now gave a limpid clarity to the voice of the strings, and the bare wall of the church tower above us served as a sounding board. In this dry land the music flowed like water: sometimes, when only the fingertips were at work, with the delicacy of a tiny stream: sometimes, when the whole hand blurred over the instrument, with the thunder of a waterfall.

Suddenly the flow stopped. The man set down the guitar and turned to us for the first time. He was indeed a stranger, a visitor from Málaga come to see his niece who lived in this house. He was here for the *feria* of San Anton. While we talked to him, two men appeared out of the darkness and walked past us into the house. They carried guns, long-barrelled shotguns, and over the shoulder of each was slung a rabbit. Two more corpses. The men were strangers to us, as had been the man who butchered the pig, and half the women round the flesh-laden table, and the woman who had brought us the chairs. How, after many visits to Dalmácija and two spells of residence, were so many of its tiny population unfamiliar to us? In the same way that the diversity and strength of a great string quartet – late Beethoven, perhaps, or Schubert – will seem to derive from more instruments than merely four, so did this small village convey to us, continually, a multiplicity beyond its meagre numbers.

25 July

Next morning there was a postscript to the demise of the pig. As Georgina and I lingered over our breakfast coffee, there was a clatter at the edge of the *cañizos* over our heads, as though some small animal was trying to gain access over the wall behind the terrace. Looking up, we saw a hand thrust through an aperture, gesticulating. Behind it was the face of Marta, she who maintained the miniature farmyard behind the wall which contributed, from time to time, to the sounds and smells of our environment. Having attracted our attention she withdrew her hand, and then pushed it through again, this time clutching a present: a string of *morcillas*, like a necklace of livid flesh. We thanked her profusely, and took them, and laid them somewhere out of sight, possibly for future consumption or possibly not.

Later, strolling at the top of the village, we met a man hobbling along the alleyway on a crutch. We had not seen him since the spring, when he had invited us in for a tour of his house. He had added an upper storey of which he was extravagantly proud, and a sweeping cantilevered flight of steps up to his front door which had the same incongruity as an avenue of limes leading to a potting shed. At that time he had been hale. Now he could barely support himself on one leg. What had happened? He told us, in short sentences: even when well, he was a man of few words. He had been working among his vines, he said. In May. It was hot, very hot. He was digging out the weeds, *poom, poom, poom* (with his spare hand he wielded an imaginary mattock). He was an old man, sixty-three. That night he had been very tired, but next day there was more weeding to be done. Again he had worked many hours in the sun, *poom, poom, poom.* Suddenly he had fallen down. He could not move nor speak. They had taken him to Málaga. (How? No villager had a car, nor a telephone.) He had been in hospital two weeks. For the first week he still could not speak. But now he was better, he said, and he smiled as though all his troubles were over.

And his fields? Who worked them now, we asked? His son José; the man replied. We knew this particular José only slightly. He was a strikingly handsome young man, sleekly muscular, with a fine regularly featured face, but like his father he was sparing with his words. He had befriended us from a distance, so to speak, through exchanges of infinitely courteous hellos and good-byes, but nothing more. His wife was even handsomer than he, and even shyer: a petite, gipsy-coloured girl from the next village, with huge liquid eyes. She and I, when meeting at the shop or in the streets, had frequently conducted extensive visual conversations, without, I believe, having ever exchanged a single syllable.

José was a good worker, his father said. It was necessary. He had much to do, even without cultivating his father's land. Every year he and another young man from the village went cane-cutting down on the plain, clearing the sugar fields after the crop had been harvested. It was hard work, very hard. They would return to their homes each day covered with blood owing to the sharp-edged leaves, and black with smoke from the burning of the debris. The work was well paid but the hours were long. Fifteen hours, dawn till dusk, non-stop. His son was a good worker, the man repeated: and as he leant against a wall in the shade, propped on his crutch, he again smiled us his bright smile.

Would we like a *copa*, he asked, gesturing towards his *bodega*. We declined, saying that we had to shop, and wishing him well we walked back down the hill. There was a stranger in Consuela's house, an affable middle-aged man who proved to be her brother. He lived down on the coast, but had returned for the next day's *feria*. I invited him up to our roof terrace for a drink.

Luis, the builder who had done the first work on our house, arrived at this moment to make some purchases from Consuela and included himself in the invitation. He looked as dapper and sprightly as ever, and I made the mistake of asking him, routinely, about his health. Immediately his hand flew to a part of his anatomy which he identified as the site of his liver. It was paining him, he said. I wasn't surprised, knowing his drinking habits. He then sat down on the doorstep and rolled up a trouser leg. The skinny white calf was covered with purple spots and I stepped back instinctively, as though the pox, whatever it was, was threatening to leap at me across the intervening space. The other leg was just as bad, said Luis, and eagerly rolled up the second trouser-bottom, like a mid-century Yorkshireman going paddling. This leg was indeed worse, not merely spotted but swollen. The spots ran right up to his waist, he said, but fortunately disrobed no further. They'd taken skin samples, he announced with relish, indicating a couple of scars indistinguishable from the rest: and blood samples too, he added, pantomiming the process in the crook of his arm. He leant back against the doorpost, well pleased with the sheer visibility of his symptoms compared with his usual heart trouble, asthma, rheumatism and eye problems. All the villagers were interested in bodily malfunctions – inevitably, since their livelihood depended on their physique – but only Luis made a full-time occupation of the subject.

He was, however, well enough to climb to our terrace for a beer. I seated him at a safe distance while Georgina and I talked to Consuela's brother, hoping to learn more about his formidable sister. But nothing new emerged. The lady had never married. Emilio (the white-haired Emilio) was an *amigo* who helped her with her land. Isabel helped her with the house and the shop, as did her mother. They all lived in the house – it was a big house. Was Consuela rich? we asked slyly. Her brother smiled, with a kind of family pride. Well, there was the shop, he said, and the *bodega* down on the road where people from down the valley came to buy Dalmácija wine, and there was land which had been left by her father and three uncles, and there were two more houses in the village, and the house on the hill. The house on the hill? The *finca* on the ridge beside the road? We knew that house, we said. We had walked around it. Once, hankering after its superb situation, we had asked Consuela if she would sell it to us.

Would we like to see inside it? the man suddenly asked. If so, he would get the key. We assented gladly. We were planning to visit the *feria* at Cabimas, the town in the next valley, and could stop at the house on the way. We finished our drinks and strolled to our respective cars. Luis decided to come too. On the tortuous drive up the side of the valley he bubbled with all the eagerness of Tigger being taken on an Expotition. *Vroom, vroom*, he trumpeted from the back seat, turning an imaginary steering wheel and working an imaginary gear-shift. He'd never driven a car but would love to try. Not now, I said, our friends were awaiting us.

Consuela's brother and his wife were standing on the ruined terrace outside the house. A withered stubble of dead thistles roughened the cracks between the earthenware paving slabs. A row of pillars stood in front of the house like sentries, but the pergola they had once supported was gone. Below us, on the steep slope that ran down to the road, pyramidal masonry protruded from the brush like Mayan ruins from a Guatemalan jungle. The house had once been surrounded by raisin racks, but now only traces of their retaining walls remained.

Around us, extending through a panoramic 270 degrees, a stupendous vista lay bathed in the afternoon sunshine. The house stood on a long flat shoulder protruding from the hillside, and apart from a short upwards stretch the whole countryside was revealed. Southwards the sea shone in the cleft between the walls of a plunging ravine. Westwards the track wound back to Dalmácija: the village was concealed behind a ridge, but the valley curved away into the distance, past the Moorish castle and on towards Málaga. Eastwards lay the way to Cabimas. It too was out of sight, but the mountain range behind it was visible, a procession of peaks as jagged as Alps, too steep and adamantine for cultivation or habitation. Georgina and I stood there for a while, on the terrace, reluctant to enter the house. Both of us were consumed with the idea of walking out onto these paving stones of a morning, and sitting beneath a recreated vine arbour and looking out at these hills. It was a spasm of acquisitiveness: we wanted to own this view. Bewitched as we were by our house in

Dalmácija, we knew it could not offer an experience like this. At such moments the old dream returned to the inward eye, distant but still insistent, the dream of a white house standing in isolation on a mountain top.

Consuela's brother inserted a key into one of the three doors that opened on to the terrace. The house consisted of a number of sub-sections laid end to end. All were immaculately whitewashed, although the place was empty. Consuela renovated it every year, her brother said, in memory of their father. The family had been reared here. This first part was the oldest – and he pushed open the door. Inside was a single room, characterized only by an ornamental fireplace and a dead rat. This was the original *cortijo*, he said: all the rest had been added later, shortly before he was born. We returned to the terrace and entered another door. Here, our eyes needed adjusting not so much to the darkness as to the scale. By local standards the room was huge. It extended the full depth of the house, except where two bedrooms were partitioned off. Their walls reached only half-way up the interior space, so that the full area of roof could be seen, a serried succession of dark beams supported, ultimately, by a single pillar in the centre of the room.

We strolled around, our footsteps echoing on the paving. In a recess in one wall stood three huge water jars, each of which would have accommodated a well-fleshed Ali Baba. Since there was no plumbing, all the water would have needed to be brought up here by mule. There was nothing else in the room except a trestle table, twenty feet long, which filled the main floor space. The man's eyes kindled when he saw it. This was where they used to eat, he said, when their friends came up to help with the harvest. In its heyday this house had been surrounded by seventeen raisin racks, the greatest array in the neighbourhood. Many men had been needed to work its vineyards. The work was even harder than today. The men would carry back the boxes of the grapes on their heads from far across the valley, many times a day. We listened aghast: perhaps men were cheaper than mules up here, in those times. Then when the work was done, our host continued, all the workers would gather round this table for food and wine, and afterwards there would be singing, and the playing of guitars. Instinctively I looked up, as though craning to hear the last of those vanished notes echoing among the tall rafters.

Now the man's wife took up the role of tour leader. She showed us the kitchen next door – a waterless sink and an open fireplace – and then led us back onto the terrace, and into a separate enclosure at the end of the house. Through the gateway was a tiny yard with a bread oven in it, and a stall at the far side. They used to keep pigs there, she said, and chickens in another stall next to it. And rabbits. We looked around us, visualizing all these activities. The little community up here must have been almost self-sufficient, like a miniature monastery. Now it was empty. The yard contained only a few sacks and boxes, the scant stock-in-trade of its brief annual use by a smaller labour force than in the old days. For a week or two at harvest time its rooms would again ring with voices, but far fewer than before. Then for the rest of the year it would relapse into silence.

Days of wine and roses, I thought, as we stood again on the terrace, looking down at the wizened rose bushes straggling along its edge. But these too were symbols not merely of pleasure, but of hard labour. Planted in fissures of the solid rock, the flowers would have needed constant watering from the jars in the kitchen. Now most of them were ruined, like the raisin racks. Why were there fewer raisins now than formerly? I asked our host. Because raisins needed much work, he said. Many of the villagers were digging out the vines and planting almonds. Especially the older villagers. Almonds made less money but were easier. The landscape and the labour-patterns of Dalmácija would change in our lifetime, I thought. They were changing already.

It was time to go. The pillars were throwing long shadows across the paving, and the *feria* at Cabimas awaited us, a half-hour's drive away over the hills. We thanked our friends and assigned Luis to them for the return journey, declining his offer to show us the best bars in Cabimas.

The track led up the ridge where we had picnicked in the spring at a threshing floor, then plunged down into the extensive valley on the far side. We passed a village on a headland above us, making a circuit around it so that when first seen its houses shone pale pink and then from the reverse side were black against the evening sky, with the church tower pointing like a finger to the first precocious star. Here we picked up a hard-top road, which wound down the hillside until at the bottom it crossed a river running with water, and with gardens of corn planted along its banks. After the barren terrain of Dalmácija this was like another country, and a more crowded one. Whereas our own valley contained not a single *cortijo,* here they were studded thickly along the slopes, with larger *fincas* positioned handsomely on the ridges, some of a generous size, with two storeys of tall windows, and all surrounded with rank upon rank of raisin racks. This was a rich place, and presiding over it at the head of the valley lay Cabimas.

Before we reached it we found ourselves at the end of a line of cars inching slowly up the road. The *feria* was evidently a big event. Finally, at the edge of the town, we parked the car and walked. The road was crowded, and among the stalled traffic were some of the paraphernalia of the fair – trucks decked with palm branches and crammed with celebrants. One contained a brass band, whose music echoed off the houses that rose steeply up the hillside. The strolling crowd included dozens of little girls like the two we had seen at Álamos, solemn of expression but resplendent of dress, with combs in their swept-back hair and beauty spots on their rouged cheeks. Their costumes, in bright – almost iridescent – tones of pink and green and blue, shone out in the twilight as with quick twinkling steps they hurried up towards the main square. All along the street stood stalls, specially erected for the day. Business was brisk, stimulated by large hand-lettered placards. Confectionery was on sale 'at factory prices'. Piles of gimcrack pottery proclaimed the strident promise: 'Every ticket a winner'. A van stood with its rear doors open and its interior stuffed with dresses: not the Andalusian dresses of the young girls but dowdy teenage finery that looked like rejects from the King's Road of ten years previously. There was no shortage of customers. Today was the major *feria* of summer, the feast of Saint James, whose name in Spanish never fails to stir my blood . . . the battle-cry of El Cid and his fellow knights in their struggle against the Infidel . . . *Santiago!*

At the top of the steeply climbing street the ground levelled to form the town square. We had once spent a night in an hotel here, but now the place was transformed. It was like a stage: or, because the dense crowd made it seem smaller, a cockpit. The windows and balconies of the houses that ringed us on three sides were filled with onlookers whose faces gazed down on us with a certain grotesqueness, lit as they were only from below by the fairy lights strung around the square from pillar to pillar and from building to building. The bell-tower dominated the fourth side. Like the faces of the aerial audience, only the lower part of it was visible: the top faded into the twilight, and was further obscured from our eyes by the strings of bunting that criss-crossed the square above our heads and formed a fluttering, many-coloured lid over the scene that confronted us.

Two bands were simultaneously playing different tunes, separated from each other by the steady hum of human voices which served as insulating wadding between them. One band was in a truck, where the performers were so tightly crammed together that each appeared to be playing two or three instruments at once. The other was on a low, ramshackle stage. This group's performance was accompanied by the capering and miming of two comics in female dress, offering another example of the role of clowning in religious festivals – whatever the religion. The comedies of Aristophanes fulfilled this function, in the Athens of the fifth century BC. And I remembered watching the antics of a pair of buffoons in sawn-off jeans mocking the shuffling solemnity of a rain-dance by a row of warriors accoutred in buskins and plumes and pine foliage – a tortoiseshell rattle strapped behind each knee – in a Hopi Indian village in Arizona.

But these Andalusian comedians had more competition than their Indian counterparts. Across the square was a parade of horses. To eyes accustomed to mules, these tall sleek animals had a magnificent elegance as they stepped daintily through the crowd, necks arched, tails twitching with suppressed energy. They were ridden by slim, upright men of gipsy mien, ferociously dark and unsmiling, wearing leather chaps and tight black jackets and flat wide-brimmed hats. Behind each one a young woman sat side-saddle, in the same costume as the little girls we had seen, with the many-pleated folds and flounces of her dress cascading down the horse's flank, and a plump dark arm around the rider's waist. Unlike the wooden impassivity of the men, these creatures were conspicuously of flesh and blood. As we watched the horses and riders, we realized we had seen them before, although under such different circumstances that the mind was slow to register the fact. At the great spring fair in Seville – one of the most gorgeous visual feasts in Europe – we had watched the Andalusians parade all day between the rows of bright marquees, arrayed just like these here in Cabimas, but in endless numbers, and accompanied by others riding in open carriages drawn by four high-stepping horses – or six – with harnesses jingling and bottles of sherry clinking on the velvet cushions . . . while all the dresses and flags and tents and lanterns coruscated like a huge flower garden in the brilliant sunshine.

Here, at night, and transposed to a small square half-way up a mountain-side, the experience was more intimate and primitive: also, as the horses bore down on us, more immediate. Removing ourselves with as much nimbleness as the crowd permitted, we made our way to a long trestle table at the far side of the square, where two overworked men were dispensing free wine from a gigantic barrel. A few yards away stood a pair of oxen, so statuesque that they brought to mind a full-scale version of those model crêches one sees in English churches at Christmas. Then a huge eye blinked, and an ear flicked away a fly. The beasts, shoulder to shoulder beneath a massive yoke, were harnessed to a brightly painted cart which had evidently formed part of a procession earlier in the evening. Now their shoulders, motionless, rose like rocks above the surging eddies of the crowd.

Sipping our wine, stunned by the music and the noise, and fuddled by the hallucinatory flickering of the bunting over our heads, we too were motionless, unable to bestir ourselves, or even to converse above the din: capable only of watching, and drinking. Yet it was time to go. Tomorrow, we knew, we had our own *feria* in Dalmácija. And that was due to last two days.

26 July

As on Easter Day, there was a perceptible excitement in the air of Dalmácija from the moment that Georgina and I opened our front door. There were strangers in the streets, darting to and fro in urgent haste, despite the heat, and friends of ours, when they appeared, were almost unrecognizable. The wives of Luis and Aurelio, whose ample muscularity was normally concealed within shapeless black frocks and all-enveloping aprons, now bulged exuberantly in bright cotton dresses which appeared to have shrunk in the wash. The men were less transformed. Some visitors were in suits, but most of the others wore what might be termed their standard drinking garb – the white shirts and slacks and trilbies into which they habitually changed when they returned home from the fields.

Down at the bottom of the village, it was evident that the little square where we used to park the car was destined to be the centre of events. The middle of it had been fenced off with a barricade of *cañizos*, around which stood a ring of poles. These were interconnected by a complicated rigging of criss-crossing ropes from which hung a dazzling panoply of flags. Against the white of the walls and the bright blue of the morning sky these pennons entranced the eye with their fragmentary brilliance – small dancing flecks of scarlet and orange and yellow that filled the air over our heads like the maple leaves of a New England autumn.

Rosalia's son Pedro, the young Aurelio and two other men were pulling on the ropes like the crew of a clipper ship, while an athletic stranger – evidently a visiting electrician – shinned up the poles to string a necklace of fairy lights. Beside the square a tiny bandstand, which we had never previously seen in use, was being filled with cases of beer and lemonade. Clearly drink took priority over music.

All day the village finalized various activities in various places. The whole population was humming with suppressed excitement, like a hive about to swarm, waiting for the festivities to begin. They began at about seven in the evening with a series of explosions that rattled our teeth in their sockets. From the platform in front of the church Emilio was discharging rockets, lethal silver-nosed monsters that looked as though they could down a jumbo jet at 10,000 feet. He fired them with casual panache from a hand-held wooden contraption which he pointed vaguely skywards over his shoulder, while hob-nobbing with a circle of friends. He lit each fuse with his habitual cigarette, from which the hot ash fell freely onto the pile of unfired rockets at his feet. Georgina and I decided to wait behind the corner of the church until he had finished.

The next event was almost as noisy. Surging up the hill came the Álamos wind band, a gaggle of boys and girls in white shirts and blue shorts or skirts, led by two large hot men similarly clad, a flushed Tweedledum conducting the music, if you could call it that, and an almost apoplectic Tweedledee playing a trumpet. The column stopped outside the church and busied itself with extricating spittle from the instruments while its leaders mopped themselves and chatted with Emilio. Inside the church the service was still in progress. The doors were shut against the rockets and tubas and male laughter, but were opened briefly to eject three dogs which, Rosalia told us later, had mounted a raid on the communion bread.

At last the doors were flung wide, and out streamed the women and children, followed by the Saint. He was a dour figure with a black pig at his feet and a bell in his hand, the traditional equipment of San Anton, patron saint of the village. (St Anthony's Hospitallers in the Middle Ages used to ring bells to attract alms, and the order's pigs were allowed to roam freely in the streets. The Pigling Bland who used to frequent our sitting-room evidently knew his rights. The tradition survives also in the word 'tantony', a diminutive applied to the runt of a litter of pigs or to the smallest in a peal of bells.)

Like the Christ figure at Easter, the Saint stood on a wooden platform which was carried by the handsome young José and three other men. The load was shared by other groups of men as the procession trickled slowly round the village. It followed the same course as before, but this time it was preceded by the band and the overall mood was more festive than religious. From time to time explosions echoed off the hillsides. Emilio had evidently replenished his stock of rockets.

As soon as San Anton and the pig were safely parked back in the church the crowd dispersed, except for the wind band which streamed down the alleyway to the house of Angel. Here its members settled like roosting starlings on the tiny platform outside the front door, some sitting on the parapet, others on chairs provided for them. Inside the house all was chaos. Ana's massive daughters, up from the coast for the *feria*, trundled to and fro, elegantly coiffed and gowned but liquescent with perspiration, purveying plates of sausage and cheese and cold omelette, and trays of lemonade and beer. Ana herself, for once speechless, directed operations in the kitchen while Angel did likewise in the *bodega*, whence proceeded jugs and glasses of wine in a mighty flood. As the food and drink circulated, the band reached again for their instruments. The music echoed off the walls with a new vigour. Erect in the midst, the conductor, with forearms the size of Serrano hams and a face flushed the colour of the evening sky behind him, performed a *pasa doble* on the trumpet; and then, encouraged by the raucous applause of the onlookers, another, at even higher volume and with more extravagant gestures of his instrument and whole body. All round the platform toes tapped and heads nodded and wine glasses waved in unison, while the clarinets squealed and the horns brayed. Empty beer bottles rolled under the chairs, long-haired dogs scavenged for fragments of omelette, and at the head of the steps, framed in the white doorway, stood Angel, a forbidden tumbler of wine in his hand, eyes flashing delightedly, the daemon of the feast.

But in between the flourishes of the *pasa doble*, other sounds were beginning to intrude. From the bottom of the village came the thump of drums and the unmistakable jangle of electric guitars. The music of the old Spain was giving place to the new. Waving farewell to

Angel across the flailing limbs of the band, Georgina and I walked down the hill to investigate.

The *zariba* in the square was filling up. It contained a number of tables and chairs, with a space left at one end for the band. The latter, familiar to us from the hand-printed posters which had appeared in the village over the past few days, were a pop group from a village over the hill, and they hopped and writhed amongst an array of electronic equipment whose cost must have transcended the entire annual income of Dalmácija. The noise was intense. We paid our 300 pesetas each to a lad sitting at the entrace, and went in. At the nearest table sat José and his young gipsy wife, and we joined them. As so often before, our communion was voiceless, this time with good cause. The din made conversation impossible. The other three watched proceedings while I watched the girl.

Compared with the other females of the village, who even in youth were compact, she seemed almost of a different species. Her limbs were elongated, and wherever they lay – compressed against the hard chair or crooked on the table top – they fell into an inevitable elegance like those of an athlete or predatory animal or any creature where physical intensity predominates. Her head, now turned away from me, alas, had a similar angularity, with high cheek-bones across which the dark skin was tightly stretched. This facial skin had begun to ripen in the Dalmácija sun, but along the corrugations of her spine, which ran a very long way down into a curved shadow where the top of her dress met her shoulder-blades, the flesh was delicate and softly furred like the under-belly of a kitten. I anticipated dancing with her, an Escamillo to her Carmen. I had only ever seen her in slow motion, and seldom in close-up.

But nobody was dancing yet, except for some tiny children, who shuffled carefully in the dust in front of loudspeakers taller than they. After a while they were joined by groups of teenaged girls cavorting together under the eyes of the young men who stood around the perimeter, beer glasses in hand. At last one or two couples appeared, and Georgina and I joined them, threading our way between the children and the poles supporting the fairy lights. For a few minutes we hopped up and down, mimicking what appeared to be the prevailing choreography. Then the music stopped, and with a quick step I returned to our table to claim a dance with José's wife. But the table was empty, nor were the couple to be seen within the enclosure. I went to find some more beer, while my pulse subsided.

The music blared on and on, and from time to time Georgina and I joined the thickening crowd of dancers. Once, during a tango, she was snatched from me by an unknown stripling who appeared suddenly from the throng and bore her irresistibly away, tossing her to and fro like a nursery toy, and leaving me tangoing with myself, not an easy thing to do. Then the youth returned her to me and vanished again. Like him, the other men were changing partners, switching from one girl to another throughout every dance, as in some giant Roger de Coverley. Not until midnight had come and gone did men and women pair off, and even then they seldom touched. Only as dawn approached and the music slowed did the bodies move together, and at last the brown hands clutched and dark heads drooped against dreamily gyrating shoulders.

By then we were tired. As we walked slowly back up the hill, the church tower and the roof lines were beginning to emerge from the dark lavender sky, and the angular dimensions of the houses were hardening. High overhead, in the greater radiance of the upward air, the swifts were already circling and flickering like sparks rising from a fire.

27 July
I was sipping my breakfast coffee when I was summoned downstairs by a banging at the door. It was

no longer early, but we were still trying to integrate ourselves after the excesses of the previous night, and gather our strength for the reprise that evening. Not for the first time I regretted the perpetual open-house policy of the village, and envied the reclusiveness of J. M. Barrie: 'Sir James Barrie, I presume,' said an uninvited visitor; 'You do,' said the playwright and shut the door in his face. There would be no unsolicited interruptions, I thought, if we lived in Consuela's house on the hill. Up there, a rattle of the door could only be the wind.

Our visitor was another José, Angel's son-in-law, the master of the previous night's revels. We had barely glimpsed him as he sped from group to group, and now he had come to make amends. He was a small man, but his personality transcended his stature. His arms flailed, his eyes flashed, and he exuded a different style from that of the villagers. He was a business man. He bought all of Dalmácija's produce – the almonds and raisins and lemons – for resale down in the valley. Only the olives went to the local co-operative for pressing. He also owned some land: not the precipitous terrain up here, but flat land down on the coast, where he grew avocados and intensive vegetable crops. Now, as he sat on our terrace, we told him of our ambition to buy the land next to our house. An excellent plan, he said, he would fix it. But Salvador didn't want to sell, we said. José guffawed. He would fix it, he said.

How had we enjoyed the *feria*? he asked, turning to Georgina. He'd heard that she was an expert at the tango. He leant towards her, eyes sparkling, and I was impressed to see how quickly her weariness fell away. She visibly melted under his gaze, or rather she crisped up, like a noodle in a hot pan. Georgina is no mean eye-sparkler herself, and from then on the conversation was entirely between the two of them. Were we enjoying our life here? The village, the house, the people? Was the house finished? Did we need any more furniture – if

216

so he'd tell us where to go. Was she planning another tango tonight? Was it true we were returning to England tomorrow? I sipped my cold coffee, and watched the hillsides change colour for the penultimate time. At last José rose to go. As he left, he looked around him. The house needed whitewashing, he said. He'd fix it. Then he was gone, after an embrace of my shoulders, politician-style, and a final laser-smile at Georgina.

Whitewashing was already on our minds. The house had not been done since we bought it, and by now the walls were, in pictorial parlance, badly foxed. The villagers whitewashed the outsides of their houses once a year, and the insides twice. Ours, by contrast, was a disgrace. It looked like a carious stump in a faceful of flashing teeth. But after our efforts on the wall overlooking the street we were not keen to tackle the entire job ourselves. We would pay someone to do it, a defter *cal*-flicker than we. But we didn't dare accept José's offer without consulting Rosalia first. We were due to see her that evening. She and Jesus had invited us to a farewell drink in their *bodega*.

Rosalia's *bodega* was more of a genuine cellar than most. At the appointed hour she led us down to it, through a narrow defile behind her house – a tiny vertical garden, with rows of flower-pots hanging from the walls – and past the entrance to her mule stable, then doubling back under the main building through a blistered wooden door. We were now under her sitting-room. At one end a hatchway showed where a ladder had once run upwards. Along one side of the room were the wine barrels, four of them. The rest of the floor-space was filled with almond boxes, mule saddles and sacks of fertilizer. Picking our way between these impedimenta, we propped our buttocks on a low shelf, an uncomfortable perch, since it was covered from end to end with small metal objects: weighing scales, carpentry tools and the spikier components of mule bridles. The only light came from a single light-bulb, and Jesus's squat figure threw an enormous shadow as he scrambled over the barrels, dipper in hand.

Rosalia, comfortably seated in the only chair, proceeded to interrogate us about our behaviour the previous day. Why had we not been in church? Had we paid our entrance money to the dancing? Where had Georgina learnt to tango – was it a common English dance? We answered as best we could, sipping our wine, and managed to shift the subject to whitewashing. We mentioned José's offer. José could never find anyone, said Rosalia. It would be a big job. Everyone was busy, especially in the summer. The only possible person would be . . . and she paused before delivering the punch line . . . Luis. *Luis?* But hadn't Luis . . . well, weren't she and Luis . . . I mean, why was she recommending Luis, of all people? We remembered the matter of the machete. Not to mention the after-shave. Anyway, was he well enough? He had appeared to be suffering from the Black Death when we'd last seen him. Rosalia dismissed such matters with a gesture that was amplified in shadowy semaphore on the wall. Luis needed the money, she said, and she raised an invisible beer glass to her lips. But if that was his, er, problem, would he do a reliable job? He knew how to whitewash, she replied briskly, in the manner of an insurance salesman skipping over the small print. Besides, his wife would help him. Rosalia would put the matter to them, and if necessary get Luis to buy some more *cal.* We agreed. We knew better than to remonstrate with Rosalia.

And tomorrow? When were we departing? Early, we said, but we would come to bid her farewell. For a moment we looked at each other in silence. For us, Rosalia *was* Dalmácija, the very quiddity of the village. Her personality grappled us to her with hoops of steel, and, through her, to the whole community. To say good-bye to her was to ring down the curtain on another act in our Andalusian divertissement. But there was no time for sentimentalities. The race would be beginning soon, she said.

We didn't know what the race was, but went looking for it at the bottom of the village. The preparations were still being made when we arrived. A small crowd was lining up expectantly along the road, which was full of mules. Across the road was stretched a high wire. A number of reels of coloured silk were being attached to the wire by a young man standing on another's shoulders. From time to time he fell off, to much applause from the crowd, but at last all the reels were attached, a dozen of them. Each one had a ring at the end, dangling down over the road.

Now the mules were lined up, and each was mounted by a pair of youths, one behind the other. The event proved not to be a race, as such, but a kind of elimination contest. In turn, with a clatter of hoofs and a tornado of dust, each mule cantered under the wire, while the pillion rider reached up with a knife which he endeavoured to thrust through one of the rings as he passed underneath. If he succeeded, the silk unfurled with a flash of colour and he rode off in triumph, flourishing it from the end of his dagger like a jouster flaunting his lady's favour. If he failed, he tried again. This continued for an hour, while the crowd shouted and the dust swirled. By the time the last ribbon had gone, the velvet night had descended.

As on the previous evening the twentieth century arrived abruptly, with a cacophonic screech of guitars. The fairy lights shone out and the little dance arena began to fill. Georgina and I repaired to the makeshift bar for a preliminary beer or two, and found ourselves standing next to Salvador. He greeted us cordially. He had not visited the *feria* the preceding night, he said, but Georgina's tango was the talk of Álamos. His teeth flashed at her out of his dark face. Georgina seemed to be on the receiving end of altogether too much eye- and teeth-flashing today, and I decided to change the subject: had Salvador thought any more about selling us the land? I asked. He shrugged, as though the matter was of complete indifference to him. He and his wife had talked it over, he said, and had decided that they might sell – at the right price. He named it. It was about one hundred per cent above the true value of the land. I said so. He smiled, a brilliant, sustained and disarming smile. Yes, his price was too high, he said, but we could afford it because we were rich. He turned away to order us a round of drinks. The frangipanis and mangoes and bottlebrush trees faded in my mind. I tried to resign myself to a prospect of stunted olives and sardine tins for ever. But Salvador seemed to be a reluctant executioner of these dreams. We must talk of the matter again on our next visit, he said, raising his glass.

He was evidently not a dancing man, so in due course we left him and entered the arena. None of our friends was there. The elder generation, again, was not taking part, and the youngsters were mostly from the neighbouring villages. I saw the fair-haired beauty with whom I had danced at our party, but she was confined to a seat at the receipt of custom, taking the money. José's wife was nowhere to be seen, although I certainly looked carefully. Nobody snatched Georgina from my arms for another tango. At around midnight we remembered being told by José – José of the flashing eyes – that the *feria* ended with hot chocolate at Angel's house.

The place was already crowded. In the kitchen the women were indeed drinking chocolate, but what was handed to me came from the *bodega*. I looked around me at the figures that filled the low-ceilinged room, some standing, some sitting, some crouching on the floor kaffir-style; and at the rough hands that held the wine glasses and the cigarettes; and at the brown faces, animated with talk and laughter. Half these people were strangers, yet all were familiar to me, as had been all the villagers from the first moment of our arrival in

Dalmácija. I recognized them from before. I had met men like them in the pages of George Borrow and Robert Byron and Norman Lewis . . . Spaniards and Persians and Cambodians and Guatemalans. I had met them in the Appennines, befriending Eric Newby and John Verney during the war, and in the Mani, walking the stony paths with Patrick Leigh-Fermor. And I had met them in the flesh on my own more modest travels, farmers in the Cevennes, fishermen in the Cinqueterre, wayside bartenders in Yucatán. Also carpenters in Herefordshire and apple-pickers in Kent. Adam had been a peasant. So had most humans since the world began. Now the peasants were in eclipse and the destiny of each country lay in its cities. Yet it was the peasants – these people around me now – who continued to embody manners and virtues that were disappearing in urban communities but which still greeted the traveller in remote places everywhere: curiosity to know where he was from and how he had come there; sincerity of welcome; stability; pride. Such things were of great value. I wondered, as I drank Angel's wine, how long they would survive.

5

AUTUMN

. . . amo tu duro suelo, tu pan pobre,
tu pueblo pobre, como hasta el hondo sitio
de mi ser hay la flor perdida de tus aldeas
arrugadas, inmóviles de tiempo . . .
tu áspero vino, tu suave
vino, tus violentas
y delicadas viñas . . .

I love your thin soil, your rough bread,
your rough people, and how, in the depths of me
the lost flower of your
crumpled, timeless villages takes root . . .
your harsh wine, your sweet wine,
your twisted
and delicate vines . . .

Pablo Neruda

31 August
It was dark when we arrived. Bad planning had combined a late flight with our bringing the children for
the first time. We guided them down the slope from
the car, fuddled and dubious, and it seemed an age
before we could find the keyhole in the front door.
Inside, the sitting-room was like an oven, and when
we tried to switch on the light nothing happened.
Stumbling through the house, we found that the other
rooms were the same. Our whole electricity system
was defunct. We had had similar trouble before,
and had stationed candles and matches in every
room. But now none was to hand. While Georgina
foraged for them in the gloom, I made a number
of return trips to the car, sweat pouring off me,

to bring down the luggage. The children were beginning to whimper.

Unpacking and bed-making in the semi-darkness was like playing blind man's buff in a sauna. At last the children were in bed, and Georgina and I were free to look around for other necessities. Like gin. No electricity meant no ice, and warm gin does not come high on our list of desiderata, but this was an emergency. However, a search soon revealed two things: first that the house was devoid of any kind of drink, although we had left it well stocked: and second, that there was whitewash everywhere, not simply on its target area, the walls, but also on the floor, the doors, the painted beams of the upstairs bedroom, and any items of use or decoration which we had been foolish enough to leave in the line of fire.

This was Luis Torres's work, of course. Crouching there in the candlelight, hot and tired and achingly sober, we cursed him with a series of terrible curses. We cursed him for an incompetent, we cursed him for a drink-taker and for a drink-stealer. And when we had finished cursing him we cursed Rosalia. Why had she recommended Luis to us, knowing his proclivities? We looked around at the blotchy walls with despair and then, inflamed with tepid tonic water, we fell to cursing the place itself. It was a hovel; it was airless, and undersized; and at the moment, not to put too fine a point on it, it smelt. Either Marta had increased the complement of her farmyard, or our drains were costive. How would our children endure a holiday here? And what about our friends? We had invited a couple to visit us in a week's time. We had told them much about Dalmácija, luring them with high-flown descriptions of its beauty and charm. I had waxed positively poetical, I recalled, at our last meeting with them. Agog to see the glories of such a paradise, they had signed up on the spot.

Now, stumbling through the paradise's nether regions, I found that adversity had not finished with us yet. The loo was not working. To my petulant manipulations the cistern responded only with a hollow and dusty groan, like an exhausted shadoof. Curiously, this cheered me up. Short of the roof falling in, there was nothing more that could go wrong. In any case, everything would look different in the morning.

1 September
Not everything looked different in the morning. The whitewashing looked just as bad. It was clear that Luis belonged to the Jackson Pollock school of interior decoration. We were grimly surveying his handiwork when Rosalia arrived. Her initial welcome was cordial, but her manner soon changed. We had caused her great trouble she said. The whitewashing. It had made much dirt for her to clean up. (There was no sign that she had laid a finger on the dirt, but we let it pass.) It was all our fault, she went on: we should never have chosen Luis for the job.

For a moment I reeled, and it couldn't have been drink. Then, speaking calmly, albeit between clenched teeth, I reminded her that it was she who had recommended Luis to us. We had been surprised, I said. The surprise had been hers, she replied looking me straight in the eye: Luis was not a good workman, a very unwise choice. But what about his wife? I cried, trying another tack: Rosalia had said his wife would supervise him. His wife had not been near the place, she replied. But what we should do now, she went on, was to get his wife to clear up the mess. There was a gleam in Rosalia's eye as she proposed this, and I began to sense the evolution of an anti-Torres strategy. But before I could respond there was a creaking of the bedroom door, and our two boys emerged, rubbing their eyes.

Immediately Rosalia was down on her knees, arms outstretched, clucking a stream of endearments.

Confronted with their first foreigner, in a form they may not have anticipated, the boys were apprehensive, but were grappled in turn in an Antaean embrace. Spaniards, like Italians, adore children. Indeed their family ties extend both downward and upward, binding the generations together. Every house in Dalmácija contained members of at least three generations, sometimes four. When asking after my mother, as the villagers always did, despite not knowing her, they could not understand why she lived alone, separate from Georgina and me. I could find no satisfactory explanation, and often pondered the alternative ways in which Spanish and English treated their old folk. Rosalia had her mother living with her. She prepared a bowl of gruel for her every day, but the old lady was never in evidence when we called in the evening. She was in a back room, in the dark. Whenever Rosalia went out, she locked the house behind her, 'because of the dogs'. Her mother remained inside. Sometimes we saw her face peering through the bars of the window. I wondered which was worse: to be treated like a superior pet in one's own house, or to be treated like an inferior human being in an English nursing home.

After breakfast we took the boys around the village. Officially we were introducing them to the place but in fact we were showing them off. The walk was like a triumphal tour. At every house the women-folk emerged and clasped Adam and Daniel to their assorted bosoms. ¡Precioso! they cried. ¡Que guapo! ¡Que gordo! How plump! This was a compliment, one of the highest, and the boys' thighs and arms were pinched and massaged every yard of the way: and at every stop, their cheeks and pockets were stuffed with sweets.

All this was satisfactory enough, and the electrical and plumbing problems soon proved tractable. But the Luis issue was unresolved. I would need to beard him. And perhaps his wife. And possibly also his daughters: Rosalia was beginning to develop the concept of a mass

Torres labour force to clear the house up in the shortest possible time. For the children's sake, she said. It was unhealthy for them to live amongst all this mess.

When I carried the tray for lunch up to the terrace, it was as though I had inadvertently released the catch on a jack-in-the-box. There, not fifteen yards away, was Luis. He was at eye-level on a ladder against Consuela's house: I could practically have shaken hands with him, if I had felt so inclined. He was whitewashing, of all things, but broke off to wave me a cheerful greeting. He welcomed us back to Dalmácija and enquired after our flight, and our children: he'd heard we'd brought them. Then, with barely a hesitation, he mentioned the whitewashing of our house: was it satisfactory? The alleyway outside the shop was one of the more public corners of the village and I did not wish to bellow grievances too openly. Could he come for a drink that evening? I asked.

He arrived with his usual jaunty step, in his straw hat and elegant sports shirt. *No, gracias*, he said, no drink for him. He was under doctor's orders: no alcohol. No alcohol? Then what had happened to all the drink we'd left in the house? Oh! he hadn't been under doctor's orders *then*, he beamed, and it had been thirsty weather. But he'd buy us some more. And without further ado, he hurried down to Consuela's *bodega* and returned with an armful of wine bottles. He knew it was the grade we drank, he said – it was the same as we had bought that morning. Outfaced, we shook hands on it, merely agreeing that he and his wife would come and clean up the spatterings on doors and floor. But the matter of the drink evidently still weighed with him. He insisted on giving us a written apologia, a kind of absolution for his lapse, inscribed in a Spanish so crudely achieved that words elided and consonant sounds were interchanged. It said: 'To Don Hugo, as I was putting my hand to whitewashing early in the morning everything was closed and for that I drank the five bottles of wine nothing else and a little gin nothing else your friend Luis Torres.'

2 September
The heat woke me early, before dawn. Next door, in Marta's toy-town farmyard, two cockerels came to life. Their refrains were identical, except that one had a rising inflexion, and the other a dying fall. They sang in meticulous alternation for what seemed like hours. I was in no mood for a concert at this time of day, but listened in fascination to their complementary responses: O Lord open thou our lips . . . And our mouths shall show forth thy praise.

It was hotter now than in July: sometimes remorse-lessly so. Through morbid curiosity we had bought a thermometer, and today I eyed it at regular intervals, with a desiccated detachment. By nine a.m. it stood at 75 degrees, by noon it was 85 degrees, and by four p.m. it showed close to 100 in the shade, moving up or down a couple of degrees according to the intermittent puffs of wind from the sea. It held this level until past six p.m. and it was not until seven-thirty that it dropped into the 80s, whence it barely declined further through the evening. At midnight it was still nearly 80 degrees – almost as hot as at midday, and hotter yet inside in our bedroom under the tiles.

This inexorable tide of heat carried all the villagers before it and shaped their day. They started work early in the morning, the coolest period of the twenty-four hours, and as we breakfasted on the terrace we could watch them labouring on the hillsides. It was the time of the almond harvest, and across the valley we could see family groups, here and there, clustered around the trees. A net was spread beneath each tree in turn, and the branches were belaboured with long sticks to dis-lodge the nuts. The tapping sounds were audible from far away: in the enveloping silence the slightest sound acquired emphasis and drama . . . like the clicking of high heels on an Oxford pavement at dawn after a ball . . . By two p.m. the hillsides were empty, and the only sound was the intermittent shrilling of the cicadas. All external signs of life remained extinguished until about seven p.m., when the sun dipped below the hill, and the population poured into the streets as though to celebrate a revolution. Consuela's shop was in action until past eleven. All ages of people were subject to this diurnal pattern of activity, and at midnight the alleyway below us still echoed with the shrill voices of tiny children.

We soon adapted to the temperature, aided by the fact that this was a dry heat. Unless we were labouring we hardly sweated, and without the sweat to attract the dirt we actually felt cleaner than in London. The children, too, adjusted both to the heat and to the Spanish hours, which they modified according to their own timetable. They stayed up late, but unlike the local children they rose late. This meant that by the early afternoon, after a morning spent playing football in the alleyways, they were still fresh and would invite their new-found friends into our sitting-room, which would fill with small excited bodies of both genders, pushing toy cars along the rough quarry-tiles or swapping plastic weaponry or playing card games with amoebic rules: chattering the while in Spanish and English with no cross-over between the two.

Our boys' Spanish coevals were mostly girls, but they also befriended two boys, both older. Luis was a lumbering lad of sullen mien, possibly through shyness, with a brow so low that his eyes were practically level with his hair-line. Georgina and I were frightened of him, if it is possible to be frightened of a ten-year-old. Ramon was altogether different, only slightly bigger than Adam, our elder son, and with a merry disposition. His hair was curly and his eyes were bright: with a pair of furry legs, he could have been one of the Botticelli satyrs attendant on Venus and Mars. He was the son of

Marta, who was slightly dotty. Rosalia quite evidently detested her, but in general the villagers contrived to stay civil to each other. Dalmácija was too small to sustain serious animosities. Good relationships were essential to survival, as in a lifeboat or a prison camp. To us, Marta was a friendly neighbour, and her love of Ramon was strong to the point of obsessiveness. At any hour of the day one would hear her calling for him: ¡Nino! ¡Nino!, Son! Son! His name was never used. (In the same way one would hear a leather-lunged labourer bellowing across the valley: ¡Primo! Cousin! Evidently these vocal shafts needed no identification to reach their mark.)

While settling in, we had discovered another setback, apart from the initial problems with electricity and plumbing. Our plants were dead. Not the geraniums outside the front door – they were all right, although past their best – but a couple of comparative rarities in pots on the patio. We had brought them back to England from a holiday in Kenya, and I think it was their outlandishness that had attracted Rosalia's hostility. There was a so-called pyjama lily, a kind of pink-and-white striped amaryllis, which we had dug up on a farm in the foothills north of Mount Kenya, where it grew wild: and a frangipani of an unusual pale apricot colour which we had purloined from the garden of a Malindi hotel (Georgina never travels without secateurs in her handbag). The lily had been easily portable, like a gigantic onion: but the frangipani cutting had been obliged to travel from game-park to game-park in wet loo paper, and had occupied half a dozen different tooth mugs during its evening sojourns. It had eventually arrived here, via London, in excellent health, and had even flowered. Now it was a wizened husk, despite our pleas to Rosalia to take especial care of it. Clearly she had not totally neglected the patio: in a prime position stood a clump of arum lilies (my least favourite flower, after African marigolds), in a galvanized iron bucket, which she had evidently introduced herself along with one or two other rejects from her own garden. No, it was evident to me that the Kenyan immigrants had received the full force of the Rosalia Evil Eye. I remembered Borrow. Collect the spittle of the aggressor, he had said. But he hadn't suggested how to set about it.

3 September

It was spiteful of Nature, that implacable lady, to organize things so that the busiest time of the Dalmácija year came when the heat of summer was still at its height. Later, in October, came the wine-making, followed by the olive-harvesting in November and December: but now was the time of the almonds and the raisins. And the raisins required the greatest labour of all.

Of course the labour had already been grinding on through most of the year, at various times. The vines required pruning in the early spring, followed by fertilizing and spraying and weeding. The only attention they did not require was tying-in. Here the vines were not trained along wires as in France, or up trees as in Italy. They were planted haphazardly on the hillsides, giving the bare slopes the pock-marked appearance of a plucked chicken-leg, and the new shoots simply lay along the ground. In this climate they only sprouted to a length of three or four feet each year – except when they were trained up a trellis, like ours, and watered regularly.

Now, in early September, the grapes were ripening. When their time was nearly come, the men went to work to prepare the raisin racks. There were about thirty of these, sited at various points around the village, each on a gentle slope facing the midday sun. They were rectangles of bare earth, which needed weeding and then sweeping, until no loose earth nor pebbles nor blades of grass remained. Each rack was surrounded by lengths of cane, anchored to the ground around the perimeter, serving as rails to which the edges of the canvas covers were tied, if ever it rained. These covers were now being checked for holes by the women, and darned as necessary, like fishermen's sails. As a further precaution each group of racks was protected by a brushwood fence, to keep the newly swept surfaces free from wind-blown dust: and for the past few days we had been watching the men gather armfuls of dried Spanish broom from the hillsides and compress them into flat sheafs which they wove into any newly eroded gaps in the fencing.

One group of raisin racks was visible from our roof terrace. It belonged to another José, who used to be mayor before Emilio. He was a diabetic, and had once shown us in his house a formidable array of syringes and needles. But this disability didn't prevent him from working as hard as the rest. We watched him now, on the far side of the little valley, plodding among his vines, stooping every couple of yards to select a ripe bunch of grapes and pack it into a box. Near him stood his mule, tethered in the shade of an olive tree. When the boxes of grapes were full he strapped them on to the mule's panniers, two each side, totalling a fifty-kilo load. Then man and beast would return down the steep tracks towards us, disappearing behind the cemetery and reappearing in the alley below our house, whence they would scramble up the path at the end of our terrace, turning off through an entrance in the broom fence half-way up the slope. We strolled over to chat to him as he unloaded. This was a bad year, he said. Not enough rain in the spring. The bunches of grapes were small and there were few to each vine. In a good season a single bunch would weigh a kilo or more and a single vine would fill a box. But not this summer. Like farmers the world over, his livelihood waxed and waned with the weather.

Once he had unloaded the grapes, his wife and daughter took over. Crouching on their haunches, they spread the bunches carefully on the ground, forming a layer one bunch deep, and continuous, so that no earth showed through. Hour by hour and day by day this layer was extended until it filled the rectangle. Then they moved on to the next rack.

For two weeks the grapes lay in the sunshine as though on a gigantic griddle, and the women tended them and turned them, meticulously exposing every part of every bunch to the metamorphosing heat. And as the days passed the green fruit changed colour, not all at once, but randomly across the racks, forming rich patterns like those of a Beshir carpet, or of the thyme walk at Sissinghurst Castle . . . greens and golds and russets and purples . . . until each rack was covered with a layer of uniform blueish umber, the colour of a bruise, and the raisins were ready to go. During this period, if one walked between the racks, one could almost sense the sugar bubbling within each grape, concentrating its virtue and releasing the inessential vapours, so that the air above the ripening fruit was denser than elsewhere and filled with fragrance.

The women were out there every day, morning and evening. They wore huge wide-brimmed hats, and as they bent double, their hands darting to and fro among the grapes, they looked like Vietnamese women planting rice. When all the raisins were dried, they packed them into boxes, sorting and rejecting any shrivelled runts in each bunch, or any that were mildewed, and José packed them onto his mule again, for transport down to the bottom of the village, where they would be collected for sale by the other José — José of the flashing eyes. And so the main commerce of the village was achieved, with much time and much labour and no great reward. We remembered our first visit to Dalmácija and our first meeting with Angel. He had been sorting his raisins then. Since that time we had always thought of this place as the refuge of a lost tribe of raisin-makers, surviving in isolation, surrounded by their ripening fruit.

We watched José's family throughout that morning, as the grapes arrived and were spread. When the work began again in the evening our consciences stirred us, and we felt guilty at lying comatose while people toiled. We decided to go for a walk. Extricating the boys from Marta's house, their faces tacky with sweets, we set out along the track which led over the ridge to Álamos, the old link with the outside world. We walked slowly: it was still hot, and windless. Beside the path stood clumps of fennel eight feet high, shrivelled to dead straw except at the tips where a glint of green still lingered among the branching seeds. The stalks were hollow, like the one in which Prometheus hid the stolen fire. Beyond them grew the vines, each bearing three or four bunches of pale green fruit. Underfoot, the dust swirled around us and coated our ankles. At the top of the ridge we stopped, glad of the excuse, and looked back at the village. From here our house was visible, and next to it the little olive grove above the cemetery – the future Hanging Gardens of Dalmácija, if we could ever persuade Salvador to co-operate.

Below the far side of the ridge stood a one-room *cortijo*. Small as it was, someone had taken the trouble, years before, to plant a vine arbour in front of it, which now shaded part of the little terrace which ran around the house. In the shade sat an old woman, surrounded by piles of almonds which she was extracting from their husks. As the path ran close to where she sat, we hailed her. She waved to us and beckoned us to approach. Typically, she showed no surprise at the sudden arrival of four foreigners in the middle of nowhere, but reacted more primitively, embracing the children and ruffling their hair and patting their cheeks. Disappearing inside the *cortijo* she returned with bunches of grapes: then, in response to a stereotyped comment on the heat, she offered us some water from a leather bottle which hung from the arbour. We all essayed the demanding business of squirting it into our mouths in the local style, which required swallowing and breathing at the same time. The water, what little I absorbed of it, had a strong animal flavour, and I wondered how long it had been hanging there.

We continued towards Álamos, but soon turned back. The children were flagging. Our returning steps had slowed almost to a halt, when we heard hoof-beats behind us, and up the path came a man leading a mule laden with almonds, heading for the *cortijo* we had just left. Seeing the children, he mounted them on the mule. Georgina, who had a camera, took the inevitable photo, and we have it still, enlarged and hanging on a wall. When I look at it, it surprises me in one respect. Against a backdrop of pale blue hills and black almond trunks, the boys on the mule are radiant with delighted smiles: but the man holding the mule is portrayed − contrary to my recollection − with an attitude and expression of nethermost gloom, as though performing his service under extreme coercion. Perhaps, like more primitive people across the world, he was afraid of having his photograph taken, believing that part of his identity was being captured by the camera. Similar fears were widespread in the Middle Ages. It was dangerous to part with fragments of oneself − nail-clippings or beard-shavings − in case an enemy used them to make a spell. Nor did these personal elements need to be concrete. Rumpelstiltzkin lost his power when he gave away the secret of his name.

I myself had a strangely destabilizing experience of a different kind, late that night. The heat in our bedroom was intense. The bed was only a few feet from the undersides of the tiles which had been absorbing the sun all day, and lying there was like being on a spit before a flame. I turned to and fro in a half-conscious quest for air, and at one point turned over my pillow,

234

to offer a cooler surface to my cheek. This simple action had an odd effect. Something opened in my mind. The last time a hand had turned and smoothed a pillow for me had been in some sick-room, when I had been a small boy. Suddenly, under that torrid roof, I had a long glimpse down the years, a faint vision of childhood, like the distant and circumscribed view of the chancel through the squint of a medieval church . . .

4 September
Today we were smitten by an event so crucial, so far-reaching in its significance, that the occasion will rank among those in history of which later chroniclers have been able to say: this was the day, this was the pivotal moment after which nothing remained the same.

The water ran out.

Not just the water in our house, but the water in all the village. The fountains ran dry, and our taps with them.

It soon transpired that nobody else regarded the event as significant. When we ran to Rosalia, like frightened children to their mother, she had few words for us. The water often ran out in the autumn. It was just that we had never visited Dalmácija at this time of year before. When buying the house, and during all our subsequent sojourns here, we had been serenely unaware of this hydrological sword of Damocles.

Rosalia quickly apprised us of the disciplines which would now apply. The water would be rationed. It would be switched on for half an hour a day. That would be our chance to fill our bath and a few buckets, on which we would have to subsist thereafter. Today the water would run in the evening at about six, because the villagers had been cut short without warning. Normally it would be switched on in the morning. Early. But the hour was apt to vary from day to day. This was because the man in control of the supply was Emilio. If he had had a couple of *copas* too

235

many the night before, he might forget, and the village would go dry until he sobered up.

Georgina and I digested this information with dismay. Would we have bought the house if we had known there was no regular water supply? It was too late to worry about that. But what about Mark and Rebecca, the friends who were due to arrive in a couple of days? How would six of us survive on such a pittance of water each day? In this weather we drank litres of the stuff – there were always bottles of it cooling in the fridge. And what if we had no ice-cubes for the gin and tonic? The mind boggled. We sped to Consuela's shop to stock up on buckets.

The children were delighted. Being told not to flush the loo imbued life with a primitive, adventurous aura, like belonging to the Swiss Family Robinson. We hadn't told them Spain was like this. They hung around expectantly, awaiting the next disaster. When the water ration duly arrived in the evening, with a primordial burping and gurgling, they sped joyfully from tap to tap, falling over the buckets and juggling the bottles, until the floors were awash with the precious fluid. Long before the bath was half full, Emilio's invisible hand, up at the top of the village, had cut us off again.

The common deprivation bound the villagers even more closely together, and us to them. Isabel lent us a big plastic container, bigger than anything Consuela had had for sale, to tide us over the initial crisis: and Remedios arrived in our sitting-room clutching a tiny jugful of water from her own meagre store – the liquid equivalent of the widow's mite.

After assembling our supplies and mopping down the floor, we went up onto the terrace. Again it was searingly hot. There was a feverish wind that seemed hotter than the air itself, and blew in panting gusts like the breath of hell, catching the fallen vine leaves that lay on the paving tiles beneath the arbour. These were so large and so dry that they rattled in the breeze with a metallic clatter, and instinctively I raised my feet, as though to avoid injury, when one of them came bowling by. It was too hot to read and there were no rural activities to watch: but there was still the scenery to admire. At this time of late afternoon, and during the early morning too, the sun shone down parts of the hillside at exactly the angle of the slope. This had the effect of detaching the trees and vines from the surface of the ground. The soil caught no light and receded to an umber or lavender backdrop: but the grey-green olive trees and the silver almond branches leapt out towards the eye in puffs of pale colour like dabs from the end-bristles of an oil-painter's brush, and the vines, smaller and brighter, formed pointillist patches between the darker folds of the mountain.

After a while we became aware that we had not seen or heard the children for a while. We went in search of them, and ran them to earth in the house below Rosalia's. Adam was seated in the lap of my blonde dancing partner, watching TV and looking, I thought, enviably comfortable against her bosom. Daniel was in the firm but fond embrace of the black-clad mother, being intensively fed like a Strasburg goose. Both boys had taken to *la vida Española* with a will.

5 September
Next morning the new routine began. Into our deep subconscious as Georgina and I lay asleep, there penetrated a distant sound, unobtrusive at first, but with a growing insistence as its significance sharpened. It was a one-word cry, repeated a number of times. *¡Agua!*

Creeping from our bed, like the whining schoolboy unwillingly to school, we turned on the bath and put a bucket to fill in the sink. Then we took two more buckets out to the fountain. It was like coming late to a party. There was a small crowd of women in the little square, lined up in front of the tap, throwing a row of long shadows in the early sunshine. We chatted to them as we waited, while the swifts flew low overhead. The air was still relatively cool, and the waiting group was charged with an energy which, we knew, would soon be dissipated in the midday heat. Every woman, it seemed, was speaking simultaneously, as though releasing a stream of essential information which had become bottled-up during the night, until her spell at the tap had come and gone, and she had staggered away along the alley, a water container in each hand, leaving a track that glistened along the ground like a snail's. Watching the scene I took great pleasure in it: but I was unsure that I wished to repeat it every morning. Not at this hour. There must, I thought, be a better way to survive the drought.

Rosalia appeared. Would we like to go almond-picking with her family? Indeed we would – we had requested as much, two days before. There was no time for breakfast. We woke the boys while Jesus saddled up his mule, then perched them both, still half asleep, on the animal's back, one behind the other, like miniature *condottieri* above the brightly coloured trappings – cascades of scarlet tassels down wither and haunch, a broad chequered band across the crupper and a girth as ornate as a sultan's sash. More tassels nodded from the mule's forehead, and an embroidered strap encircled his velvet nose. He was a sleek and powerful beast, well fed and dutifully maintained, as were all the mules in the village. They were essential to the rural economy, and they were valuable. Jesus told us they could cost up to 100,000 pesetas – more than a third of the price we had paid (admittedly some years before) for our house. What was this mule's name? we asked in a gush of British sentimentality. Its name was Mule, he said.

Our cortège took the track up the hill towards Cabimas. The mule was followed by a small black goat, a recent acquisition which accompanied Rosalia's family everywhere like a dog. Untethered, it roamed energetically beside the road, cropping vine leaves and the few barely visible blades of greenery that survived among the dead grasses on the earthen slopes. When we had almost reached Consuela's house – our unattainable dream-house – Jesus turned off into the trees, dismounted our boys, and unfolded the two large nets on which they had been sitting. These he spread on the ground beneath one of the almond trees which stood, dark-limbed and almost leafless, along the thousand-year-old terraces. On the lower side the nets were tied up to branches to create a belly: on the upper side they were weighed down with stones.

Then Jesus went to work with his long cane, knocking the almonds off the tree and into the net. Click, click, click, the sound we had been listening to from our roof terrace. Most of the almonds rained down still in their husks, to be separated later, one of the year's more back-breaking tasks. Others shed their husks as the cane struck them, and skipped down the netted slope like Danaë's golden shower. Some of these we cracked open between two stones and ate, creamy-white, sweet and juicy.

We asked Jesus how he could tell his trees from other people's, especially as his land, like everyone's, was scattered in small parcels around the valley. All the boundaries were marked, he said, sometimes by barely visible stumps and stones. He knew every tree of the hundreds he possessed. As he spoke he was furling his nets and gathering the sacks. The great heat would soon be upon us. Before loading the mule he led us a little further down the slope to a fig tree, and urged the boys up the knobby white branches. They threw the fruit down to us, and cupping them in our hands we sat down in the densest shade we could find, beneath an ancient olive. The warm, fleshy succulence of the figs was delicious after the tang of the almonds, and when we had finished them Rosalia scrambled out into the sunshine to cut us a bunch of grapes.

The scenery outside our circle of shade was bleached almost to invisibility. Lolling against the trunk, with grape-juice dribbling down our chins, we asked Jesus about the different types of olive, and how to prune almonds, and what the mule ate, and about the value of his crops. Around us nothing moved except a sudden flock of small brown warblers, nicknamed *almendritas*, little almonds. We had seen few other birds during the summer, except the swifts and martins. It was too dry. A few wheatears and goldfinches, a green wood-pecker and a hoopoe, that was all: except for a solitary, enormous bird of prey which had circled slowly over the village and drifted away down the valley. A griffon vulture. What about partridges? we asked Jesus. Yes, he had shot several: and rabbits. There were foxes, too. Also, he added, looking among the roots of the tree, snakes. He had seen a huge black one the other day, on this very slope. What did they eat, I asked idly. I was quite fond of snakes, at least English snakes. They ate rabbits, he said. Georgina and I rose quickly, and gathered the children. It was time to return to the village. We hadn't known that Andalusia was in-fested with boa-constrictors.

Back on the terrace, sedated with wine, we turned our minds to our most pressing and disturbing pre-occupation: the arrival of Mark and Rebecca next day. Visualizing them in London, as though peering at them through a mental telescope, we tried to imagine them peering the other way, at a miniature and infinitely dis-tant Dalmácija, dusty, waterless, primitive, surrounded by a bare and apparently serpent-ridden wilderness. I remembered a quotation that the Dutchman Jacob had once shown me in his library on the pine-clad knoll above the sea. It was from an inscription on a tomb in Cádiz, carved at a time when Andalusia was at the very rim of civilization: 'Heliodorus, a Carthaginian madman, ordered in his will that he should be put into this sarcophagus, at the farthest extremity of the globe, that he might see whether anyone more mad than himself would come so far as this place to see him.'

After meeting our friends at the airport, we decided to have lunch on the coast before venturing up to Dalmácija. A large meal with plenty of wine would raise group morale. We would withhold the first exposure to the village until it was cooler, in the evening. Or possibly after dark.

We had two favourite beach restaurants. The first was almost invisible of access. A narrow track turned off the main road and led for half a mile through fields of sugar-cane to a thatched bar which, in this setting, looked more Caribbean than Andalusian. Because of its seclusion it was always half-deserted, and the long straight beach, backed by high dunes which excluded all sight of the land, conveyed an aura of utmost isolation. We thought of bringing Mark and Rebecca here, to counteract any preconceptions they might have had about the Costa del Sol: but at the last minute our stomachs took control. The food at the other restaurant was better.

This one was at the extreme end of the big beach at Teles Pires, at a safe distance from the high-rise flats. Like all the other *merenderos* along the coast, it consisted of a shack containing the cooking facilities, and a bar. In front of the bar, laid on the sand, was a long cement floor filled with tables. Over the tables was a roof of bamboo slats, through which the sunlight fell in slivers onto chequered table-cloths: and on three sides grew ten-foot canna lilies, filling the space between ground and roof and creating a jungly shade within. Outside was the beach, and peering through the cannas one could see a dozen fishing boats drawn up above the high-water mark. There were few bathers here: yet half a mile away, towards the town centre, they were packed as densely as ants.

We ordered gin and tonic, quadruple measures by English standards, and took them out onto the beach. A strong breeze blew off the sea, and it was hard to reconcile this cool air with the heat of Dalmácija, only a few miles inland. *Couchant* upon our towels, we surveyed our fellow-occupants of the shore. They were all Spaniards. This was recognizable from their physiques, at least in the case of the women. Up to the age of about sixteen, these local girls had the sleek fragility and ecstatic grace of impalas. Daintily they paced the water's edge in chattering groups, or stretched their pliant bodies in games of beach tennis, or emerged from the sea shaking their long dark hair, bejewelled with beads of water trapped in the down of their rich brown skin . . . But by the age of twenty, something had happened. The gazelles had turned into beef-calves, and soon thereafter they turned into oxen. The older women sitting in the shade of their umbrellas, or waddling up to the bar for a glass of lemonade, had massively protuberant bodies which, when squeezed into tight black swimsuits, gave them the dimpled corrugations of a Michelin Man. I averted my eyes, and watched their daughters.

A little later, returning with more gin, my eye was caught by the behaviour of two men further along the beach. Each would walk a few steps up the sand, then return to the same spot and repeat his walk. They were pulling on a rope which ran out to sea. Each man had a leather harness round his shoulders, to which was attached a short length of cord terminating in a bolas. Every time he took up position he twirled the bolas, and the weight spun round the rope, giving a secure grip to the cord which led to the harness. Then, like a dray-horse, he bent his shoulder and dragged the rope a couple of yards up the beach. His partner took turns to do the same. They repeated these actions for a quarter-of-an hour, while a boy coiled the upper end of the rope as it came in. At last, out of the sea came a net, gathered together to form a pocket. As the final belly appeared, the two men were joined by several more, some holding buckets, others carefully turning the net inside out to disgorge its contents. Alas, there was little enough within: half a pail of jumping, flashing fry, none bigger than a finger. How often, I wondered, would these men have to repeat this labour each day in order to earn a livelihood?

By now it was past three o'clock and time to eat. There were two slates displayed above the bar, one giving the meat menu and one the fish. We opted for the fish. There was no shortage of choice, belying the local fishermen's scant catch. On the counter stood flat dishes of anchovies in oil: succulent slivers, well-garlicked, which we nibbled on crusty bread as *tapas:* alternatively there were pungent mugs of gazpacho to sip while we debated the main dishes. We could have a paella, a massive cornucopia of fish and chicken and rice and prawns and mussels and olives and peppers. We could have *calamares* or *calamaritos*, two sizes of squid. Or there were *jibias,* cuttlefish chopped and fried. There were also clams and mussels and grilled prawns. There were baby soles. There were *pescadillas*, mini-hake, and *boquerones*, mini-anchovies, and *salmonetes*, mini-mullet, and various other kinds of small fish to whose identity the dictionary gave uncertain clues: *morralla*, for example, and *rosada* and *herreras*, defined respectively as 'little fish', 'hoar frost' and 'blacksmiths' wives'. Also *jurelillos*, 'carangoid sea fish'. More familiar, and compulsively delicious, were big sardines which were transfixed with bamboo spits and grilled in front of a driftwood fire on the beach: they were sluiced from time to time with sea water, which gave them a sparkling salty crust. We ordered some of these, together with a selection from the rest of the menu, avoiding the blacksmith's wives, and we washed them down with a couple of bottles of Manchegan white.

While we ate, the restaurant filled up. The only non-Spaniards were two Dutch girls, whose pale flesh, unguented with sun-lotion, was unpalatably reminiscent of the anchovies in oil. Children ran between the tables. Waiters bustled back and forth with bread and fish and salad and frothing jugs of sangria. The flags of all nations except Britain fluttered from the cane roof (the owner's wife made the flags herself, said the waiter, and the Union Jack was too difficult). The chatter of voices, the animated faces flecked with shredded sunshine, the smell of grilling sardines and the glimpses through the floral walls of the blue of sea and sky – that cogent Mediterranean blue – conspired to give the scene a carnival atmosphere, and to turn a meal into a celebration.

Afterwards, as we drank coffee and brandy, an old man who was sitting near Rebecca plucked her by the sleeve, and started to fumble with the waistband of his trousers. She turned away sharply: but the objective of the man's action was the disinterment from some inner pocket of a box of dominoes. Would Rebecca like to play with him? he asked with the eagerness of a child. She went and sat at his table. He played his pieces with panache, slamming them down on the table with a crash, as though squashing flies: and he was no less cavalier when it was Rebecca's turn, rejecting a number of her moves as infringements of the rules – his rules. In a few minutes he had won, and leant back with an air of relaxed superiority. Would he like a drink? No. Another game? No. He stuffed the dominoes back into his waistband, gave a nod of farewell, and limped away between the tables.

There was another distraction a few minutes later. Standing at the bar awaiting the bill, I spotted a small movement in the sand outside. A little creature was slowly walking along the edge of the beach, pausing after every couple of steps and rocking to and fro in a kind of slow-motion tango. It was a chameleon. It

244

carried its tail high over its back like a foxhound, and oblivious of its obligations as a natural history lesson it was bright green against the dun-coloured sand. Our children squeaked with delight when I brought it to them. It walked experimentally up Daniel's arm, gripping his flesh with a strange two-toed clasp, and rolling its eyes in contrary directions simultaneously.

By now it was evening, and the whole scene around us was unified in a monochrome haze. The mountains had disappeared, and so had the offshore horizon. Halfway up the sky hung a yacht, as motionless as a constellation. Nearer, a fishing boat slid down towards us, its oars dipping at long-extended intervals. In the prow stood a dog and a man, both graven details in an image where nothing moved except the oars, while the boat, foreshortened, grew gradually larger. When it nudged the sand, man and dog descended and were joined by a group of people of all ages, including a waiter from the restaurant, evidently in search of additions to the menu. In unison a dozen pairs of hands laid hold of the gunwales, while a boy applied a series of smooth wooden blocks beneath the bows as the boat slid slowly ashore. It was painted bright yellow with a red under-belly and a blue prow: the only bright-coloured object in a seascape of silver and lavender. Two final heaves, slow and ritualistic, and it was safely beached. All over the world, at this hour, similar fishermen were doubtless performing similar tasks. The practices of those who live from the sea are as unchanging as the sea itself.

The boys insisted on taking the chameleon back to the village. We put it on the vine, where we could vouch for a rich diet of flies. Next day it had gone. Or perhaps it had belatedly mastered the art of camouflage.

7 September
Mark and Rebecca were swiftly initiated into the *agua* ritual at dawn the next day. Rebecca, despatched to the

fountain, found herself centre-stage amid the village's female cast. She performed admirably. Although unable to speak or comprehend a single word of Spanish, she evidently held several diplomas in sign language, and over the next week she regaled us with a stream of detailed and intimate information about the villagers' private lives, none of which was known to Georgina and me.

Rosalia was not at the pump. She was inside our house, directing operations with a heavy hand. After a while I asked her, a trifle petulantly, why she wasn't gathering water for herself? It was not necessary, she said: she had a *depósito*. A *depósito* was a water-cistern. Rosalia's was the only one in Dalmácija, since most of the other houses lacked plumbing, and those that had water-taps drew directly from the village supply. But as she explained, a *depósito* was useful during water-rationing. It automatically filled up when the supply was turned on. She was still limited to those 500 litres for the rest of the day, but there was no need to fill other receptacles. This meant, I astutely realized, that there would be no need to rise at dawn, when the dreaded cry of *¡Agua!* rang out.

We warmed to the idea of a *depósito.* If we wanted one, said Rosalia, José was our man, *el Chico de Álamos.* He would buy us one and bring it up on his lorry. Emilio could do the necessary building work to install it. José the plumber could connect it to our plumbing.

Having satisfied herself that we understood her instructions, Rosalia took her leave. She had much to do, she said, and it was true. At this time of year she spent every morning and evening picking almonds or sorting the grapes on her raisin racks. In between, during the torrid spell from lunch to dusk, she was in her house preparing the almonds for sale. Her kitchen was full of them. Sometimes Georgina went to help with the dehusking. The piles of nuts gave the little room the appearance of a sandpit, and our boys soon learnt to treat it as such. They scrambled to the top of the heap and slid down, hooting with glee, half-buried in the soft, furry, grey husks. These outer jackets of the almonds smelt wonderful, like hay. Everything in Dalmácija had a smell, the jasmine, the herbs of the hillsides, the mule-dung, Marta's farmyard, and of course the wine. Even the dust had a fragrance of its own, a kind of spiciness akin to those mysterious powders which fill the sacks in oriental bazaars.

While our children cavorted, Rosalia and Georgina would sit at a table, extracting the nuts from their husks. Sometimes a neighbour was there too. With so much work to be compressed into the harvest season, the villagers helped each other as much as they could. If one household had a momentary respite they would offer their labour elsewhere. The work was all manual, and all slow. The almond husks, those that had not opened of their own accord, required trepanning with a small knife, one after another, for hours, gradually creating a golden mountain of nuts on one side of the room and a grey mountain of empty husks on the other. The debris rolled among the feet of the women as they worked, and their hands became abraded by the edge of the knife and blackened by the stain of the fruit. There was little talk: the repetitive work was too tiring and the dark, enclosed space was too hot.

At dusk I drove down the hill in search of Chico de Álamos. I entered his tiny parlour, feeling as usual like Alice after nibbling the wrong edge of the toadstool, and found the room full of children looking at television. The man himself was in the kitchen behind. He sat alone at a table, watched by his wife who stood beside the entrance while he ate. Whatever food had inflated her over the years, she had evidently not shared it with him. He was finishing an artichoke stew when I arrived, and moved quickly on to a ham *tortilla*, round and greasy, with upturned edges. He gave me a slice. It was delicious. He also poured me a glass of sweet

Málaga wine from a bottle on the table. There was an empty bottle of Catalan white next to it. He was clearly not a patron of local wine. Finishing the omelette, he pushed back his chair and patted his belly. He had not eaten since eleven in the morning, he said: just the two meals per day. No breakfast? No, none to speak of, only some ham and cheese, washed down with beer.

We proceeded to business. I still owed him for the building materials he had brought me in the spring. Since then, I had never succeeded in meeting him at a moment when he had the bills and I had a chequebook. But he appeared to be indifferent to payment. This time he had his bills to hand. They were well organized and clearly scripted. I was impressed. Almost nobody in Dalmácija could read or write: Rosalia's occasional letters to us in England were written in two or three different hands, according to whichever scribe she had found to execute them for her. I settled the previous bills and added the order for a *depósito*, together with a couple of angle girders and some cement for the platform. Emilio had taken one look at the site chosen for the installation and specified the precise materials immediately. Our villagers might not be scholars but they were born engineers.

I drank another glass of José's wine, agreed a delivery time for the *depósito*, and drove back up to Dalmácija. It was nearly dark. Halfway up the hill I passed a long procession of mules, plodding slowly under their loads like a camel caravan in the foothills of the High Atlas. As always they were richly decked with trappings of scarlet and their panniers were piled with the produce of the day's labour: sacks of almonds, boxes of grapes, packages of shopping from Álamos, water-jars that had sustained the workers during the day. Amid these bundles sat small boys or old men, and lagging at the rear, many paces behind, walked a pair of elderly women carrying buckets. I offered them a ride in the car, but they shook their heads.

Up at the house the children, as usual, were nowhere to be seen, but the adults were gathered on the terrace in some disarray. Supper had been causing problems. Georgina and Rebecca were dubiously eyeing the *pièce de résistance*, a chicken procured from Consuela. It did not look quite as other chickens. It had apparently been skinned, rather than plucked, which gave it a shiny redness, like styrene: and its attitude on the plate – wings widespread – suggested that rigor mortis had set in while it was still in flight. It looked as big as a pelican, but Georgina had decided that it might be inadequate for six of us, and had also bought a string of sausages. Leaving them in the kitchen, she had returned to the house a little later to find them emerging from the front door in the jaws of Luis's dog. After a short chase round the church the survivors had been rescued, and the worst of the dust sluiced away under the tap. General opinion was that a spell on the barbecue would cauterize any other impurities.

Spectacular as was the daily view from the terrace, it was even more dramatic at night. The surrounding hills were black, but the roofs below us were lit by the bulb of a street light. This single source of illumination created a chiaroscuro of simple extremes: clear sugary whites and deep ebony shadows in a composition of sharp-edged divisions – the lines of wall and roof and street-corner. The same bulb inked all our table setting in silhouette on the wall behind us, a Matisse-like arrangement of table and chairs and bottles in pure black outline except in the centre, where the candle-flame softened the black to sepia.

Up from the patio below came a steady flood of perfume from the *Dama de noche,* a shrub whose unobtrusive yellow-green florets smelt only at night. The fragrance broke over us like waves, and the warmth of the midnight air was almost as tangible, lapping around us as we sat there motionless, replete with food and wine. Out of the corner of my eye I watched the shadows on the wall waver infinitesimally, as the candle-flame flickered. Is it the flag that moves, or is it the wind, asked the Buddhist Patriarch Hui-Neng: neither, he answered – it is your mind.

The sound of cicadas was deeper at night, as though they had tuned down their instruments by a few tones. And at this hour they played more steadily: during the day they were apt to stop their trilling suddenly and simultaneously – at a flick of the conductor's baton, as it were – leaving the listener, fuddled by the heat, uncertain as to whether the sound had been real, or whether it had been a buzzing within his own ears. Now, the music was strong and continuous, as pervasive as the heat and the fragrance. If Sydney Smith's definition of paradise was eating *pâté de foie gras* to the sound of trumpets, murmured Mark, reclining at full length like a Roman feaster, then perhaps the Andalusian equivalent was drinking brandy to the sound of cicadas.

8 September
Today we had our first crisis involving one of the children. The possibility had been on our minds ever since we decided to bring them out here: Dalmácija's isolation, and the lack of a telephone in the village, were liabilities as well as attractions.

The boys were playing with Ramon and Luis and a couple of other lads, racing through the house and out of the front door and back in through the rear entrance, in a Spanish version of cops and robbers. We adults were reading on the terrace above the battle, when suddenly there was a scream. Adam had closed the patio gate against the Spaniards, and then, peering through the key-hole, had received a toy dagger in his eye. Fortunately the blade was made of rubber.

We soon found that it was not just the sound of clinking ice-cubes that brought Rosalia to our house. She was in our sitting-room quicker than we could

250

descend the stairs, and seconds later she had Adam on her knee and was sponging away the blood with cold water. Her calm and resource served to anaesthetize our panic. The wound was nothing serious, she told us: a view endorsed by the four other women who had appeared in the room almost as quickly as she. They were right: and the reassurance they conveyed was broader than the matter of Adam's eye. That morning we realized the rallying power of the villagers in an emergency, the collective strength and concern that was available to us, especially when the children were involved. We saw another instance of it later the same week. Searching for Daniel, to go shopping in Valdez, we could find him nowhere. We asked at Rosalia's house and several others, and as we hurried through the alleyways, with mounting alarm, we realized that the village – normally empty at this hour – was filled with the black figures of what seemed to be the entire female population. They were searching amidst the rubble of the half-dozen ruined houses, and peering over the steep escarpments where the ground fell away into the ravines around us. Like crows they flapped among the white buildings, until a cry from Georgina brought a halt to the activity. Daniel's disappearance was accounted for: Adam revealed, belatedly, that he was with Mark and Rebecca, who had gone on to Valdez ahead of us.

As for Adam's eye, his own desire for its recovery was heightened by the fact that the *feria* of the *Candelaria* was to be celebrated that night. This was a purely local festival. Although the name means Candlemas, it was not held in February (like the normal Candlemas) but in September, on the day of Málaga's patron saint. It had its own rituals: pyrotechnically, it was the Spanish equivalent of Guy Fawkes Night. A huge bonfire had been built in the arena at the bottom of the village, topped with a pumpkin-headed figure. This signified Judas, and his consumption by the fire represented the purging of the sins of the world. Brenan tells of similar ceremonies in his time – the 1920s – but attributes them to Midsummer Day, or, in Northern Spain, to the Saturday of Holy Week.

We were summoned to the festivities at dusk, by a volley of shots. The fire was lit as we arrived, and the flames licked up through the olive-prunings and broken fish-boxes to curl around the figure above. To us, in that country, the effect was momentarily horrifying, conjuring up images not of Fawkes but of the Inquisition. But such thoughts were quickly dispelled by the clapping and laughing of the audience. The square was full of girls. This *feria* was more of a party than a religious ceremony (there had been no church service), and as we had already discovered, parties were for girls. Mark and I were almost the only males there, apart from our boys. I had no objection to this.

As the flames died down the music started: but unlike the other *ferias* we had attended, there was no band, only the girls' voices. While they sang, the singers formed themselves into a ring, and the songs became dances. These whirling-dances, or *remolinos*, are of great antiquity (an early example is depicted by a Cretan clay model dating from about 1350 BC in the Heraklion Museum), and many are relics of courtship rituals. Such was this one, no doubt, since the ring broke up into pairs at various stages of the choreography, but the words of the songs had wider provenances: '*Miaou, Miaou, Miaou,*' we cried as we linked arms, and threaded in and out, and regrouped, and circled around. The firelight shone on the excited faces and tinted the flailing arms and legs, and as each chosen pair plunged into the gyrating circle it vanished from sight in the deep shadow within, until it broke out and reappeared, brightly lit, dramatically reborn.

Gradually the dancing moved away from the fire, and up the hill. By now we were following the format of 'Oranges and Lemons', with each couple passing under the raised arms of the couple above, over and over again, up and up, past Luis's bar and Rosalia's house, while the girls sang and sang, and Rosalia and her neighbours stood at their front doors to watch us pass. We were in the darkness now, dancing as much by touch as by sight, brushed by the soft warm bodies of the girls and the flick of their long hair as the human skeins formed and reformed: but ahead of us was another glow of light. A second bonfire had been lit at the top of the village, bathing young José's house in a copper glow that softened its modern silhouette, and transformed the ruin next to it into one of those golden towers that shimmer, distantly, in a Claude sunset. Here we regrouped and danced some more, until distracted by cries from the far side of the village, by Angel's house.

There was a third fire down there, and this one was out of control. It had been built beyond the cluster of houses, in the gully below Emilio's house, and instead of dying down after the initial blaze the flames had spread through the dead grass surrounding it. A clump of prickly pears was being consumed, with a fusillade of sharp reports as the heat exploded the sap inside the fleshy flanges: undermined by the creeping holocaust, the grotesque jointed plants collapsed with the despairing gestures of drowning men. The flames raced up the slope. Already they were singeing the first of the olives and ahead of them lay Emilio's little grove of orange trees, their fruit shining like lanterns in the light of the fire. A number of children – headed by ours – were clapping and shouting with excitement, but at the edge of the blaze a group of men were working silently and urgently, beating at the flames with shovels and branches. No 'Miaou, Miaou,' for them: their livelihood was at risk. At last the fire was out. The scene reverted to the darkness of a summer night, through which tired and exhilarated figures peered at one another. The hillside was sprinkled with embers, as though with glow-worms. Judas had been dispatched, this year, with extra drama.

9 September
After the *agua* procedure the next morning I strolled around the village. It was the painter's hour. All the buildings were strongly side-lit by the sun's new arrival over the edge of the valley. The view from the far side of the village was best, the east side, where the smell of last night's brush fire still prickled in the nostrils. From here the church tower showed distinct against the mountain, white against purple, the colours of a consul's toga. The gate to Angel's patio was open, and as I passed it his voice hailed me, inviting me in.

Four men were sitting around a table: Angel and young José's father, his crutch propped against a wall, and the old Aurelio and a man from the house where the pig had been slaughtered. They were playing cards. The table was set under the vine arbour, next to the shed containing the wine press. The vine tendrils hung around the players like a canopy, creating a separate enclave within the coolness of the patio, a shade within a shade. I tiptoed towards them, loath to interrupt their game, and peered over Aurelio's shoulder. The cards gleamed with unfamiliar images – mounted warriors and swords and florid gold coins and outlandish clubs: not the stylized clubs of English cards, but brutal great shillelaghs, carbuncled and sprouting with foliage. Despite the idyllic calm of the scene, and the age of the participants, they played the game in aggressive style, slamming down the cards with the *élan* of the domino player on the beach. Coins flashed, red and green clubs went spinning across the table, and Angel took the final trick with a single enormous sword, extravagantly hilted, in a multi-coloured scabbard from which straps and buckles and swivels dangled to the four corners of the card.

Leaning back in temporary triumph, he offered me a drink. It was eight o'clock in the morning, an hour at which, in my own experience of such matters, a drink can have a most signal effect on one's system. Spanish brandy is excellent for this purpose. Being heavy and sweet, it is an admirable replacement for a glass of orange juice, although the impact is different. Labourers' bars in Spain – as elsewhere in Europe – are full of men downing *coñac* with their early morning coffee. However, it was not *coñac* that Angel now poured me. It was a clear, colourless liquid, strong and sticky. *Anís*. Due to its local pronunciation, dropping the final consonant, this fluid became known to us as 'Annie'. Just as Victorians nicknamed champagne 'the Boy', mimicking the Prince of Wales's habit of ordering up a glass from an ever-present page, so did we become close friends with Annie, at any appropriate moment of day or night.

Clasping my Annie, I watched the card-game proceed, through patterns inscrutable to me. Fortunes alternated at a bewildering speed – no-one but me had time to drink – and the cards flashed from one side of the table to another, while the illumination of the scene grew brighter as the sun rose. A ray reached over the patio wall and caught the topmost twig of Angel's custard-apple, giving warning that the coolness of this little yard would soon be gone. I put down my glass and bade the players farewell and went home for breakfast.

The remainder of the day was centred on a momentous event: the arrival of the *depósito*. José El Chico delivered it to the bottom of the village, and four of us carried it up the hill. It was relatively light but awkwardly large, with no hand-holds. We clutched the thing in a sweaty embrace, and pawed its bulging flanks, and levered it upwards with shoulder and knee. By the time we reached our house a small crowd had assembled. There was a clear consensus of opinion that whatever difficulties we had experienced in carrying the *depósito* up the hill would be as nothing compared with the problem of raising it up to our roof terrace. Debate was brisk, orchestrated by Angel, who had arrived to supervise the further modernization of his old house. After much discussion, someone went to get a rope.

The project was slightly less complex than raising the *Titanic*, but taxed us fully. The rope was tied around the *depósito* like a howdah-girth round an elephant, and the loose end was passed up to Emilio, the strongest man present. Other hands raised the *depósito* from beneath. I myself, according to a surviving photograph of the scene, was perched on the bathroom roof, roped to Emilio mountaineer-style, a position which was self-evidently both hazardous and useless. Despite my efforts, the load rose steadily. It cleared the bathroom tiles and the parapet. Emilio powered it into position on the platform he had built. Then José the plumber went to work and connected the *depósito* to the rest of the water system. By dusk the job was done. Wine was dispensed to the labour force. We also partook freely of it ourselves, in celebration of the fact that tomorrow we would not need to rise at dawn: the *agua* would fill the *depósito* automatically.

Night fell as the big straw-covered wine-bottle was passed round. Our helpers had gone, but the mood of exhilaration persisted. After supper we decided to go for a walk, arm in arm, with the bottle in a free hand. All was quiet, but not for long. We raised our voices in song as we stumbled along the route of the processions, up the precipitous alley behind the house and along the upper track towards Emilio's house. Here, for a few yards, we lowered our voices for fear that he would join us, but crescendoed again as we passed down beside the eastern raisin-racks. Still Dalmácija lay silent, nacreous in the moonlight, the rough whitewash and hard outlines softened and ennobled so that it glowed on the hillside like a Rajput palace.

Overcome by the experience, and slowed by a slight sprain to Mark's ankle incurred on the downward slope, we lay down beside the road. This position was bad for singing but good for moon-watching, and we remained there for a while. The wine had run out, but there were other entertainments to keep us there: the tracer-tracks of two shooting stars across the sky, and the dusty fragrance of the dry herbs on which we lay. At last we bestirred ourselves and walked back up through the village, tiptoeing past Rosalia's house like truant children.

10 September
Today, thanks to the new *depósito*, there was no need to rise early to collect water. But this did not mean a long lie-in, as we soon discovered. There was another reason for an early call. The reason was, inevitably, Rosalia. We had promised to take her to the Valdez cemetery today, to visit her grandparents' grave. We had assumed the project to be a mid-morning one, but the dawn pounding on the door soon disabused us. Georgina was quickly elected to discharge the task, and she went to shake the children into consciousness, as they had asked to go too. The rest of us decided to stay behind. There wouldn't be room for us in the car, we explained to her, as we settled back into our beds and smoothed the pillows beneath our throbbing temples.

We were certainly right about the car. As Georgina propelled the sleepy boys up the hill to the parking place, Rosalia casually announced that she had arranged to take several ladies to Valdez and hoped it would cause no inconvenience. Somehow four black-clad crones were shoe-horned into the back of the car, underneath the boys and a number of shopping baskets. Rosalia sat in front. Unfortunately this gave her a better view of the road. Being unaccustomed to anything faster than a mule she was almost as nervous a passenger as

José the plumber: she crossed herself at every bend, and repeatedly asked Georgina how long ago she had learnt to drive. After a while she closed her eyes, and didn't open them again until the car reached Valdez. There she resumed command, told Georgina where to park, bought some red and white carnations in the market, and led Georgina and the boys to a café. She had planned a treat for them.

The place was the size of a hat-box, and crammed with women and children. Rosalia quickly ejected a family from their seats, swept their table-top litter to the floor, and sat down. Georgina followed suit. Rosalia ordered hot chocolate and *churros*, the deep-fried local doughnuts. The boys watched fascinated as yard-long tongues of batter spewed from the gleaming machine, were cut into sections, tossed into a cauldron of boiling fat, then dusted with sugar and nutmeg. But there was no time for lingering. Rosalia had arranged to meet some friends who were also visiting the cemetery, and Georgina was dispatched to collect the car again. Rosalia did not care to walk too far because of her bad leg, although this had never inhibited her shopping visits to Álamos.

When Georgina returned, two of the friends had arrived, and a third was collected on the way out of town. All had large bunches of flowers, and by now the car smelt like a hearse. Daniel had virtually disappeared beneath a sheaf of lilies, which brought on a prolonged sneezing-fit, but at least offered him some protection against the habitual kissing and pinching and cries of *¡Que gordo!* Following Rosalia's directions, Georgina drove a few kilometres out of Valdez and up on to a shoulder of the surrounding hills, on which stood a small church. It was of some age – perhaps eighteenth century – and the whitewash was flaking off like sunburnt skin, but the simplicity of the solid stonework was charming and the situation spectacular. Everybody disembarked from the car, Georgina dusted the pollen from the boys, and Rosalia led the way to a gate in a wall beside the church.

Inside there lay, at first sight, a small town. Streets were laid out on a grid system, and each was lined with tall constructions of whitened stone. These, as Georgina soon saw, were graves, piled up four or five layers high. Our cemetery at Dalmácija was similar, but on a much smaller scale. The design was a direct descendant from the Roman occupation. In a rocky land the dead could not be buried, and so were slid into these concrete filing-cabinets above ground. The docketing, here in Valdez, was very thorough: every path had a name and every grave a number. To finalize identification, faded photographs of the more recent occupants were attached to the cell-openings, next to the vases of plastic flowers that jutted from the masonry on brackets like toothmug-holders. The roofs of the older rows of graves were rounded and roughened, and this fractured skyline, together with the irregularity of the deep shadows of the grave-apertures – eye sockets in a row of skulls – contributed to the overall impression of a ruined city abandoned on this cypress-studded hilltop: in literal truth, a ghost town.

Rosalia's grandparents were evidently late-comers to their street, since they reposed in a garret, so to speak, high up on the top storey. Georgina wondered how Rosalia, who lacked the build of an alpinist, would be able to scramble up there to perform her duties. The answer lay further down the path in the form of a massive iron step-ladder on wheels, like the mobile stairways which are trundled against the doorways of airliners, and to Georgina's eyes not much smaller. Standing in the shade of a cypress, Rosalia commanded Georgina to bring it to the grave. This took several minutes. The path was uneven, the sun was hot, and these particular graves appeared to have been built at the top of a slope. This meant that when Georgina, panting and scrabbling, at last clinked the contraption into position, she was compelled to stand there, shoulder braced against an iron limb, to prevent the thing from rolling away down the path under Rosalia's considerable weight.

Rosalia mounted the steps and proceeded to polish the glass pane which sealed the vault. Time passed. Only the vibrations of her activities prevented Georgina from falling into a stupor. Suddenly she was roused by yells of juvenile mirth, accompanied by angry voices and the sound of rushing water. The boys had discovered the tap used for watering the flowers, and were hosing each other and everyone else in sight. Leaving Rosalia clinging to the eaves of her sarcophagus, Georgina sped away down the path to make apologies and retrieve the sodden culprits. Returning to her post, she asked Rosalia how much longer her task would take. It was necessary to arrange the flowers rightly, was the answer, and then she must search the cemetery for her friends. Meanwhile the children had escaped again. Crouching in the dust, they peered into every accessible glass-fronted grave in search of skeletons, and then took to playing hide-and-seek, racing down the silent paths and flickering in and out of the cypress shadows and slipping between the solemn cliffs of masonry: the very personification of life among the dead. It was half an hour before Georgina succeeded in assembling everyone for the drive back.

Up at the house the rest of us were by now much strengthened, thanks to the healing ministrations of Annie. Georgina found us on the terrace with our feet up. We enquired cursorily about her experiences in the graveyard and returned to our books. Rebecca was reading Gerald Brenan's *South from Granada*, describing his life in a small village of the Sierra Nevada a few miles east of here. Coming fresh both to the book and to Dalmácija, she was well placed to compare the two. Georgina and I had always been aware that we were, in a limited way, following in Brenan's footsteps, but now it was interesting to sit for a while and muse on the distinctions between his village, Yegen, and ours.

Although Yegen lay in another part of the mountains, and despite the fact that sixty years had passed since Brenan's sojourn there, the similarities were striking. Both villages were primitive, without plumbing or any amenities such as markets or inns or restaurants. Both functioned without the internal combustion engine, whether in the streets or in the fields. Both populations were largely illiterate, though thanks to television our neighbours no longer believed – as did Brenan's – that the World Wars had been fought against the Moors.

The rituals of religion – Christian and pagan – and of courtship and husbandry were richer in Yegen than in Dalmácija. Here, the overall patterns remained – the processions at the *ferias*, the whirling-dances, the graven images and the basic beliefs – but many of the details had fallen away, as sophistication crept in from the outer world. The greatest loss, to our mind, was the music. Nobody here serenaded his girlfriend with *coplas*, or sang the *cante jondo*, or played the lute, or even the guitar.

Otherwise the main difference was one of size. Dalmácija was one-tenth the size of Yegen. This made it more compact: not merely geographically (there was no division into *barrios*), but also socially. There were no separate classes here – everyone was a land-owner. And apart from the mayor, there were no key role-players: no doctor, priest, nor prostitute.

But overall we had been entranced by the same things as Brenan: the beauty of this 'yellow, ox-hide land', the dominating presence of the mountains, and the protected isolation – the purity – of the little community who lived here. Visually, and in much of its way of life, Dalmácija was medieval, Arab, immutably rustic. This made it, to us, something very wonderful.

We had been seeing much of the boy Luis on this visit. Although older than our boys, he was one of the few male children available, at any rate on our side of the village, and was prepared to join in the games of kicking tin cans around the alleyways. (Balls were useless for the purpose: they had too much velocity for the limited space, and soon disappeared irretrievably down the hillside or into the courtyards of aggressive old ladies, whence recovery was hazardous.)

His relationship with Adam and Daniel was, nevertheless, a faintly alarming one. We never saw him smile, and his lowering brow and fixed scowl were not the only indications of a primitive violence. Once the boys came running home in tears. Luis had got angry with them, they said: he had pulled open the front of their trousers and spat inside. I rushed to Borrow to see if this could be some localized application of the Evil Eye.

Today Luis arrived later than usual. He had his hands in his pockets. He withdrew them to reveal two tiny bundles of fluff. On the table in front of the children he laid two kittens. They were a present, he said. We could take them back to England when we left the day after tomorrow. That would not be possible, said Georgina quickly, and she made a sketchy attempt to explain the laws of quarantine. It would be kinder, she said, to return the kittens to their mother. He couldn't, said Luis, with his usual paucity of words. Why not? we asked. Because, he said, he had found them on the rubbish heap. But if we wished he would put them back there: and he reached over to pick them up. This was too much for the boys, who burst into tears.

Attracted by their wailing, Rosalia appeared and took control. The kittens must be washed, she said, and dispatched Georgina to bring soap and water. Both, on their arrival, were rejected. The water was too cold for such young animals, and the soap too coarse. Georgina returned with a bar of the finest complexion soap the household could muster, and was sent downstairs again to find a towel. The nearest to hand, in the emergency, was a finely worked Harrods face-towel. Rosalia found this acceptable, and went to work. Luis extracted a comb from Rebecca's handbag. The kittens were titivated beyond recognition. They were now, said Rosalia, ready for their food.

After several minutes Georgina reappeared, sweating freely by now, with a bowl of bread and milk. She should have known better. Such crude fare was instantly rejected, not merely by Rosalia and Luis, who had formed a solid axis on all matters feline, but by the kittens themselves. Rosalia strode over to the barbecue, where a large rabbit lay awaiting its final preparation for supper. This would do, she said, in a tone of modified rapture which implied that filet mignon would have been more suitable. She proceeded to dismember it, and to dice what looked like an inordinate amount. The kittens wolfed it down. They were evidently going to be expensive house-guests. Being, myself, no cat-lover at the best of times, I was glad that we would only be entertaining them for two days. Meantime there was the problem of their premises. I fenced off a corner of the terrace with a double row of bricks. Rosalia and Luis quickly dismantled this and replaced it with a massive barricade which utilized all the deckchairs, leaving us standing. For the rest of our stay in Dalmácija, the terrace became an obstacle course, and every activity, however simple, revolved around the kittens. I came to dislike Luis even more than before.

By nightfall an acceptable coexistence had been achieved. The remains of the rabbit had been enjoyed and the stresses of the kitten episode had been assuaged with wine. Despite the heat the night was very clear. The moon was down. Across the centre of the sky the Milky Way ran like a skein of smoke, and the constellations, especially when viewed with a wine glass in hand, had a particular insistence. Their collective brightness seemed to be the most important part of the firmament, and the darkness between them mere negative space, an obstruction, as if the earth lay beneath an upturned colander, through the holes of which penetrated shafts from some immeasurable brilliance which lay behind. Orion bestrode the southern horizon, with his left foot resting on the castle ruin across the valley. Beside him shone Taurus, centred on its biggest star, Aldebaran, the Eye of the Bull. An Arab name, I observed to my reclining guests, and therefore appropriate to our situation here. There were many other Arab titles up there, I continued sonorously: Alcaid, Algenis, and Algol (El Ghul, the Ghoul, the Gorgon star in Perseus) not to mention the Latinate constellations, the Canes Venatici, the Corona Borealis, Piscis Australis . . . In fact, said I, warming to my theme and gesturing widely with my glass, there was no collection of names as divers and curious as those of the stars. Betelgeuse, Famalhaut, Ophiocus, Deneb . . .

Exhausted by my little lecture, I lay back in my chair and tried to focus on the Seven Sisters. One should never start night-fishing for sea trout, I had been told, until one could count seven stars. Seven for the seven stars in the sky, and six for the six proud walkers . . . five for the symbols at your door and four for the Gospel makers . . . I hummed my way to the end of the old song and then launched into a reprise, *mezzo forte*, throwing in a bit of descant. Three, three for the ri-i-i-vals . . . Looking around, I saw that the others had gone to bed. Two, two for the lily-white boys, clothed all in gree-een, oh . . . one is one and all alone and ever more shall be so.

12 September
This morning we went up to watch Rosalia working on her raisins. It was the last day of our holiday, and we

had seen less of her than usual, owing to the demands of the harvest season. Now we felt sorry about it. We tended to admire Rosalia more in her absence than in her presence.

Her raisin racks were high on the hillside behind Emilio's house. We picked our way up there with care, using all the available cover of gullies and prickly pears to ensure that Emilio would not spy us if he was at home, and invite us to sample his terrible wine. The stuff was demanding enough in the evening: at ten in the morning, the prospect was unthinkable. We reached the enclosure with safety. Passing through the brushwood fence, we saw the figure of Rosalia ahead of us, dark against the eastern sun, squatting on the ground. She wore one of the wide-brimmed hats that the women seemed to wear only for this purpose, and a rough over-skirt. Embarrassed, perhaps, by her appearance, she gave us only a brief greeting, and continued with her work.

Beside her stretched twenty feet of grapes, almost filling one of the racks. Those bunches at the bottom of the slope, which had evidently been harvested first, were already a purplish brown. Those beside her were mottled pink and copper. Higher up, they were still a bright sappy green. Leaning over this variegated tapestry of fruit, Rosalia picked at the half-cured bunches, turning and rearranging them, slowly and gently, almost caressingly. When she had tended those within reach, she shuffled her body further up the hill, with a grunting and a creaking of joints, doubling her legs awkwardly beneath the wide skirt in a deformed crouch like that of a Calcutta street-cripple. Her face was invisible beneath her hat. The sun was hot, by now, and there was no shade for her or for us. We attempted an occasional pleasantry, but Rosalia was too busy or too tired to rally in her usual style, and after a few minutes we turned to go. But then came the sound of a rhythmic clinking further along the hillside, and her son Pedro appeared, leading a mule.

He was a fine athletic lad of twenty, who had been given leave from the army to help his family with the harvest. He flashed a smile at us, whirled up one of the boys in a swooping embrace, and commiserated with us on our return to England next day. Then he turned back to his work. As the mule stood there, docile and motionless, Pedro unstrapped the four boxes of grapes and laid them on the ground. He gave us each a bunch, and watched us briefly while we crunched into the new warm fruit and the muscat juice ran between our teeth. The other bunches he passed to his mother, one by one: and one by one she laid them on the earth, each in its place, grape against grape. Thus every bunch from this family's land – all the produce of several acres of hillside – passed through their individual hands not once but many times on its way to the shops of the north: from vine to mule, from mule to raisin rack, where it would be turned again and again, and from raisin rack to the merchant's crate. And so it was with all the raisins of Dalmácija.

We had planned a picnic for that night, and after leaving Rosalia Georgina and I drove down to Álamos to buy sausages and potatoes, since Consuela was out of stock. Parking the car below the town we saw Salvador emerging from his mule shed. We had looked for him several times without success, so here was our first opportunity to reopen the issue of his land. We greeted him, and invited him for a beer in the bar across the road. Had he thought any more about selling? we asked. Would he come down on his price? What did his wife think? Surely he was not even planning to harvest the almonds and olives there – we had not seen him near the place? What good was the land to him? He interrupted us in mid-flow. Why didn't we kill the matter? he said, and named a substantially lower price. It was as though he had suddenly wearied of the game. Honour, or the natural rhythm of Spanish life, was satisfied by the amount of time which had already elapsed. We had a deal, if we wanted it.

I shook Salvador's hand, and hugged Georgina, and ordered another round of beer. We were land-owners. We possessed three-quarters of an acre of hillside, and three almond trees, and a dozen olive trees, and a regiment of prickly pears, and still had space enough for the bottlebrush trees and frangipanis. I would be able to dust off the tropical flower book again. But meantime a thought struck me: we were leaving tomorrow, and would have no time to deposit money in a bank. There was no need for money, said Salvador. We could pay next time. And the *escritura*, the title deed? Next time, he said: but the land was ours *now* – and he shook my hand again.

Thus was our ambition accomplished at last. Georgina finalized the *escritura* on her next visit. It was a standard form, procured from the post office. The signatures on it came first, hers and Salvador's, and El Chico's as witness. At this stage the form was completely blank: all the specific information was filled in later at the tiny bank in Álamos. The acreage was tallied in some obscure Arab unit of measurement.

We returned to the house in high glee, to find it transformed into a local produce stall. The sitting-room was full of boxes of raisins and bags of almonds, and bottles of wine and olive oil, and dishes of grapes to be transferred into containers of our own. Our neighbours knew we were leaving early tomorrow, and were bringing us their farewell gifts. There were presents for us and for the boys, and for Rebecca and Mark, and for my mother and Georgina's sister, neither of whom had yet visited Dalmácija but who had formed the subject of conversations. All these things had to be packed. There was no chance of leaving any of them in the house for future consumption: Rosalia would find them. While we deliberated, and looked for impermeable wrapping for the olive oil, Isabel arrived with a bottle of vinegar, followed by Marta with a string of *morcillas*. We hoped there would be no customs check at the airport.

All was confusion. Georgina was negotiating an alternative residence for the kittens. Some of us were compressing raisins into corners of suitcases and encasing wine bottles in underpants. Others were preparing for the picnic. At last everything was ready, and both cars were loaded with food and drink and rugs and chairs and fire-making equipment. The site for the picnic was close behind the village, over the ridge above us, but it was easier to drive than to walk. The only navigable track was via Álamos. It was the same way we had taken to visit the stupenduously sited *finca* with three owners and a malodorous bedroom. We drove up the hillside and through a cleft at the crest of the ridge, and suddenly the whole valley was revealed before us. On the far side, the mountain range was lit from the west, so that the shoulders which thrust out towards us were given strength, and the whole massif had weight and a formidable presence. It dominated the view, not merely through its size but also its colour, purple shaded with indigo. Down in thevalleytheinterveningridgeswerelessdistinct,ingreys and muted golds, and the white *fincas* and *cortijos* were barely perceptible in the shadows, except where they stood on raised ground and caught the evening sun.

We parked the car beside the track and walked out on to a level platform of hillside a few yards away. Here we dragged together some stones to make a hearth, and sent the boys to gather twigs. Soon the sausages were grilling nicely, and we settled back to watch the sunset. Around us the big plumes of sun-dried broom were tinted yellow and copper, and far away to the west the many-layered mountains softened and blushed. As we sat in silence, sipping our wine, our eye was caught by a dusting of black flecks in the sky towards the coast. They were birds, a long way off. To be visible at this distance they must have been huge, and there were many of them, at least a hundred. Perhaps they were griffon vultures. We had seen them locally, but only singly or in pairs. Now they were gathering, in this great convoy, for their migration south to Africa.

Suddenly we were distracted by a commotion behind us. The fire was out of control. Despite the encircling rocks, a spark had kindled the grass around it, seared tinder-dry by months of summer sun. Tongues of flame were spreading down the hillside like rivulets of lava, glowing in the dusk. It was like a rerun of the *Candelaria* episode. Frantically we beat at them with branches of broom, fearful of setting the whole landscape ablaze. As we stamped out the last of the embers a white mule appeared out of the twilight, led by an emaciated old man: a stranger, perhaps from Álamos, returning home after a day of harvesting a distant crop. He trudged incuriously past us, apparently impervious to the sight of this group of blackened dervishes dancing around a fire. Before we could shout a greeting, or an apology, he had gone.

Thirsty from fire-fighting, we opened another wine bottle. The sausages, well dusted with the ash which our activities had stirred up, were nearly cooked. So were the potatoes. The eggs were quickly scrambled, and the long loaf segmented. As we ate, we became aware that again we were being watched, this time with more interest. Just outside the circle of firelight stood the boy Luis. We hailed him and offered him a sausage, and beckoned him to join us, but he remained motionless, unwilling either to move nearer or to leave. He stood there throughout our meal, gradually fading from sight as the dusk darkened. By now the mountains were black and flat, paper cut-outs against the sky. It was still too bright overhead for stars. The great birds had gone. Perhaps they had already crossed the water. Tomorrow we too would be migrating, but in the contrary direction.

6

WINTER

Hoc erat in votis: modus agri non ita magnus,
Hortus ubi et tecto vicinus iugis aquae fons
Et paulum silvae super his foret.

This was my dream: a bit of land–
nothing much – with a garden near
the house, and a spring of ever-flowing
water, and a few trees.

Horace

As the globe tilted past autumn, the farming activities in
Dalmácija diminished and slowed until by January the
villagers had largely withdrawn within the thick walls
of their houses, sheltering from the weather in mid-
winter as they had in mid-summer. Not that the winters
were cold, by English standards. Rosalia had once told
us, on our first visit, that in February the hillsides were
white. With snow? we had asked, dismayed. No, with
almond blossom. The renewing of Nature's cycle, and
the work that accompanied it, began early, after only
a short break during which the temperature seldom
dropped below 50 degrees, and the sky released the
only appreciable rain of the year.

Before the winter rest two tasks remained: wine-
making and olive-gathering. The wine was made in
October. By then, the last of the raisins had been sent
down the valley in their flat wooden boxes, and the
raisin racks had been swept clear of the lingering debris
of stalks and shrivelled skins. That done, the mules

were again busy bringing in grapes, but this time they took them to one of the two presses in the village, Angel's and Consuela's.

The grapes for raisin-making had all been muscatel, but for wine the villagers used a mixture of four or five grape varieties. Everyone had a different recipe, dependent partly on his preference and partly on the types of vine planted in his various plots of land. Only Angel made wine of pure muscatel. As such it was probably unique, at any rate locally. Nobody in the surrounding countryside made such wine, he said: the muscatel of Málaga was made from raisins, not from fresh grapes, and muscat vines were seldom planted elsewhere in Spain. He was justly proud of it. He had just a single barrel of it, topped up with new wine each year, on the *solera* principle employed at Jerez. He sold none of it. It was for his friends. He himself, the warm-eyed host, the very Bacchus of the village, could no longer drink wine. Hobbling on a stick, he was an ill man.

But in October his house was a centre of activity. With barrels to fill under every home in the village, and only two presses to deal with the tons of grapes converging from the surrounding hillsides, the pressing went on non-stop for a month. The gate into Angel's little patio was open all day: the table and chairs were put away, and the caged goldfinch had been hung from a higher shoot of the vine to leave clear passage for the boxes of grapes that were unloaded from mules standing in the street outside.

The press was in a shed on the far side of the patio. The axle for the revolving handle rose vertically from the concrete floor. Each wine-maker, when his time came, spread his bunches of grapes around the axle until they lay several inches deep. Then he kicked off his sandals and rolled up his trousers and stepped over the raised threshold onto the grapes. Three or four of his friends did likewise. For the next few minutes the group

271

of them trudged to and fro, advancing and retreating and rotating as though participating in a slow-motion saraband, trampling the fruit beneath their feet. On a few occasions I joined them. The sensation, despite the thrill of performing so atavistic an activity, was not wholly pleasant. Treading each big new bunch of warm grapes was like crushing some living thing, and as the structure and vitality of it was trampled into submission, the disjointed relics – the skins and stalks – thrust up between my toes and clung to my ankles, while the sticky liquid, like life-blood, ran about my feet.

When the fruit had been thus pulped it was shovelled around the axle in a low pile which was topped with a mat of esparto grass. Another layer of pulp was added and another mat, and so on until the stack was nearly a yard high. Then the big wooden lid of the press was slotted over the axle, and the handle twirled onto the screw. Down it came, revolving easily until it pressed against the lid. Two men leant against the ends of it, and began to walk slowly round.

And so the last of the precious juice was released, with a crunching and a sluicing, and a creaking from the primitive mechanism, and a grunting from the men who operated it, and a murmuring from the women who watched, and a buzzing of flies. The pale liquid gurgled down a hole in the corner of the floor, into a small well outside in the patio. This had no exit. As it filled, the wife and daughters of each wine-maker reached down into it with buckets which they emptied into the big plastic containers normally used for collecting water from the fountains. These were loaded onto a waiting mule and transferred to the family's *bodega*, where the requisite number of barrels had been emptied and scrubbed and purified with sulphur in readiness.

Splashing from well to bucket to container, the juice soon bespattered the whole small area within the patio, and ran down the path beside the fruit trees which

Angel had grafted, and out into the street, where queues of wasps battened onto every runnel, enjoying the first taste of the *vendange*. Angel had once said that rain was the blood of the soil: now we saw, not for the first time, that wine was the blood of the village. Angel himself, most days, was there to see it flow, propped on his stick in the doorway of his house, on the bank of the lake of juice.

Rosalia invited us to watch Jesus press his grapes. He used the other press, in the *bodega* behind Consuela's shop. It was entirely appropriate that Angel and Consuela, the two characters (apart from Rosalia herself) who, for us, most clearly personified Dalmácija, should control one of the village's most vital activities. Consuela's press was more enclosed than Angel's, standing in the cool, dark undercroft of her building. In this confined space the fragrance of the grapes was intense. Moreover, next to the press was a row of barrels, where Consuela's own new wine was beginning to work, so that the fumes of the furiously frothing liquid mingled in our nostrils with the syrupy sweetness of the fresh fruit. In the half-darkness the sense of smell was intensified, and within a few minutes it seemed that our lungs were filled not with oxygen but with vaporised must. It was like being inside a wine barrel. Nor was there any escaping it. Our clothes were impregnated with the smell of a pulled cork, and when we returned to our roof terrace, only a few yards away, the breeze blowing up from the sea had a vinous breath.

During November and December came the olive harvest. All across the hillsides the olive trees had increased their presence, retaining their foliage while the almond trees withered to sculptured stumps. Now at last the olives were ripe. The technique for gathering them was the same as for almonds. A net was spread under each tree, and the family of its owner gathered round, belabouring the branches with long poles. But the fruit

273

was more reluctant to leave the twigs than had been the almonds, and children were sent up the branches to pick the stragglers by hand. From our seats on the roof terrace, still shirt-sleeved at midday on the sunnier days, we watched these scenes being enacted around the village. By evening, as the sun dipped below the rim of the valley, the mules would return down the steep tracks laden with four sacks apiece. Behind them strode the family, swinging their poles like lances, followed by groups of dogs, tan or beige or dark brown, the colour of Andalusian goats. During this time the village was filled with sacks of olives, stacked in every *bodega* or at street corners, awaiting collection by the co-operative. It was the black olives that went for pressing. There were also pink ones – the prettiest but the least palatable – and green ones, which were stored in water for eating. Ours, on our newly acquired patch, were mostly pink. But there were also some accessible green ones, which we picked and processed according to Rosalia's instructions. First we split them, by pressing them with a heavy weight, then we subjected them to several changes of salt water at intervals of four or five days. Finally they were ready for tasting. They tasted vile.

This was just as well, because we had decided to grub out most of our olive trees, especially the ones at the near end of the plot, which had been cut down at some time in the recent past, and consisted of shapeless thickets of young shoots. At the far end, where the Arab terraces were more distinct, the olives stood tall and elegant, and were accompanied by three almond trees. All these we planned to leave. But nearer the house we needed to do some levelling of the land in case we ever wanted to build an annexe, and to open up the view over the new garden. Not that we planned to do anything too drastic: a rearrangement of the slope was what we had in mind . . . the removal of some of the rocks and prickly pears . . . the creation, perhaps,

of some new terraces, with steps between them . . .
new sight-lines and perspectives . . . a reshaping of the
terrain which would cunningly preserve the vernacular
of our Andalusian hillside while also giving scope for
boldness of design and dramatic sitings of exotic trees
and shrubs. I had a vision in my mind, admittedly not
altogether clear in its details, of something like an
Assamese jungle in the up-country, with a prospect of
descending paddy-fields. But all of this required some
fairly drastic earth-shifting. It was no mere pick-and-
shovel job. We would need a bulldozer.

The whole village latched on to the idea of a bulldozer with alacrity. Like any manual society, they were
impressed by machinery. Their enthusiasm far transcended our caution. For our part, although we could see
the need for a bulldozer, we could not for the life of us
understand how it would ever gain access to our land.
The only approach was via a narrow mule path which
descended a one-in-four slope from the track above
the village. Our neighbours saw no limitation in this.
Only Rosalia observed, with relish, that if the bulldozer
struck the corner of the house adjoining the narrowest
part of the track, it would prove to be a very expensive
garden. This it was likely to be in any case. We already
realized we would need to wall it off. Apart from the
rubbish, the prevalence of mule-droppings indicated
that the place was providing pasturage in our absence:
and similar evidence suggested that it was frequented at
night by those of our neighbours who lacked plumbing
in their houses.

Finding a bulldozer proved to be a major project.
As usual, everyone proffered plenty of advice. Bulldozers had various known habitats in the surrounding
neighbourhood, but could never actually be tracked
down when needed. Rumours began to fly, like reports
of yeti-sightings in the Hindu Kush. A bulldozer was
spotted in Valdez, but vanished again. A bulldozer
was said to be finishing a job at Álamos: we set up

a road-block to intercept its return to its lair, but it got away. A bulldozer was available in Cabimas, owned by a man who actually had a telephone. This was only a limited bonus, since there was no telephone in Dalmácija. I had to use one in a bar at Álamos, which meant that the quest was fragmented and occasionally alcoholic. Finally a bulldozer arrived. It was too big. Even the villagers admitted it was too big. After much further telephoning and extensive use of the bush telegraph, a second one appeared. I was assured it was smaller and well used to mule tracks. To me it looked gargantuan. It filled the road at the bottom of the village, and as it set out to climb the route of the processions the hillsides shook with the thunder of its engine.

Its appearance at the top of the footpath was one of the most terrifying single moments of my life. Facing me as I stood below, it blacked out the sky. Its blade was raised in a gesture of naked aggression. Its motor rumbled eagerly. Suddenly it fell upon me like glistering Phaeton. Giving me barely an instant to leap out of the way, it hurtled down the track at what seemed like forty miles an hour. It missed the neighbouring house by two inches, thereby saving me about 200,000 pesetas, but sliced off a number of the agaves sheltering the raisin racks of José the ex-mayor. In a moment it was at the edge of our land, and sat there looking pleased with itself.

On top of it, as distant as Nelson on his column, sat a man silhouetted against the bright sky. He wore a woolly hat, and his lunch dangled from one of the many knobs of the controls. He looked down at me expectantly, for orders. Vying inadequately with the roar of the engine, which he had not seen fit to switch off, I tried to bellow our intentions at him, but the Assam concept now seemed hard to explain, especially the bit about paddy-fields. I began to make rice-planting motions, in desperation, but the man lost patience with me, slipped the machine into gear, and tore into the hillside.

Immediately the landscape of this corner of Andalusia began to change out of all recognition. The bulldozer's steel blade proceeded, in a horrifyingly short space of time, to gouge out a beetling cliff, above which José's raisin racks teetered precariously. Rocks tumbled down the slope, to be buried later by tons of earth. Whole trees disappeared beneath the surging debris. A wide expanse of prickly pears vanished as though they had never been. The motor roared high and low as the demented machine ranged to and fro, turning and doubling back, raising its blade as though questing for its next victim, then plunging it viciously into the rapidly vanishing soil. A column of dust rose hundreds of feet into the air, like smoke from the fiery furnace. Georgina and I staggered around amid the debris, wringing our hands, occasionally making futile gestures at the small dark figure in the epicentre of the tornado. Our Assamese dreams were obliterated within minutes. There would be no subtle changes of level, no flights of steps, no opening vistas – the entire hillside was disappearing. As the deluge of earth neared the cemetery below, the watching villagers clustered defensively, pointing down at the tombs of their ancestors which now looked likely to be converted into catacombs. At last, with a final triumphant pass along the very coping of the graveyard, the bulldozer stopped. The driver switched off the motor and reached for his sandwiches.

Silence descended. It was like the silence of the Somme when the guns stopped: or like that bit in *La Belle Dame Sans Merci* where the sedge was withered on the lake and no birds sang. Georgina and I looked around us, stunned. A large piece of landscape had simply disappeared. We had to reorient ourselves with some care to realize where we were. Instead of standing in an olive grove we were standing in a flat desert of bare soil. We had started the day expecting to contrive a garden. What we had now got, instead, was a parking-lot.

The villagers were delighted. They wandered to and fro, digging their toes into the fresh tilth and muttering *¡Muy rico! ¡Muy fuerte!* They had been sorry to see the olive trees go, but were confident that this rich new earth would sustain a fine plantation of almonds or citrus. I decided not to tell them, at this point, about the frangipani and the bottlebrush tree, let alone the wine palm. I concentrated instead on trying to rearrange my features so as to look as though the garden had emerged exactly as planned. We could see that Rosalia was impressed. Apart from pointing out the decimation of José's agaves, she said nothing. She could find nothing to criticize in this new scheme of things.

But for us the sudden arrival of the Gobi Desert on our doorstep had a pivotal significance. This mark on the hillside was like a cross on a voting paper — a signal of intent. Our initial purchase of the house had established a bridgehead in Dalmácija: now, like invading infantry, we seemed to be digging in for a long stay, perhaps for ever. Curiously, we had never been entirely certain of our future plans. Perhaps the strangeness of life here had had a disconcerting effect on us which precluded precision of thought. We had always found things to love in Dalmácija, but also things which we sometimes wished were otherwise. The all-pervading friendship of the community, stronger than anything we had known elsewhere, was offset by the total lack of privacy. The house itself, charming though it was in its indigenous style, was dark and cramped, with small rooms and inadequate space. Even now that we had land in which to build an extension, the mule track still intervened: any annexe would have to be separated from the house by the local equivalent of a motorway.

Moreover, the siting of Dalmácija itself, albeit sheltered, partook of none of the grandeur of the surrounding landscape. It was frustrating to know that, invisible behind the protective wall of our miniature valley, lay the magnificent vista of a 6,000-foot mountain range. For years Georgina and I had hankered after every hilltop *finca* we passed. The tour around Consuela's house above the track to Cabimas had unsettled us further. Would not that be a far more suitable and impressive house for us? It would be within easy visiting and shopping distance of the village – not too remote a refuge for our old age. Perhaps the time had come for us to withdraw, or semi-withdraw, from Dalmácija? Perhaps – dismaying thought – we had had the best of it?

For indeed a change was coming upon the place. It had been changing ever since our arrival. On almost every visit there were new developments to be seen, few of them welcome to our conservative eyes. For a start, it was becoming less inaccessible. The dirt road from Álamos was now hard-topped, and continued past Dalmácija to Cabimas, linking our valley to the next one. Electronic communication came next. Shortly after my telephone pursuit of the bulldozer, the village was given its own telephone. It was installed in Consuela's house, in one of her inner rooms, on a wall next to a mezzotint of Christ crucified. It had a modern perspex canopy, and was surrounded by large bright signs giving operating instructions in several languages. The villagers regarded it with awe. Two old ladies sat beside it like guards of honour at a catafalque. They came to life at every incoming call – which only Consuela was allowed to answer – cross-examining her on the precise subject-matter of each conversation. The telephone added greatly to Consuela's status: already a powerful figure in the village, she now embodied, in her massive person, the link with the outside world. Could I telephone England from here? I asked, half-joking. I could telephone anywhere, she said grandly (and, as it proved, truthfully). It was very simple. There was a meter on the wall which told you how much to pay. If it said nothing, she added optimistically, you paid nothing.

The arrival of the telephone was welcome to us. With young children in the house, we were glad of a potential lifeline in an emergency. But other changes in the village were disconcerting and disfiguring. For the first time in hundreds of years, new houses were being built which did not continue the style and materials of the old. Instead of contributing to the rich corrugations of the other earthenware-tiled roofs, they were flat-roofed cubes, like Emilio's, or garish sprawling villas, like young Aurelio's. These two new carbuncles were on the outskirts of the village, but the most intrusive new addition was in the centre. It was Rosalia's. She and Jesus had added an *almacén* – a work-shed – to the side of their house facing the church. It had given them valuable extra space for dehusking and storing their almonds, and a flat roof for hanging out Jesus's trousers to dry, but it had eliminated the little square. The acacia tree, the one splash of green in this part of the village, had gone. The doors of the *almacén,* which loomed opposite our own front door, were gaunt slabs of metal. Nobody used wooden doors any more. Further down the slope, below the vanished square, another new house had been built, slowly, rising stage by stage over three years, until its flat concrete pate blocked out what little view Rosalia had left us.

The village alleyways were now bordered, here and there, by new wrought-iron railings, artfully curlicued, with the ornamentation picked out in white. The government was putting more money into the countryside, and the results showed in little touches like these: also in the evidence of greater prosperity – not merely the new houses, but also new machinery. In Dalmácija, this took the form of mechanical almond dehuskers. Many families now had them: they were the latest status symbol. For hours their motors clattered away all over the village, shattering the autumnal calm, spewing out piles of discarded skins and saving hours of back-breaking labour.

But it was the roof-tops – whether tiled or cemented – which betrayed the greatest change of all. The television aerials had long been there, but now they were joined, on houses all over the village, by white cylinders which perched like over-sized cotton-reels on the highest points: the water-cisterns of the occupants beneath. When we had bought our house, it became the first in the village with plumbing, except for Angel's. Everyone else drew their water from the fountains, and the queues of bucket-toting women were one of the sights of Dalmácija. The fountains were meeting places . . . women's clubs; and when the women were joined by the men watering their mules, these gatherings offered a visual summary of life in the village, a local *Cavalleria Rusticana.* In those days the water might run short, but it never ran out. Now Dalmácija, which had originally been settled here some time before Christ, because of the excellence of its springs, had become dependent on water-lorries which grunted up the hill from the valley below.

Rosalia and Jesus had installed a bathroom far grander than ours, filled with every kind of appliance including a bidet. Many of the other houses were similarly equipped: Remedios and her wine-sodden son were amongst the few that still had no water. The overflow from Emilio's washing machine ran across the dusty track. Even on the hillsides the changed attitudes to water-conservation were evident. Some of the men now used weedkilling sprays on their land instead of grubbing out the spring weeds by hand, and the slopes around the village were variegated with patches of bare earth and patterns of dun-coloured dead grasses, according to the method used. Other agricultural habits were changing too. Fewer vines were being cultivated and almond trees were being planted instead. Almonds required less work than raisins, especially now that the machines had arrived.

Even the villagers' diet was altering, not fundamentally but at the edges. Rosalia no longer cultivated her bean patch in the gully bottom below the cemetery: the strip of level ground was needed for a new garage for her son's car. A fish-man still came up on a motor-bicycle with his panniers brimming with dollar-bright anchovies, but he was facing increasing competition from the frozen hake which now found a place in the villagers' new refrigerators. As with bathrooms, our fridge had been one of the first in the village, and space in it had been on permanent loan to our neighbours: at any time our tonic bottles or chilled gazpacho might be displaced to accommodate a leaking bundle of nameless offal from Rosalia or a bowl of greasy broth from Remedios. Now they had their own resources, and seemed to be modifying their eating habits accordingly. To judge from the ever-increasing froth of plastic rubbish that lapped around Dalmácija, yoghurt and margarine and pre-packed delicatessen foods were becoming staples on the menu.

Georgina and I viewed all these changes with mixed feelings. When we had first arrived here the village had been in decline. Houses on the fringe of it had collapsed and not been replaced. The church school was closed and the children sent to school in Álamos instead: after which, when they reached adulthood, they drifted away from the region altogether, and looked for work on the coast. Now, after less than a dozen years, Dalmácija was transformed. It was growing, and it was prospering. Its young were staying and planning to make their lives here. They had more money, and a more comfortable existence. And yet . . . and yet . . . what had originally enthralled us, from our first day here, had been the discovery of a community where the juggernaut of time had creaked almost to a halt. Except for the arrival of television, the twentieth century had not yet made its way up the hill. It was Dalmácija's immutability which had made it precious to us, and to those of our friends who had visited it. But that immutability was now crumbling. Moreover its erosion had coincided with our presence here. Was this a coincidence, or were we in some way responsible for what was happening? Perhaps our arrival here, like that of the conquistadors in the Caribbean or of Cook in the Pacific, had tainted the very culture we admired. The fatal impact . . .

On our roof-top eyrie, around which the life of the village seemed to revolve, we debated the matter, and re-debated it. To stay? To go? But to go was, ultimately, unthinkable. We were in here too deep. And what had changed in the village was less important than what had remained unchanged. The people were the same. Their good nature was unvarying. But in other ways time had left its mark on them too: the cast of characters was modifying its role, or stepping off the stage. Luis the boy had become Luis the man. He no longer had either the time or the inclination to play with our boys, but went off on mule-back every day to work in the fields. Luis the barman had died, although he was not old. His weight and his lame leg had immobilized him, and the immobility had weakened him, and pneumonia had carried him away. Georgina and I had gone to his funeral. The *Cura* had come up from Álamos and preached a very long sermon that was all about God and not at all about Luis. Down on the coast Jacob the Dutchman had also died. We went to his funeral, too.

But Angel, although infirm, was still here. Now, like us, he was a bird of passage. He and Ana spent most of each year alternating between a daughter in Valdez and another near Marbella, but they regularly returned to Dalmácija for several weeks each summer for the *ferias*, and for the harvesting of the grapes and almonds and the making of the wine.

These great activities, the main forces that drove the Dalmácija year, continued as before. So did the lesser activities that contributed to them. The fields were still cultivated by hand. Every morning Jesus and the other men still saddled their mules, and returned with them at dusk. The grapes might no longer be brought back on two legs, as they had been a generation ago, but they were still brought back on four. Mechanization had made no inroads here, apart from the almond machines and a handful of cars. Whatever the minor changes, Dalmácija was protected from major flux by its situation.

This much was clear to anyone who stood on the ramparts of the castle and looked about him. Down on the coast the skyscrapers continued to proliferate, and the plastic-sheeted farms, with their three crops a year, crept across the flatlands towards the mountains. Within the hills themselves there were developments too, to left and right, where the water was plentiful and where the *cortijos* and *fincas* that scattered the slopes were being sold to foreigners at the rate of several dozen a year. But straight ahead, directly below the castle, was a valley of a different kind. It was brown for much of the year, and there were no *cortijos*, only a single village, Dalmácija. The drought kept the foreigners away, and the intensive farmers, too. The isolation and the convoluted approach road discouraged tourists. The steepness of the hillsides and the paucity of the crops precluded any major change in the method of agriculture. By all these things the village was protected . . . sheltered from the winds of change. Surely it would remain intact, at least for our lifetime.

As for the deficiencies of our house, the acquisition of Salvador's land would alleviate some of them. The place would never be the *hacienda* of our dreams, with cool verandahs and tall shuttered windows and a fragrant patio within: but we could build an annexe with a verandah and, well, tallish windows, and the garden would be as fragrant and almost as sheltered as any patio. Admittedly the enlarged estate would have a mule track running through the middle of it, dividing the old from the new, but we could cope with such minor inconveniences.

And there would certainly be plenty of room for the preconceived oleander thickets and citrus groves, plus selected curiosities from my tropical plant book. The only problem was an almost total lack of water. Many of my favourite dream-plants needed forty inches of rain a year, according to the book. This part of the Costa del Sol normally received about ten. There was only one thing to do. We built a cistern, to be filled by water-lorry. After our earlier troubles with Luis the builder, we entrusted the job to Emilio. It formed part of a larger project, including the construction of a wall around the near end of the garden. (The rest of the boundaries were secured by the drop into the cemetery, the cliff up to José the ex-Mayor's raisin racks, and a steep falling-away at the far end, protected by a thicket of prickly pears.) The wall was much admired by the villagers. It rose to an impressive gateway, necessary for the discouragement of four-footed and two-footed trespassers. The cistern, however, was a less immediate success. It was built according to Emilio's own design, with a tiled roof and, to our surprise, windows. The end result, after it had been painted swimming-pool blue inside, was a cross between a summerhouse, a bomb shelter and the Blue Grotto at Capri. The filling of it by a water-lorry driven by Chico de Álamos was a solemn occasion, well attended. We would have cracked a bottle of champagne on one of its smartly whitewashed corners, had we had one. Instead, we plunged into its shaded depths and floated indolently on air-mattresses, admiring the view from the windows. The next morning Rosalia pounded on our door even earlier than usual. She had news for us. The cistern was leaking.

For a short while we were, after all, the owners of a small paddy-field, but we ignored the irony of this and persuaded Emilio to make another attempt to create a water-tank that actually retained water. Time passed. More lorry-loads of cement came up the hill. Extensive and detailed advice was provided by the rest of the village: it seemed that everyone was steeped in the lore of cistern-construction, except Emilio. At last it was done, and the garden was ready for planting. Georgina and I pored long hours over our plant book. Some of the more esoteric items were available at the Surrey nurseryman we had visited previously. We packed them into a suitcase and brought them out on the plane. They survived the journey well, but we immediately discovered, on touring the local garden centres, that we could have bought most of our specimens here in Spain at a fraction of the price, and doubtless in sub-species more suited to the climate.

From various sources we assembled a motley cast of flowering shrubs and fruits, and lined them up in the garden like a would-be chorus line auditioning for a show. The mint bush was there, and a strawberry guava and a jacaranda and a fruit-salad tree and two mandarin oranges. An acquaintance on the coast had given us two cuttings of frangipani . . . but feared that our garden would be too high above sea level. There were a pair of papayas . . . though the site might be too windy. Also a couple of avocados . . . which would only thrive with regular water. Other candidates similarly faced meteorological extremes which were alien to their nature. Almost none of them, now that we reviewed them, seemed to be ideally suited to our arid hillside in southern Spain, 1,500 feet up, served by a leaky cistern and an ignorant gardener. The latter was Jesus, who had been induced to minister to our garden in our absence. He now stood by, watching the consecration of his see with an expression in which apprehension was nicely blended with incomprehension. He viewed the sickle-shaped thorns of the coral tree with particular mistrust, and who could blame him.

We picked the bottlebrush tree as the first contender. Anything from Australia must have a certain robustness. Like us, it was an immigrant to this country, but we hoped that – again like us – it would settle in well and adapt happily to local conditions. It had a preposterous flower, but would provide a cheerful splash of red if sited at a safe distance. We selected a spot for it at the far end of the garden, above the cemetery, where there was a view down the valley and across to the castle. The position was romantic, but the ground underfoot, even now in mid-winter, was like adamant. As I spat on my palms I thought of that other corner of Iberia, along the banks of the Douro, where the vintners used dynamite to blast holes for their vines. All I had, here, was a pick. I took hold of it. The bottlebrush tree sat beside me, expectantly. Georgina was on the roof terrace, semaphoring the optimum spot for the hole, where the tree would not impinge on the view. Adam stood by with the watering can. Daniel had a wheelbarrow of mule-dung. Rosalia was ready with the Evil Eye. I swung up the pick and brought it down with all my strength. It rang like a bell.

THE END

A SELECTED LIST OF FINE WRITING
AVAILABLE FROM BLACK SWAN

THE PRICES SHOWN BELOW WERE CORRECT AT THE TIME OF GOING TO PRESS.
HOWEVER TRANSWORLD PUBLISHERS RESERVE THE RIGHT TO SHOW NEW
RETAIL PRICES ON COVERS WHICH MAY DIFFER FROM THOSE PREVIOUSLY
ADVERTISED IN THE TEXT OR ELSEWHERE.

99526 6	RHYMER RAB: AN ANTHOLOGY OF POEMS AND PROSE	ed. Alan Bold	£6.99
99572 X	STRANGE ANGELS	Andy Bull	£5.99
99493 6	COAST TO COAST	Andy Bull	£5.99
99479 0	PERFUME FROM PROVENCE	Lady Fortescue	£6.99
99557 6	SUNSET HOUSE	Lady Fortescue	£6.99
99558 4	THERE'S ROSEMARY, THERE'S BLUE	Lady Fortescue	£6.99
12555 5	IN SEARCH OF SCHRÖDINGER'S CAT	John Gribbin	£7.99
99364 6	VIDEO NIGHT IN KATHMANDU	Pico Iyer	£6.99
99507 X	THE LADY AND THE MONK	Pico Iyer	£5.99
99585 1	FALLING OFF THE MAP	Pico Iyer	£5.99
99505 3	TRUTH TO TELL	Ludovic Kennedy	£7.99
99637 8	MISS McKIRDY'S DAUGHTERS WILL NOW DANCE THE HIGHLAND FLING	Barbara Kinghorn	£5.99
99504 5	LILA	Robert Pirsig	£6.99
14322 7	THE MAZE	Lucy Rees	£6.99
99566 5	THREE-QUARTERS OF A FOOTPRINT	Joe Roberts	£6.99
99579 7	THE HOUSE OF BLUE LIGHTS	Joe Roberts	£6.99
99638 6	BETTER THAN SEX	Hunter S. Thompson	£6.99
99601 7	JOGGING ROUND MAJORCA	Gordon West	£5.99
99666 1	BY BUS TO THE SAHARA	Gordon West	£6.99
99366 2	THE ELECTRONIC KOOL AID ACID TEST	Tom Wolfe	£6.99